The Just Economy

Richard Dien Winfield

Routledge

New York London

First published in 1988 by

Routledge
an imprint of
Routledge, Chapman & Hall, Inc.
29 West 35 Street
New York, NY 10001

Published in Great Britain by

Routledge
11 New Fetter Lane
London EC4P 4EE

© 1988 Routledge, Chapman & Hall, Inc.

Printed in the United States of America

Library of Congress Cataloging-in-Publication Data

Winfield, Richard Dien, 1950–
  The just economy.

  Includes index.
  1. Distributive justice. 2. Social justice.
3. Economics—Moral and ethical aspects. I. Title.
HB523.W55   1988   323.4′6   87-28719
  ISBN 0-415-00185-4

62, 411

British Library Cataloguing in Publication Data

Winfield, Richard Dien
  The just economy.
  1. Wealth
  I. Title
  339.2   HB251

ISBN 0-415-00185-4

For my wife, Sujata

Contents

Introduction

With ever growing urgency, the modern age has tied the fate of justice to the design of the economy. From the rise of secular industrial society out of feudal Europe, through its global expansion under colonial and imperialist venture, to the outbreak of worker revolution and fascism, and the latest contest of communist and capitalist blocs, hardly anything has figured more prominently in the struggles of the times than the question of how the economy should be organized. Instead of being left lie as a neutral domain outside the realm of right, the arrangement of need and labor has everywhere become a contested issue of public affairs. If little agreement has been reached as to what the economy ought to be, the antagonists of left and right and north and south have all concurred in treating economic relations as normative structures playing a key role in the constitution of a just society. Whether they promote bourgeois independence to uproot feudal serfdom, civilizing commerce for the developing world, free enterprise to counter communist oppression, or socialized production to end all exploitation and class division, on one point all are agreed: The economy is an integral domain of justice with its own rightful relations.

This view has become such a modern prejudice that it is surprising to discover that the vast majority of thinkers have conceived economic relations such that normative questions are excluded from economic inquiry. Far from treating economic relations as features of social justice entailing their own rights and duties, most theorists have rendered the economy a normatively neutral sphere by conceiving it in either natural or monological terms. Both of these approaches rest on undeniable aspects of economic reality, yet both unduly assume that these aspects play a privileged role in determining the character of economic relations.

The Natural Approach to Economics

Conceiving economic relations in natural terms amounts to portraying them as a metabolism between man and nature, or, to take a less species-specific viewpoint, between living agents and the natural world they inhabit. It can hardly be denied that some such metabolism is an ineluctable feature of the human condition as well as the condition of any rational creature whose biological needs must be met through purposive dealings with nature. However, recognizing that biologically limited agents are subject to this law of survival is one thing; taking it as the key to understanding an economy is another.

If the essence of economic relations is sought in the metabolism between man and nature, the economy gets reduced to a sphere of necessity, having as little to do with right and wrong as mechanics or physiology. On these terms, economic relations become defined as functions given by nature, rather than as conventions ordered by the free will of all or any economic agent. So conceived, the economic order comprises an inescapable condition of life underlying all action, save for that of some divine demiurge or creator of nature who might be thought to impose natural law upon the inhabitants of the world. Whether or not an appeal is made to divine determiners of nature, the natural approach leaves those who participate in the economy as members of an economic system for whose design they can have no responsibility. Although their economic activity might affect other spheres where normative issues enter in, its own working would no more involve issues of justice than would that of any other natural process. If the "economic" metabolism of man and nature were to have any laws of its own, these could only be matters for an economic science describing the nature of the economy rather than prescribing how it should be ordered. Any search for a "just economy" would be folly, involving the category mistake of treating an ethically neutral domain as if it were a normative affair. Although this consequence has all too often been ignored, it lies at hand the moment the natural conception is employed. Thus, when classical political economy roots economic need in biological requirements, bases commodity exchange on a natural inclination to barter, and construes capital as the stock of goods necessary to sustain the worker's life during production,[1] when neoclassical economics treats the factors of production as naturally scarce resources,[2] and when Marx[3] and Arendt[4] characterize production as a fact of the human condition, the natural conception is at hand, undercutting any normative concern with the economy.

The Monological Approach To Economics

The same result follows when the monological approach is adopted and economic relations are conceived as functions of a single agency. Like the natural approach, the monological conception seizes upon an undeniable element of economic reality which it then assigns a privileged role. Here attention is focused on two indisputable facts: first, that the participants in any economy do not act merely instinctively out of natural urge, but engage in economic activity to satisfy psychologically determined needs; second, that in laboring to satisfy such needs, agents engage in a technical activity of making products, wherein an individual acts upon a given material, impressing it with a new form. Once again, there is little controversial in acknowledging these components of economic relations. What is disputable is the assertion that these features not only figure within economic activity, but define the economy that contains them.

The monological approach commits this reduction by determining economic relations in terms of how the self relates to objects. The forms this reduction may take are as varied as they are familiar. The psychological aspect of need can be elevated to a governing economic principle, as marginal utility theory has done in determining the values of commodities through estimates of consumer desire. On the other hand, economic relations can be defined in terms of their technical component, where the economy's reigning paradigm becomes that of a single agency acting upon objects according to causal laws. This has its most obvious application in conceiving the production of goods, which commonly gets represented as a technical process where a laborer employs an instrument to transform a given material into some desired product. The technical model can, however, equally be extended to distribution. When this is done, the multilateral process of the market gives way to a unilateral assignment of goods, whose consumers are treated just as much as ordered things as the objects they thereby involuntarily receive.

However the monological paradigm be applied, the outcome is the same: economic activity is deprived of all intrinsic normative character. By being reduced to functions of a single agency and objects, the economy is stripped of the relations between individuals wherein rights and duties have their play. As a consequence, the monological approach joins the natural approach in leaving justice an utterly extraneous concern to economics. This may not be realized by marginal utility theorists when they draw their demand curves, by Heidegger[5] and Habermas[6] when they reduce production to technique and instrumental action, or by econometricians and social planners when they attempt to guide economies with models for technically allocating given resources. Nevertheless, by adopting the monological paradigm, they all effectively exclude considerations of justice from what is inherent in economic affairs.

Although this common outcome of the natural and monological

approaches to economic theory opposes the assumptions underlying the central strifes of modern times, such discrepancy is not a count against their respective paradigms. Indeed, since both approaches render economics a descriptive science, they stand wholly indifferent to the conflicts embroiling representatives of different visions of a just society. By addressing economic reality as something consisting in relations of nature and the self that no joint action can change, these approaches are in no position to offer any normative critique of existing economies. Accordingly, if their theories were not to fit the reality they purport to describe, what would warrant change would be not economic institutions, but their conception.

This suggests how the very problem of an intrinsically just economy would cease to exist if economic reality could only be conceived in natural or monological terms. If they were the only theoretical options and theory had claim upon objective truth, then all striving for an intrinsic economic justice would be fundamentally absurd, seeking normative value in a type of activity that really had none. The economy might provide a domain in which normative claims originating in other spheres made themselves felt. Yet, whereas these might entail property entitlements, moral duties, family rights, and political prerogatives, economic activity would be unable to foster any justice specific to its own relations.

The Option of a Prescriptive Economics

If, however, economic relations are not reducible to natural or monological functions, but can comprise in their own right normative social relations, the situation is entirely different. In that case economics would have to be a prescriptive, rather than descriptive science to do justice to its subject matter. Instead of turning a blind eye to normative issues, such an economics would fall within the theory of justice. Its task would be to provide the concept of the just economy, in light of which the legitimacy of existing economic orders could be called into question. When an economy did not accord with this concept of economic justice, what would warrant alteration would not be theory, but economic reality.

As the natural and monological approaches can testify, the possibility of such an economics, which the makers of modern history have so pervasively assumed, can hardly be taken for granted. In practice, the rise of a distinct economic justice depends upon the emergence of an economic order divorced from and not engulfing other institutional spheres, such as the family, tribal associations, religious orders, caste groups, estates and other political bodies.[7] So long as the place of individuals in noneconomic institutions already determines their participation in exchange and production, whatever norms govern their economic activity equally pertain to their household, kinship, religious, political or other social roles. Conversely, if economic institutions have engulfed all other social institutions, then the norms governing the economy apply equally to these other relations and lose their economic specificity. Only when an economic order arises neither engulfing nor engulfed by all other institutions, does the economy win a discrete institutional existence, so that entitlements and obligations figuring within economic relations can have a uniquely economic character, allowing for a prescriptive economics.

However, it would be wrong to maintain, as does C. B. Macpherson, that any economic justice that thereby arises represents a defensive action against the newly disengaged economy's encroachment upon traditional values.[8] The historical advent of a disengaged economy may elicit ethical objections that aim at subordinating economic activity to norms conforming to traditional arrangements. Yet such norms cannot comprise a distinct economic justice, for all they represent are rules for restricting economic activity in terms of principles rooted in other institutional spheres. What sets traditional institutions at odds with a discrete economic domain is that they order economic activities as part and parcel of their noneconomic affairs. Hence, whatever principles they apply in self-defense leave no room for a prescriptive economics that could mandate independent canons for a just economy. For this reason, the triumph of a disengaged economy, such as the market system, over the ethical opposition of tradition does not signify the fall of economic justice, nor the elimination of all other institutional norms that are not economic in character, as Macpherson suggests.[9] Rather, it establishes the framework within which ethical claims of a purely economic kind can be realistically raised for the first time, without eliminating the distinct ethical norms of other coexisting spheres, such as the family and state.

Whether such claims have validity is an altogether different matter depending upon the resolution of several conceptual challenges that must be met before a prescriptive economics can have any plausibility. To begin with, if economic relations are to be ascribed any intrinsic normative dimension, their structure must not be conceived independently of the relations between agents in which justice has its place. On the one hand, this entails that economic relations not be determined in terms of natural or monological functions, which by definition have no normative character. On the other hand, economic relations cannot be characterized as functions of some other normative sphere, such as the household or the state. If economic activity were relegated to their domains, there would be no specifically economic issues of justice. Instead, the economy would be left an adjunct arena in which rights and duties deriving entirely from elsewhere would play themselves out. Taken together, these requirements mandate that if economic relations are to have any independent normative character, allowing for talk of a just economy, they must irreducibly consist in relations between agents involving matters of justice specific to their own economic activity.

Conversely, if the economy is to comprise a normative domain in its own right, then the reality of justice must incorporate an economic sphere distinct from other normative institutions, such as property relations, the household, and the state. For this to be the case, justice must somehow accommodate within its universal norms the implacably particular factors of need and its attendant provisioning.

As the history of ideas has shown, meeting these challenges in theory is no easy matter. Not only have the proposed solutions been plagued by bitter controversy, but the very thought of a prescriptive economics has been rejected out of hand by the most influential traditions of practical philosophy: the praxis theory initiated by Plato and Aristotle, and social contract theory. Not surprisingly, their common exclusion from ethics of any separate branch of economic justice has involved conceiving economic relations in terms of the natural and monological paradigms. By contrast, the interaction theory of justice established by Hegel has admitted the economy into the reality of right, and in so doing, has undertaken to conceive an economic order determined entirely in nonnatural, nonmonological terms of free relations between agents.

In order to investigate the problem of a just economy, the following book will seek to uncover and evaluate the respective logics of these divergent approaches. Chapter 1 will examine how and why praxis and social contract theorists are driven to systematically exclude economics from the theory of justice. Chapters 2 and 3 will show how those theories that incorporate elements from praxis and contractarian frameworks fail when they attempt to consider economic relations from a normative point of view. Part II will scrutinize to what extent the interaction theory introduced by Hegel resolves the difficulties of the preceding approaches and furnishes a satisfactory normative conception of economic activity. It will be argued that although Hegel provides a viable framework, his economic theory is both incomplete and significantly flawed. An attempt will be made to indicate how these shortcomings are to be overcome. In conclusion, the resulting concept of commodity relations will be examined in light of its bearing upon the just economy and the competing economic ideologies of modernity.

PART I

Economic Justice as a Problematic
Idea

1

The Systematic Exclusions of Economic Relations From the Domain of Justice

Praxis Theory

Praxis theory seeks to conceive what justice is through contemplation of a highest good providing the rationally prescribed end that conduct and institutions must realize to be normatively valid.[1] This strategy has an immediate appeal, as would be expected of the seminal form of Western practical philosophy. If justice comprises justified action and justification must rest on reasons, rather than arbitrary opinions, valid conduct must ultimately lie in abiding by some highest norm whose own validity lies no where else but in its own given content. Little else seems feasible, for if the reason validating actions and institutions had authority through some further norm requiring similar justification, an infinite regress would result, leaving legitimation an insoluble problem. Accordingly, it would seem that justice is possible only if a highest good can be conceived that grounds itself, possessing validity solely in virtue of its own character. It would thereby provide an immediately valid standard, whose given content would have the exclusive privilege of mandating what is right and wrong, extending subordinate normative value to whatever other activities and ends contribute to its realization. To the extent that only reason can provide access to such a self-evident and universally valid norm, the highest good would provide the foundation of a system of practical norms prescribed by reason to which willing should conform. On this basis, right conduct would consist in rational willing, where the will obeys reason by restricting its own liberty in accord with the given norms comprising the rational order of the good life.

Where this leaves economic activity only becomes clear once it is recognized that if the good life consists in realizing ends antecedently prescribed by reason, politics must play a paramount role. The founders of praxis theory, Plato and Aristotle, consistently emphasized this primacy, and came to common conclusions regarding the role of economic affairs. Admittedly, achieving the rational goals of the good life requires performing specific functions, including activities of production and commerce providing for survival and the conveniences required for the good life. However, fulfilling these functions with excellence cannot be guaranteed through their performance alone. Not only may agents be ignorant of the proper forms of conduct, but those that are not may still decide to disregard them. Consequently, if the greatest justice is to be achieved, the activities prescribed by reason must be supplemented by a ruling activity empowered to insure that those best able to perform the rationally mandated functions actually do so. This need for rational government, which moves Plato to introduce his guardians, transforms the problem of justice into a preeminently political problem of establishing the just state.

Aristotle leads us to the same result simply by thinking through what action can count as valid, when the validity of action is sought in the achievement of rationally prescribed ends. If the value of conduct lies in the end it achieves, then action will have validity only if an end can be attained which is both for its own sake, and the end to which all other goals should be subordinate. Unless there be such a master end-in-itself, the value of all action will be hopelessly relative. Either all action will pursue goals whose only purpose lies in serving other ends of equally dubitable finality, or there will be a plurality of ends-in-themselves, leaving each agent in an insoluble quandary as to which to seek. Yet, if normative conduct requires that there be a highest good, what could it possibly be? Certainly, no product of action could count as a master end. Products for use and consumption must be disqualified, for they serve as means to other ends, rather than as ends in themselves. By contrast, products possessing value in themselves, such as objects of fine art, may exist for their own sake, retaining worth solely for their beauty, rather than for their utility, entertainment, or any edifying or educational benefit. However, such products lack the subordinating character of master ends. Their existence is utterly indifferent to other activities, for not only can the work of art be created without subordinating all other affairs to it, but, once produced, the work of art not only has no hold on other activities, but is properly left alone to be regarded for its beauty rather than as a rule for life. Moreover, no work of art can preclude the existence of others. Hence, even if art were to count as the good, the plurality of art works would signify a diversity of ends in themselves condemning ethics to an inescapable relativity.

For these reasons, if anything is to be a master end, it must not be a product of activity, but a type of activity performed for its own sake and subordinating all other affairs to its own. No economic activity can have this sovereign character. Production and trade aims not at itself, but at providing the goods and wealth to satisfy particular needs. Similarly, nothing in economic endeavor essentially entails subordinating all other activities to its satisfaction of need. The required master activity must instead be political, provided that politics be understood as a sovereign activity of governing properly pursued as an end in itself. Such government may indeed require other pursuits including economic activities to provide finances for the state and means of subsistence for its members. Yet if a highest good be realized, government must make its own governing its raison d'être, and subordinate all other affairs accordingly. Only then will these subordinate pursuits have any justifiable value, for unless they contribute to the good life, their worth is baseless. Hence, the good life is ultimately the life of the citizen who engages in ruling, subordinating all other activity to no higher end than that of making possible the political life.

In these respects, as guarantor of the fulfillment of all functions necessary for justice and as preeminent activity of the good life, politics assumes a privileged role within praxis theory. How this relegates economic activity to not just a subordinate, but ultimately a nonethical endeavor is patent in Plato's and Aristotle's complementary theories. As far as both are concerned, the good life begins precisely where concern with need and work ends. Those activities rendering services and producing goods to satisfy particular needs are relegated either to slaves or to artisans who may contribute to the life of citizens, but stand excluded from the preeminent affairs of citizenship. Whether they provide for household wants or serve the needs of luxury and the accumulation of riches, these economic activities are all tainted by a shared commitment to particular ends of appetite.

By contrast, the political community realizes the good life by having its citizens follow the prescribed norms of virtue, which comprise universal ends antecedently given by reason. Any individual activity that independently creates its own end, whether as a self-serving private pursuit or as a free volition, is incompatible with the fixed norms of *praxis*.

Plato's dismissal of economic action

Plato explicitly recognizes this disharmony and constructs his ideal republic in conscious opposition to all manifestation of a self-determining particular agency. In the course of making the wisdom of the guardians the final arbiter of political life, he bars every conceivable womb of private endeavor, prohibiting personal property, eliminating the household, and restricting the exercise of crafts to a subordinate class whose tasks are allotted not in deference to individual need and preference, but according to what the rational rulers impose as best for the state.[2]

Thus, when the *Republic* comes to discuss a hypothetical association issuing from the interdependence of individual need and consisting in a division of work and commerce patterned after the naturally different talents of its members, Plato wastes no time in having it declared a City of Pigs, more fit for animals than citizens.[3] Although the organic unity of such a community might provide for the survival of its members, its organizing principle is utterly indifferent to the concerns of the good life. What joins its members is simply the drive to satisfy their particular desires by pursuing whatever needs and occupations may complement those of others. Each participant aims at his own welfare whereas no one aims at the common benefit that may result from their complementary occupations. Not only does this subordinate the community to the blind necessity of appetite, irrespective of the rational ends of virtue, but it leaves room for a fevered state where the divisions of commerce foster cravings for riches and disparities in wealth that threaten its own unity. On both counts, the economy has no affirmative worth in its own right.

Therefore, when Plato finally erects his threefold division of the polis in place of the organic unity of the City of Pigs, the rule of the guardians groups the different crafts into a single administered body where their duties lose all semblance to a self-governing economy. Not only do these occupations now proceed as tasks laid down by ruler-wisdom independently of the immediate wants of appetite, but they do so without in themselves exercising any fee-earning art.[4] Here in the one recess of the ideal polis where economic relations might have sway, all deciding role for need and its satisfaction is actually effaced. The productive class labors as but a subordinate tool of guardian political wisdom, leaving individuals with no freedom to choose what their needs shall be or how they will satisfy them. If they are driven by any motivation it is just as noneconomic as the external rule that oversees their production. Not surprisingly, in Plato's analogous division of the soul, the third component, whose appetitive nature allegedly makes money its chief instrument,[5] gets branded the most despicable and godless part.[6]

In the *Laws,* Plato repeatedly draws the lesson to be learned: Since riches are for the service of the body, as the body is for the service of the soul, wealth must take the lowest place in our esteem, as but a slave to both.[7] So he decrees: The pursuit of wealth for its own sake can have neither sanctuary nor abode in our city.[8] Not only does it threaten the attainment of those common ends prescribed by reason, but it mistakenly treats wealth as an end in itself, when in fact, the pursuit of riches has no ethical value. Only when production and trade are stripped of their consuming passion for wealth and constrained by political rule to satisfy the limited needs of the good life can work and consumption coexist with virtue.

With this last chastisement and banishment, Plato gives final seal to the exclusion of any independent normative value from economic activity, consummating what his departure from the City of Pigs had already heralded. Although the governing restraint of the guardians' rational will may permit labor to be performed in service of the good life, economic affairs provide no norms of their own worthy of recognition. Because praxis aims at realizing the universal aims of the just state, which are prescribed by reason independently of personal preference and initiative, the particular pursuits of commerce can be allowed no affirmative autonomy.

Aristotle's exclusion of economic affairs from *praxis*

Aristotle comes to a like conclusion without following Plato's extreme course of sacrificing both household and market in favor of a ruled class of craftsmen. Preserving mention of the *oikos* (the household), Aristotle is careful to distinguish the utterly noneconomic *praxis* of household management from the normatively neutral *poeisis* (making) of slave work, just as he admits the existence of markets only to radically separate their untrammeled trading and artisan industry from the proper affairs of the citizenry.

In Book I of the *Politics,* he puts economic activity at one remove from the ethical concerns of citizens by having households and markets emerge as successive stages in an explicitly natural process generating the material conditions for the good life of the polis. Although both households and markets get subsumed under state rule once the political order arises, the worth they gain by serving politics as their final end does not make their economic arrangements ethical institutions in their own right. Their very existence as antecedent conditions of politics leaves their essence already defined in terms of preethical principles, which is what allows them to exist in an identifiable form before any state has emerged.

Hence Aristotle has the household arise as the unifying result of the two elementary associations that produce and sustain life without regard for the further considerations of justice. The natural impulse to preserve the species joins man and woman in procreative bond and when the survival needs for their union are rendered secure through the subsequent addition of master and slave relations, the household comes into being as their composite unity.[9] With its aims rooted in nature and its emergence requiring no contribution of any conventional institutions, the household comprises a type of association that of itself is naturally instituted for no higher purpose than the satisfaction of the daily recurrent needs on which the life of the species depends.[10] These needs are limited by the given requirements of subsistence rather than the caprice of personal preference. Hence, to the extent that the natural environment provides sufficient possibilities for human survival, the availability of the goods these wants address need not be characterized by scarcity in the way in which commodities might be said to be scarce in relation to the conventional boundlessness of market need.[11] In all these respects, the affairs endemic to the household are defined simply by the necessities of subsistence in utter indifference to the further concerns of the good life.

Nevertheless, Aristotle accords household management its own integral virtue. This does not compromise the normatively neutral status of domestic occupation with natural need, however, because household management attains ethical worth by being integrated within a political association where its activity obtains a new normative value transcending its own resources. In this political surrounding, household management can acquire virtue in its own right provided it aims not at the needs of life, but at sustaining the domestic ties of husband and wife, parents and children, and master and slave so as to afford the household master the minimal freedom from natural necessity enabling his participation in the good life of citizens. Under these extrinsic conditions, household management can use the household property of goods and slaves as a genuine instrument of *praxis*, serving action for its own sake.[12] In so doing, household management does not engage in the productive work of *poeisis,* creating an end distinct from its own act of management, but rather reproduces the entire association of the family, including its own activity as a self-enabling participant in politics.[13] Instead of fabricating goods, household management simply employs what has been naturally provided in order to maintain the household in line with the overriding goal of allowing the household master to devote the majority of his time to the public affairs of the good life.[14] Therefore, Aristotle can suggest that the form of acquisition most suited to the ethically limited household is not any open-ended pursuit of wealth in the market, but the hunt, that mere finding of fruits and animals, of goods naturally at hand ready for use.[15] Whatever its dependence upon natural abundance, it at least introduces no further complications such as those conventional necessities of the market that can be at odds with political aims.

Accordingly, the ethical management of the household does not elevate economic action to its own level of conduct, but observes the fundamental distinction that *praxis* is an end in itself, whereas *poeisis* is merely for the sake of what it produces.[16] Consequently, household management shuns labor, leaving all direct production for need to those entirely beneath participation in the good life, the household slaves.

When Aristotle looks outside the household to address the economic affairs of the market, they too invariably lack any ethical dimension of their own. Although these market activities provide a wealth of luxury transcending the natural subsistence that the household can insure, they still offer no more than material conditions for the good life. Admittedly, the interconnected commerce of tradesmen and craftsmen can sustain a life of convenience above and beyond all survival needs, as well as provide the surplus wealth with which public institutions can be financed. However, left to itself, the market gives its participants free reign to follow their separate pursuits with neither knowledge of the common good, nor any regard for virtue.

Not surprisingly, Aristotle conceives the blind compound of the market to arise entirely independently of the guiding light of rational rule. As Book I of the *Politics* recounts, market activity results from the succession of natural associations where first household relates to household, then village to village, until finally the set limit of their natural needs is broken and separate trades emerge to sustain and foster a new conventional livelihood.[17] Although its artificial wants and luxury make possible a new level of self-sufficiency, this may just as well support public works as private dissipation.

If good deeds are not necessarily entailed by this new association, what are, are its own economic relations where transaction emerges as an exchange mediated by currency and wealth becomes all that has its measure in money, shedding the fixity of household property and assuming a form without limit.[18] Commerce, investment at interest, and service for hire here become the modes of the new, unbounded *chrematistik*, whose quest for wealth equally engenders such intermediate forms as extractive industry, where nature's gifts are seized in their raw abundance, but used only through the mediation of exchange, as vehicles for the accumulation of riches.[19]

All this forms but a useful equipment for the polis. The moment political association is established, it relegates the market to a subordinate role, delimiting and regulating its affairs without accepting them into the ethical domain of *praxis*, whose activities are ends in themselves. The law of the polis may well organize slave production and define the value of money,[20] but in doing so it hardly consecrates economic activities. On the contrary, the political order actually distances itself from the occupations it oversees, separating the exercise of *praxis* from instrumental dealings with property,[21] as well as shutting the ranks of the citizenry to those very mechanics, slaves, and freedmen who provide the material sustenance of the state.[22]

Commerce acquires an ethical form only when the market formation of prices is overridden by set terms of trade proportional to the merit of the parties to exchange and promoting the self-sufficiency and bonds of goodwill holding the state together.[23] Solely when these extraeconomic requirements are satisfied can prices be considered just and trade be honorable. When, on the contrary, individuals go to market activities out of purely economic motives of personal want and gain and then let their transactions proceed according to purely economic mechanisms of supply and demand, they have left the good life behind.

Consistently enough, the only other occasions where Aristotle allows *praxis* to involve even the vaguest reference to need and its satisfaction are in such acts as retributive allotment according to merit, expenditure for other ethical ends, and the adjustment of the relations between the wealth and political authority of the different classes of citizenry.[24] In each of these cases, economic relations are impinged upon from without, in pursuit of ends completely extraneous to the economy.

Consequently, Aristotle has little alternative but to conclude that wherever economic activity occurs outside the household, it is still a normatively indeterminate affair whose production and commerce remains untouched by any indwelling ethical concerns. Just as domestic toil failed to possess any independent ethical stature, so every other economic pursuit finally fails to attain the dignity of *praxis*. Only as an instrument of politics can economic affairs borrow some redeeming value.

Thus, for all the discrepancy of Plato's and Aristotle's portrayals of the good life, they each arrive at the same exclusion of economic relations from ethical activity proper. Although both have conceived a concrete political community, reigning over all commerce and industry, neither can sanction any independent pursuit of particular ends. Since the valid interrelations of individuals are taken to consist in activities aiming at the rationally prescribed, universal ends of politics, all occupation in service of the particular ends of need must stand deprived of its own justice.

Social Contract Theory and the Economy

Praxis theory could hardly have a more radical opponent than liberal social contract philosophy. Rejecting the authority of all antecedently prescribed ends, liberal theory founds justice on the very principle that Plato already augured spelling ruin for the unity of the polis. This principle is the right of the individual will. With its advance, the choosing will is elevated to the position of a privileged determiner whose liberty supercedes all teleological claims by figuring as the sole source of justice. Liberal theory grants the will this exclusive privilege out of scepticism that reason can prescribe any fixed ends to which the will should be subject. Instead, liberal theory leaves the individual will unbeholden to any authority issuing independently of its choice, such as the rational rule of experts in virtue, the given means of *praxis*, or the prescribed norms of the good life.

However, liberal theorists are perfectly aware that the right of individuals to realize their liberty has no guarantee in a state of nature, where legitimate authority has yet to be established. Under such conditions, person and possession stand in constant jeopardy due to the natural license of each will, which gives each the power to hinder the actions of others. To overcome this incipient state of war where every individual's liberty stands threatened, liberal theory calls for the establishment of a civil order with no other legitimate aim than securing the liberty of its members as embodied in their person and property. Since the authority of any such regime must derive from the choice of individuals if it is not to violate the very liberty it is called upon to protect, liberal theorists appeal to a social contract to bring it into being. Through the unanimity of its founding agreement, a civil government is born, enjoying a legitimacy rooted in the consent of the governed and serving no other end than to guarantee the law-governed coexistence of their liberty.

As much as liberal theory develops this argument in express opposition to praxis theory, it arrives at virtually the same verdict concerning the normative character of economic activity. Although it is commonly held that liberal theory offers an apology for capitalism by granting commodity relations normative legitimacy under the banner of "free enterprise,"[25] liberal theory can consistently provide no more support for a distinct economic justice than it can for democratic government.[26]

In rejecting the authority of teleological ends, liberal theory does free economic relations from subordination to norms that prescribe independently of personal decision and voluntary agreement what count as "rational" needs, "just" prices, "fair" exchanges, and "equitable" distributions of wealth. Given its embrace of liberty, social contract theory cannot retain the classical and medieval doctrine that the satisfaction of wants should be restricted to those needs that have legitimacy in virtue of being dictated by reason, rooted in human potential or commanded by divine law. Nor can liberal theory accept the traditional view that prices are just to the extent that they conform to values given by nature rather than convention and that exchanges and distributions of wealth are fair to the degree that they reflect both natural price and the different merit and status of the parties to exchange. The traditional principle of commutative justice, according to which an exchange is just not because its terms have been freely agreed upon, but because the goods exchanged are of equal value, where value is measured by natural price, is just as antithetical to the right of liberty as is the Aristotelian principle of distributive justice, according to which what individuals are due is in proportion to their merit.[27] In both cases, conduct is subject to values that neither issue from the consent of individuals, nor operate in function of their equal liberty.

Certainly, liberal theory does not encounter these impositions upon liberty in market relations, where prices, exchanges, and the distribution of wealth are determined through the voluntary agreements of commodity owners. Yet, even if commodity relations may uniquely provide an economy ordered irrespective of any independently given teleological ends, liberal theory does not grant markets any affirmative value beyond the property and contractual relations they involve. Hence, however tolerable certain economic arrangements may be for social contract theory, it does not give them their own integral place within the pantheon of justice. Instead, liberal justice touches upon economic affairs only extrinsically, either by affirming the property relations at play in commodity relations, or by intervening upon the economy to insure that civil government is well financed and person and property are secured against internal and external adversity.

Admittedly, the original standard-bearers of liberalism never openly exclude a distinct domain of economic justice as if that were a necessary consequence of their contractarian approach. However, they all do reduce need, labor, and commodities to matters of the individual and nature that may at best become the given object, rather than the intrinsic normative exercise of contractual and contractually derived relations. Why they are led to this common path is made plain by examining one by one their treatments of economic relations.

Hobbes

Hobbes, great innovator that he is, sets the stage for all subsequent liberal conceptions of economic activity. He does so in two respects. On the one hand, he conceives economic relations in monological and natural terms. On the other hand, he repudiates the teleological norms traditionally imposed upon economic activity by conceiving the price of goods, the worth of individuals, and the equality of exchange to be determined by the exercise of liberty specific to contractual relations.

Hobbes begins his economic analysis by grounding the drive to accumulate wealth in the monologically defined pursuit of power germane to the state of nature.[28] He then conformably determines commodities as mere nutritive matter, defined and limited by nature, and appropriable through an immediate exertion where an individual need not enter into any relation to others.[29] In accord with these natural and monological parameters, Hobbes next lets labor proceed as an individual act upon nature occurring outside the conventions of the enacted commonwealth. Only the laborer's legal ownership of the resulting product enters into the affairs of justice as something subsequently guaranteed and insured by the rule of the sovereign.[30]

Thus, when Hobbes elsewhere ascribes the commonwealth a nutrition involving natural plenty and the concoction and conveyance of its products to the public use,[31] he is not conceiving economic relations as if they themselves involved independent rights and duties. He is instead merely describing the natural affairs presupposed and posteriorly regulated by sovereign rule. Although the distribution of naturally available materials and produced goods involves property relations, which can only derive their force from the laws of the commonwealth,[32] the legal enforcement of property leaves entirely untouched the essence of nourishment and labor, which have already been defined entirely in terms of the relation of the individual to nature. Consequently, the commonwealth's distributive justice does not constitute need and the activities insuring its satisfaction, but only adds a separate public regulation involving the lawful division of the land according to equity and the common good,[33] the public enactment of the contract procedures by which exchange may be legally guaranteed,[34] the institution of legal tender with a fixed value,[35] the impositions of public finance,[36] and legislation to encourage thrift and the development of science and technology.[37]

In the same vein, when Hobbes notes that merchants not only perform commercial exchanges as acts of contract,[38] but also enter contract to form their own corporate body politic and exercise a monopoly power,[39] what again comprises the normative dimension of their commerce is the act of private covenant and not the economic activity that their contract concerns.

As in those few other instances in *Man and Citizen* and *Leviathan* where Hobbes deigns to mention things economic, the normative bonds of commonwealth extend only to acts of contract and what impinges upon the person and property of individuals. To the extent that occupation with need and labor involves more than taking ownership, it falls outside the purview of justice.

However, if the role of property relations within economic activity does not give Hobbes a basis for conceiving positive norms for a distinct economic justice, it does give him the means for excluding the teleological restraints upon economic activity that traditional notions of distributive and commutative justice entailed.

The primacy of liberty requires this exclusion in several respects. To begin with, insofar as the commonwealth is erected for the sake of protecting the person and property of individuals, the liberty of subjects extends to all affairs that need not be regulated in order to defend personal liberty and the rights of private ownership. Hence, Hobbes lists among the freedoms citizens are entitled to the choice of what to consume, the choice of occupation, and the liberty to enrich themselves so far as can be done without jeopardizing public security.[40] Although this still prohibits citizens from any economic activities that might endanger the commonwealth's enforcement of property relations, it otherwise liberates them from any externally given prescriptions regarding what to need and consume, what trade to undertake, or how much wealth to earn.

Similarly, when Hobbes turns to consider what constitutes fair exchange, his appeal to liberty overturns the traditional view of commutative justice which considers an exchange to be just only if the goods traded have an equal value determined in proportion to the relative merit and skill of their owners and/or producers. Hobbes maintains instead that the value of any exchanged goods is simply determined by the appetite of the parties to exchange. Hence, the just value of traded goods is equivalent to whatever terms to which their owners happen to agree.[41] Here as elsewhere in the commonwealth, what reigns supreme are the considerations of liberty. Not rationally prescribed standards of virtue and skill, but the free willing of contractual agreement determines the value of goods.

This applies equally to the value of labor power, which Hobbes not surprisingly equates with the relative worth of individuals. To the extent that all man are equal in respect of their capacity to be property owners and no teleological standards of merit are recognized, the only measure available to Hobbes by which the worth of men might be distinguished is that of their labor power's market price.[42] Like all other commodities, its value depends upon the need others have for it.[43] Hence, when Hobbes speaks of the worth of men in these market terms, he is both excluding the standard of merit underlying teleological distributive and commutative justice, and once again affirming the right of will to determine what has value.

Although, as Macpherson emphasizes, this assertion of liberty at the expense of traditional limitations gives market relations relatively free scope to develop,[44] what has affirmative value within economic affairs remains the exercise of willing specific to contractual relations. Consequently, Hobbes's acceptance of the market forces of supply and demand, albeit within the limits defined by public security, does not introduce any separate norms of economic justice, but merely reiterates the same liberties of contract to which civil justice is devoted. This is equally true of Hobbes's mercantilist suggestions for state action to promote husbandry and fishing, penalize idleness and wasteful consumption, and reward industry and thrift.[45] Again, the governing aim remains not any independently given economic ends, such as capital accumulation, but furnishing the commonwealth with the means to protect the life and liberty of its subjects.[46]

Locke

Locke, by contrast, might appear to give economic relations their own privileged place within the sphere of right, for he invests labor with the power to establish the normative entitlement of property. In truth, however, this move brings him no nearer to granting economic activity a separate integral justice.

From the outset, Locke firmly sets the elements of economic relations within the frame of the natural approach. In *The Second Treatise of Government* he introduces labor as an act of the individual upon nature, predicated upon Godly command and the wants found in the state of nature,[47] rather than upon any relations between individuals in which justice might lie. Although serving God's command to preserve life and propagate the human species might seem to root labor in a normative endeavor, the God in question is the creator of the world. Since His commands are laws of nature, they have a necessity quite unlike the human laws on which justice must depend. If they are laws of nature in the sense of operative rules of necessity, there is no justice in conforming to them, since no choice is involved. If however, they are not immediately effective, but only immediately given to reason, they lack the actual enforcement without which human law is only words. Hence, when the naturally defined agency of labor is said to institute the individual's right to the possession of the resulting product,[48] this can only be by a purely natural law, which, though emanating from God, can have no force unless it later be enacted through human institutions. By themselves, its strictures are natural rules whose effective role in justice remains to be established. Accordingly, though Locke's labor theory of property purports to set a limit on ownership, it does so in line with the explicitly natural bound of men's labor and the requirements of their survival together. At best, these provisos can receive an indirect justification once the normative activities life makes possible get established in their own right. Insofar as labor has been defined as the conduit of man's metabolism with nature, it can hardly be included among those activities that give life normative status as a life of liberty.

This leaves the character of the object of consumption just as independent of relations between agents as the character ascribed to need and labor. Since the consumption good is here the product of an act between man and nature and the means of satisfaction of a naturally defined need, the corresponding value it bears will be equally nonconventional. Although Locke accounts for this value in different ways, sometimes deriving it from the technical fact of the labor expended in the good's production[49] and other times simply considering it an intrinsic natural quality,[50] in each case it stands within the scheme of man's relation to nature.

However, with the invention of money and the tacit agreement of men to put an artificial value upon it, wealth is driven beyond the limits of the state of nature.[51] Nevertheless, as much as this may bring man to desire more than he naturally needs, and toil for more than survival,[52] the mutual consent establishing the conventions of money does not raise economic activity to a civil affair with its own justice. On the contrary, as Locke consistently observes, what follows from the introduction of money is an unnatural, unequal partage of things pursued wholly outside the due affairs of civil society and without prior compact. In civil society proper, money has no constitutive place, for there the right of property is regulated by law, just as the distribution of land is determined by positive constitutions.[53] The conventions of a money economy not only play no role in the public enforcement of person and property in which civil justice consists, but actually threaten the aims of its legal regulation by setting in motion a redistribution of goods that may well undermine the security of individuals.

Recognizing this predicament, Locke hardly offers an apology for free enterprise. Instead, he demarcates economic activity from the ways of justice in a manner no less complete and final than that of Hobbes.

Rousseau

Rousseau's "economic" analysis is even more telling, thanks to his explicit reference to the differences between his own discussion and that of the classical Greek founders of praxis theory.

In his *Discourse On Political Economy*, Rousseau distances himself from the concerns of the ancients, who centered so much of their economic inquiries upon the particular economy of the household. Rousseau vows to leave aside this purely domestic activity and instead address the eminently civil sphere of general or political economy.[54] With its universal reach and civil character, this political economy would well seem to enjoy the normative stature that would place it firmly within the purview of the theory of justice.

Yet, when Rousseau proceeds to investigate political economy, he openly conceives it as nothing but the administration of government,[55] established to protect the preexisting property of individuals.[56] Instead of delineating the social reality of commerce and industry, Rousseau begins by dividing political economy into popular and tyrannical constitutions, each entirely lacking in economic character.[57] He then decrees the first principle of political economy to be that government administration conform to the law.[58] Not only does he further avoid all mention of any civil market activity, but he explicitly argues that the most vital task of political economy consists in effectively countering the free play of particular interests characterizing economic endeavor.[59] To prevent civil society from collapsing due to the substitution of private interests for the universal public good, government must strike at the economy, constraining the development of wealth, limiting the gap of rich and poor, and insuring the subsistence of those industry leaves indigent.[60]

This repudiation of any positive normativity in economic activity receives its crowning development in *On Social Contract*, where Rousseau extends his gaze beyond government administration to consider the entirety of civil life. Beginning with an analysis of the state of nature, Rousseau reaffirms Locke's labor theory of property, in which labor and need are reduced to relations of the individual and nature.[61] In line with this natural conception, he then conceives production as a precondition of society, existing prior to and outside the very sphere of right whose material prerequisites it supplies. Noting that all government requires means of subsistence for public servants who consume but produce nothing, Rousseau argues that civil life can only proceed if individuals already produce more than they need to survive.[62] Since such surplus production must precede the civil life it makes viable, it falls within the state of nature and is subject to all the nonconventional features determining that condition. Hence, Rousseau reasons that the activities of production are unavoidably and essentially determined by given climactic and geographical factors.[63] With this judgment, Rousseau brings his natural reduction to its quaint conclusion: However universal be the wish to enter social contract, only under fair weather and on fertile soil will genuine civil association ever arise.[64]

Rousseau complements this natural confinement of production by once again setting civil society in an irreconcilable struggle against the disruptive influence of economic gain. Wealth is once more denounced as the corrupter of rich and poor alike, tearing citizens away from the state to serve instead each other's private interest.[65] Commerce, the passion for gain and the hunger for commodities are all taken to degrade civil conduct to a service for money and so bring government toward ruin.[66]

Accordingly, Rousseau can only conclude with a last sweeping pronouncement against any civil role for economic affairs: The word of finance, he declares, is a word of the slave, a word thus unknown in the polis. In a state truly free, however, it too can have no place, for here in genuine society, citizens do all with their own hands, and nothing with money.[67] To foster the public good and hinder the play of private interest, the social economy of the market must be sacrificed in favor of self-sufficient households, living the natural idyll of an Alpine autarchy, yet bound together in an unforgiving general will.

Following the trail of Hobbes and Locke to this hinterland, where communist utopias are easily cultivated, Rousseau brings to an extreme liberal theory's exclusion of economic activity from the justice of civil society. Nevertheless, in so doing, Rousseau has no more spelled out the necessity of this exclusion than did his two predecessors.

Kant

Not surprisingly, resolving the issue falls to Kant. He is able to pose the problem in its purity, for he brings the contractarian tradition to fruition, honing its logic down to essentials and laying out the consequences with least compromise. Steadfastly refusing to appeal to any teleological givens that might be disguised in laws of nature and human species being, Kant grounds ethics on the autonomous individual will, stripped of all the extraneous psychological, anthropological, and otherwise naturally defined baggage previously saddled to it. Recognizing that the validity of conduct cannot lie in any ends sought for their own sake, nor in any feelings accompanying action, nor in resulting consequences, but only in the form of willing, Kant advances freedom of a special kind. Instead of sanctioning the liberty consisting in the natural capacity to choose among given alternatives, Kant ascribes normative validity only to an autonomy that wills according to self-imposed rules that are universal in character. Since this autonomy directly determines solely what maxims the individual will attempt to follow, neither the external world nor inner desire need feel its effect. Instead, the categorical imperative to which autonomy subscribes comprises a purely inner law of freedom that by itself can never guarantee real results. Given this radically individual and internal character of Kantian freedom, it is hard to see how it should bear upon economic relations, let alone any other real activities.

However, the very universality of the categorical imperative implies that there be an objective plurality of autonomous persons to whom the validity of the general maxims of the will can apply. Therefore, Kant is compelled to conceive of justice as the external reality of freedom, where persons can interrelate as recognizable and respected autonomous agents, whose external liberty is not violated. Since autonomy, like natural liberty, is an individual capacity given prior to all interaction, the logic of social contract provides once again the only available procedure for consistently erecting an order to secure the outer realization of that freedom. Only through mutual consent can a legal order be imposed to protect the external liberty of individuals without violating their choice. Hence, Kant appeals to social contract to institute a civil society ruled by a civil government whose sole legitimate aim is to permit the external autonomy of its members to be concurrently maintained.[68] The legal order that results is thus nothing but the regulative system legislating the coexistence of each person's volition with that of every other.[69] This means that civil justice has no other content than assuring the compatibility of individual actions under general rules. Consequently, all reference to the particulars of need and its satisfaction must fall outside the workings of justice. Although public authority must insure that individuals survive and have their property respected, any other dimensions of economic activity are irrelevant to civil affairs.

Kant seizes upon this conclusion and spells out just how it follows from the justice inherent in liberal theory. In the introduction to the *Critique of Judgment*,[70] he hands down the full and final verdict: Economics, whether of the household, agriculture, or the state, cannot be reckoned a normative science. Unlike practical philosophy with its categorical imperative and corollary duties, all these forms of economics contain only hypothetical rules of skill for bringing about an effect that is possible according to natural concepts of causality. Since such concepts belong to the theoretical philosophy of nature, these technical rules are mere corollaries of natural science. Economic principles thus have no place in the special science of ethics, for they fall among the laws of what is and can be produced according to causal necessity, rather than among the laws of what ought to be, as determined through the laws of freedom. With justice lying in the lawful coexistence of individual willings, occupation with need has no direct connection to the normative relations between free persons, but only involves the bond of an individual's empirically conditioned biological and psychological being with the mechanism of external nature. Since this leaves economic activity an essentially technical process, where the individual employs an understanding of causal rules to fashion natural objects for the sake of satisfying some psychologically determined desire, the economy cannot figure within the Kingdom of Ends. Although there may well be hypothetical imperatives mandating how particular economic measures will lead to certain results, there can be no question of any categorical imperatives making the pursuit of some economic aim a matter of duty. Indeed, given the technical character of production and the psychological necessity of need, no economic act could possibly be ascribed any ethical validity in itself. On the contrary, labor, Kant remarks, is inherently unpleasant and only worth undertaking on account of the end in view furnishing its wage.[71]

If this result leaves the liberal approach with little more to say concerning the normative status of economic activity, it does provide the formal basis for economics to develop as a modern "social" science, constructing empirically verifiable models for the technical allocation and use of scarce resources in relation to psychologically determined needs. Max Weber gives perhaps the classic, most bare and honest statement of this relegation of economics to a descriptive discipline. Excluding the theory of justice from social science proper, he restricts talk of economic action to the value-free context where the satisfaction of a need takes place as a technical undertaking predicated upon an agent's personal estimation that satisfying the need requires doing something making use of relatively *scarce* resources.[72] Although such positive science has all too often overstepped its proper bounds by illicitly assuming a priori principles of desire and need, as famously the case in marginal utility theory, its economics has provided the logical counterpart and modern sequel to the liberal exclusion of the economy from the preeminent affairs of justice.

In securing this legacy, liberal theory joins praxis thought in at least exhibiting the virtue of internal consistency when depriving economic activity of any independent normativity. Since both approaches arrive at this verdict by remaining true to their own conception of justice, it can be expected that any attempt to conceive an intrinsically just economy with principles borrowed from praxis or liberal theory will suffer from category confusion. Be this as it may, just such a fatal course has been followed by the political economists, Fichte, Rawls, and Marx. All in their own way illustrate the basic inconsistency characterizing and undermining the unsystematic conceptions of prescriptive economics. In order to clarify how the just economy should be conceived, it is first necessary to unmask their failings.

2

Unsystematic Ethical Conceptions of the Economy

Political Economy

Political economy presents perhaps the first sustained attempt to conceive the economy as a sphere of justice. As classically represented by Adam Smith, political economy advances the wealth of nations as an independent normative domain, whose economic system is what separates genuine civilized society from the brute struggle for survival of savages.[1] Granting the economy a worth of its own, political economy turns to analyze an economic order freed from domestic confines and direct political regulation. What it discovers is a market economy driven by laws of its own making that are the unintended result of the self-seeking of individual commodity owners. They engage in market activity simply to satisfy their particular needs, yet they end up establishing an economic system reproducing its own relations according to laws that operate without being expressly willed by anyone.

It is not merely the economic developments of their day that lead the political economists to direct their novel science at a market economy. With a market system, economic relations are disembedded from other cultural and institutional structures, allowing the economy to stand as an independent object determined in its own right. Once markets prevail, individuals cease to have their livelihood ordered by kinship relations, local custom, legal compulsion, religious mandate, political decree, or supernatural omen. Instead, participants in a market economy interact from strictly economic motives of need and enrichment, following wittingly or not laws of supply and demand endemic to the market's own self-regulating mechanism. Dependent upon little

more than respect for property and contract, requiring no other motivation than fear of destitution and desire for gain, the market system
affords economic relations a motivationally distinct, institutionally
discrete character, allowing the economy to order itself independently
of any familial, political, religious or other noneconomic factors.[2] By
so providing economic relations a radically disembedded reality, the
market system is particularly suited to be the object of an independent
economic science.

The significance of the market's unintended lawfulness

Of equal significance for political economy's development as a distinct
discipline with normative concerns of its own is the unintended law-
fulness of market activity. In the first place, it allows economic laws
to have an objective character, which would be lacking if the laws of
the economy were produced as a result of a conscious decision to order
production according to some particular plan. If economic relations
were governed in this purely technical manner, there would be no laws
inherent in economic activity, nor any possibility of an economic science. Instead, there would be as many economic laws are there were
economic planners with different schemes. By the same token, if economic activity represented merely a habitual pattern of customary
behavior, there could be no general economic science, but only particular descriptions of historical economic arrangements, each relative
to the culture of which it is a part. Only because economic laws are
not matters of technical choice, expressly willed by agents, nor historical artifacts of custom, but unintended results of any all-sided effort
to satisfy personally chosen needs, can the economy have a lawful nature of its own deserving separate study.[3] Hence, it is no accident of
history that the economic order political economy addresses is a market
system of commodity relations.

   Further, insofar as political economy views the economy as an
independent domain, resting upon its own nature, it conceives the laws
of the market system as laws of reproduction, whereby the economy
sustains itself through its own workings. Thus it is only to be expected
that political economists will advance the principle of laissez-faire as
a means for preserving the economic order, especially given the normative standing they grant the market economy.[4]

   Finally, because the laws of such an economy are realized by a
conventional activity that aims not at them, but at particular satisfactions, they are fundamentally different from moral or political laws,
which both can only be made actual when agents make them their

goal.[5] Hence, if the economy conforming to such laws has normative validity, it must be on very different terms than moral action and political engagement, whose performance depends upon agents consciously aiming at the laws they implement. Accordingly, the affirmative value that political economy locates in the market economy should involve a justice sui generis, involving something other than an application of principles originating in other normative domains. On all these counts, the laws of the market warrant treatment by a new theory irreducible to either a natural, moral, or merely political science, a theory to which political economy aspires by standing on its own and addressing an independent subject matter.

The equivocation of political economy

Nonetheless, when political economy makes its novel effort to conceive the workings of the economy, it bases its presumably normative findings upon "natural" relations. This is not entirely surprising given the unique character of a market economy. Since the market has a nature of its own, independent of technical plans and noneconomic institutions, natural relations readily suggest themselves as appropriate means for distinguishing the inherent character of the market economy from the accidents of historical convention.

However, political economy's appeal to nature injects a fatal ambiguity. It may be that a market economy is the only economic order that can be an object of an independent economic science. Further, it may be that market relations have, subject to proper background institutions, a special normative validity. In these respects, the laws of the market would have a descriptive universality for the object of economic science, as well as a prescriptive universality. Nevertheless, neither of these universalities entails that market relations are universally given by nature, such that if men are left to their own private devices, free of political interference, they will automatically engage in the economic activities specific to markets. By treating market relations as natural in this sense, political economy attaches the feature of given necessity to their scientific and ethical universality.

This rooting of commodity relations in natural necessity clashes with the conventional character of the market and undermines whatever normative character it might have. Commodity relations may have a fundamental order given for all time, yet still be products of convention that come into existence only in the particular times and places where men voluntary enact them instead of some different economic arrangement. By treating market relations as products of natural necessity, political economy excludes this aspect of their conventional character, as well as the elements of freedom and responsibility which could bring markets within the field of justice.

In taking this route, political economy conceives the nonconventional character of market activity to reside either in natural factors given prior to the interactions they determine or in the agency of a freely choosing, self-seeking individual defined independently of all social engagement. In the first instance, political economy effectively reverts to the praxis framework of privileged givens, without recognizing that this excludes the particular occupations satisfying need from the domain of justice. In the second case, political economy appeals to the free person of social contract theory, without realizing that economic relations thereby get reduced to monological affairs of technique whose only worth can lie in their harmony with the property rights of individuals. Either way, political economy falls into the sorry confusion of giving an incipiently asocial, normatively neutral characterization[6] to its otherwise eminently civilizing subject matter.[7]

This is true even though political economy is quite emphatic in situating the economy within a civil society. Selecting that context is not enough to guarantee the economy a justice of its own, for what political economy envisions as civil society is an association whose economic relations are not only natural and monological, but as political as their moniker would suggest. Political economy ends up conceiving a naturally determined "political" economy because the civil society it adopts is ultimately the same construct at which liberal theory arrived. According to the liberal framework, justice lies in a civil association where securing the natural liberty of individuals comprises the common end of society and government. On these terms, society is civil to the degree it provides a community whose members are able to exercise free choice in disposing over property and pursuing their personal interests. What makes this possible is the protective rule of a government whose own civil legitimacy resides in its unalloyed dedication to ensuring the person and property of each civilian. By embracing this natural right model of civil society and its corresponding reduction of government to a civil regime, political economy has good reason to name the economic order a "political" one. Here the society to which the economy belongs revolves around the same pursuit of particular interests whose realization provides government with its sole legitimating aim. Hence, the economy is all at once natural, civil, and political. Whereas the civil society containing the economy is defined by the monological liberty all individuals possess by nature, politics has no other end than safeguarding the same liberty that is at play in the civil market.

Although this conflation of the social and political dimensions obscures in what sense economic relations are to have an independent justice, the normative validity of the political economy is directly called into question by the very shape its own commerce and industry assumes as part and parcel of liberal civil society. Insofar as the members of civil society labor and trade in function of their natural liberty to choose their ends as they will, their economic endeavor is cast in the same natural and monological mold that typifies the civil order of liberal thought. However, whereas the classical liberal theorists were consistent enough to avoid all talk of any specifically economic justice, political economists are still intent in treating the economy as a civilizing order in its own right.

There is no more classic example of this equivocal pursuit than the political economy of Adam Smith. However persistently Smith seeks to chart the economy that makes society civil, again and again he subverts his own efforts by rooting economic relations in functions of human metabolism and the technical mastery of nature.

Early on in *The Wealth of Nations*, Smith draws attention to the civil dimension of the market economy by identifying its system of needy interdependence as the very aspect of civilized society distinguishing it from the natural state of savages, where life, to paraphrase Hobbes, is nasty, brutish, and short.[8] In quick succession, Smith points to the division of labor, the market, and the corresponding accumulation of stock as key factors raising civil association above the bare subsistence life of the wilds.[9] With their emergence, the satisfaction of need no longer proceeds as a solitary affair of the individual and nature, outside the realm of justice. Once labor gets specialized, goods become universally possessed by buyers and sellers, and means of production are amassed in private hands, consumption can only be achieved through a socially entwined work and exchange, where civil relations of person and property are duly honored.[10]

Nevertheless, when Smith proceeds to specify these basic features of the reputedly civil political economy, he reverts to natural and monological factors equally at hand among the uncivilized.

To begin with, he presents labor as the technical process of an individual working directly upon objects of nature. Since this leaves labor defined completely independently of convention, Smith readily admits that it is an activity common to both civilian and savage.[11] Accordingly, although society may improve labor's productivity, laboring itself remains something fundamentally given by man's natural condition.[12]

Inasmuch as the division of labor is thereby left to differentiate an asocial activity involving no relations of justice, it can come as little surprise that Smith next derives this division not from any civil mediation, but from the propensity in human nature to truck and barter.[13] Once this natural inclination somehow conjures up the existence of a market, individuals are supposedly led to apply themselves to different complementary occupations.[14]

In line with these natural origins, Smith lets the actual division of labor develop not among workers organized in the social settings of factories and firms, but between private producers. They each first work individually upon nature and only subsequently enter into exchange, trading the portion of their specialized products that they themselves do not consume.[15] Admittedly, Smith does go on to argue that the extent of this division of labor is limited by the extent of the market demand, whose power of exchange occasions it.[16] Nonetheless, the origin of this power in a natural propensity and the concomitant reduction of labor to technique firmly undercut whatever civil determination the market might here have implied.

Thus, just when Smith's division of labor introduces a market whose exchange relations would seem to involve the mutual exercise of freedom in which justice enters in, he subordinates them to a labor theory of value that sets prices not according to the agreements of the parties to exchange, but in line with the labor expended in the commodities' production. Since Smith conceives his labor theory of value in terms of the ability of private producers to command each other's embodied labor, where the labor in question is a technically defined toil mandated by the natural necessity of human metabolism, it leaves the presumably social category of exchange value incongruously strapped to a naturally conditioned principle.[17]

This anomaly takes an even sharper form when Smith turns to capital, whose accumulated stock ceaselessly challenges all natural limits to the expansion of wealth. As eager as Smith is to recognize capital's civil role as chief conventional mainstay of civilized society, he appeals once more to his scheme of private producers to provide an account. Capital, he explains, arises from the fact that the private producers within the division of labor require a stored-up stock of goods to tide them over until they succeed in exchanging their products with one another.[18] Hence, for all Smith's subsequent analysis of how stock functions as a capital for the employment of a multitude of specialized laborers within a single enterprise,[19] accumulated stock's baptism in the scheme of private producers stamps it with the physical being of a subsistence good, a being whose naturally defined limit contradicts and mystifies its attested social power as capital.

Such is the constant equivocation wracking the political economy so illustriously championed by the *Wealth of Nations*. As insistently as Smith addresses economic phenomena as just relations of a market society, he is ever undermining their civil validity by casting them as outgrowths of normatively neutral natural tendencies and technical operations. In this respect, Smith's difficulties represent an extended play of the categorial inconsistencies that praxis and liberal theories intimated and sought to avoid by leaving the economy at one remove from justice.

Fichte's Contractarian Autarchy

If the travails of political economy indicate the difficulties of adopting a liberal framework to determine the civil character of economic relations, Fichte brings these problems to a head by attempting to derive the just economy directly from social contract principles.

He is led to this endeavor by taking to heart the notion that the contract instituting civil government only really secures the coexistence of free individuals if it inseparably guarantees the life on which everyone's own liberty depends. He reasons that social contract cannot merely aim at protecting the person and property of individuals from injury by others; it must also address the positive task of guaranteeing the assured livelihood of all prospective members of civil society, since otherwise, the insecurity of subsistence will put their liberty in jeopardy.[20] Admittedly, other social contract thinkers were already well aware that the defense of liberty requires insuring that the survival needs of individuals be met[21] and Kant even had suggested that a lack of economic independence deprives an individual of the autonomy prerequisite for active as opposed to passive citizenship.[22] Yet Fichte goes one step further by presuming that the achievement of this goal entails subsuming all economic relations under public civil control.

In the *Grundlage des Naturrechts* and *Der geschlossene Handelstaat*, Fichte accordingly constructs a contractarian state that provides the necessary conditions for the realization of liberty by ordering within itself a self-sufficient economy.[23] Here civil society is inaugurated through a contract whose parties mutually assume not only the rights and duties of property owners and legal subjects, but the further prerogatives and obligations that entitle them to satisfy their needs while fulfilling their duty to join particular classes, in which they exercise specific occupations under the unifying governance of public authority.[24] By virtue of this covenant, civil society incorporates an economic dimension where the relations between individuals are ordered to insure a harmonious satisfaction of everyone's personal need.[25]

To this end, the exercise of liberty is sanctioned provided it promotes the livelihood of all. Hence property enjoys legal protection only as an object of utility that contributes to the livelihood of its owner without compromising that of others. What makes this possible is the subordination of property to public laws regulating exchange and distribution.[26]

These have effect, as Fichte elaborately details, by having civil government legally prescribe and insure all satisfactions of personal need. Through public legislation, each person enjoys the guaranteed right to live from his labor while being legally required to labor in order to live.[27] Whereas the social contract already defined and legitimated the different professions through its covenant,[28] civil government now enforces their organic integration by mandating a comprehensive system of exchanges. This system guarantees producers raw materials, sustenance during production, and a market for their products while legally obligating them to produce and sell their goods as public authority sees fit.[29]

As Fichte emphasizes in *Der geschlossene Handelstaat*, this regulation involves not only fixing the value of money and setting all prices and production levels, but ultimately sealing off the economy's entire mechanism of planned interdependence from the external influence of indiscriminate foreign commerce.[30] Only with this achievement of independent autarchy, can civil government secure the full economic self-sufficiency that allegedly is needed to realize the liberty of its members.[31]

Although Fichte believes he has hereby brought liberal theory to a successful conclusion, his entire conception of the just economy remains hanging on very precarious assumptions. For all the ingenuity of his constructions, Fichte's efforts are all cast in doubt by his guiding premise that the maintenance of life is not only necessary for the coexistence of free persons, but an aim whose fulfillment absorbs all economic activity. Admittedly, survival is a precondition of the exercise of liberty, and economic activities of labor and exchange can provide subsistence. However, insuring the survival of individuals is a very different matter from meeting the conventional needs and standard of living fostered by the market and its division of labor. Satisfying these artificial wants is not a necessary prerequisite for realizing the naturally defined liberty of property owners. So long as they are alive, they can dispose over the property they own, regardless of their level of wealth and the availability of luxuries in the market. Conversely, if economic activities involve a freedom irreducible to the liberty of property owners, it is unclear why social contract should enlist it under the banner of civil society. In order for the satisfaction of conventional needs to become a matter of justice, some further principles must be introduced.

If, however, all economic relations are publicly restricted to serving survival needs, Fichte's lot is no better. In that case, the economy has no justice of its own, but only warrants indirect salute as a means to life, good, bad, or indifferent.

Fichte entirely ignores these problems in constructing his contractarian autarchy. As a result, his effort testifies once more to the dilemma of conceiving the just economy with the natural principles of liberal thought.

Rawls

Like Fichte, John Rawls employs social contract notions to determine the outline of economic justice. Although Rawls remains committed to the basic strategy of liberal theory, he seeks to eliminate the formality and metaphysical character for which contract principles have been criticized and recast them so as to determine the basic social and political structures of justice.

To this end, Rawls reconstrues the procedure of social contract in terms of an original position in which individuals are presumed to be motivated by rational self-interest, yet ignorant of the particulars of their natural endowments and given social position. Rawls proposes that under these restraints, whatever principles these individuals agree to abide by will comprise the fundamental norms of justice, which can then be applied to determine what social and political institutions should be.

To determine the guidelines of a just economy, Rawls's argument thus proceeds in two basic stages: the first determining what principles will be chosen in the original position by self-interested individuals ignorant of their given particular advantages and disadvantages, the second determining how social and political institutions must be constructed in order to conform to the chosen principles of justice. Accordingly, Rawls's conclusions can be evaluated by considering three questions: 1) Is his move to the original position warranted? 2) Are the inhabitants of the original position compelled to agree to the principles of justice that Rawls presents? and 3) Do these principles prescribe the social and political institutions that Rawls claims comprise the basic structure of a well-ordered society?

Dilemmas in justifying the original position

For our present purpose of judging the coherence of Rawls's prescriptions for the just economy, all that need be considered are the second and third questions, focusing their answers upon whether the original position mandates principles specifying the relations of economic justice to which Rawls subscribes. Nevertheless, it is worth briefly noting how Rawls's move to the original position suffers from the same dilemma of justification afflicting all versions of social contract theory as well as all procedural theories of ethics.

By embracing the constraints of the original position while giving its choice procedure the exclusive privilege of determining norms of justice, Rawls must avoid injecting into the original position any antecedently given normative terms. If any entitlements, rights and duties, notions of the good, or any other ethical precepts were to enter in in determining the choice procedure of the original position, the latters' privileged primacy as the exclusive source of the principles of justice would be defeated. For this reason, Rawls goes to pains to limit the bases of choice in the original position to the putatively normatively neutral terms of rational self-interest, where what is at stake is the purely technical matter of deciding the means for achieving whatever ends are given by self-interest. Any ethical guidelines prescribing what ends should be aimed at or proscribing what means should not be adopted are specifically excluded.

Granted that his whole approach requires such measures, two problems remain. First, although the appeal to a choice procedure based on considerations of rational self-interest might seem to eliminate ethical presuppositions, the restraints imposed by the veil of ignorance are not themselves the result of any calculations of self-interest. Rather, they rest upon an antecedent commitment to fairness and equality that requires preventing individuals from using knowledge of their own natural and social assets to establish rules favoring their own particular position. To the extent that this predetermines the original position according to independently given ethical norms, it robs the original position of its archimedean status as the privileged source of a pure procedural justice. Any principles that are decided in the original position are therefore secondary to the unargued notions of justice already defining its choice procedure.

Second, even if the choice procedure of the original position were somehow defined independently of any ethical assumptions, what grants it its exclusive privilege to determine the principles of justice? Why should any common agreements based on rational self-interest have any ethical primacy? By its very character as the source of ethical principles, the choice procedure of the original position cannot already enjoy legitimacy by conforming to any antecedently given norms. Since it establishes a pure procedural system of justice where what is right is what is in conformity with principles decided by its choice procedure, the move to the original position can neither be justified by itself, which would beg the question, nor by appeal to any other principles, which would contradict its privileged role. This problem is generic to any social contract theory, and more generally to any procedural theory of justice. The moment appeal is made to some privileged determiner of ethical norms, be that determiner characterized as free and equal individuals in a state of nature, noumenal selves, or some special procedure of choice, neither the characterization nor exclusive status of that determiner can be coherently justified on any ethical terms. Because the move to a privileged determiner renders normative validity equivalent to being determined by that determiner, the chosen determiner simply cannot enjoy the very validity it grounds since its own character is given antecedently to its act of determination. This logical problem is what Robert Nozick refers to in pointing out how any theory which bases norms on a privileged process starts out with something that is not itself justified by being the outcome of that process.[32] Although Nozick fails to recognize how this problem applies to liberal principles in general, we shall see when we turn to Hegel's reconstruction of the theory of justice how the solution to this dilemma requires abandoning the liberal framework.

Although Rawls does not dwell on these difficulties, he does appropriately qualify his theory as merely a theory of justice, which serves to show how our considered judgments about social and political justice can be arrived at through a procedure fitting our moral assumptions. Hence, on Rawls's own terms, the unjustifiability of his move to the original position is not so much a bone of contention as is the consistency of what follows from that move.

Rawls's conception of economic justice

Whatever be the legitimacy of the original position, the two principles of justice that Rawls claims are there agreed upon provide the basis for his structuring a just economy. The first principle, that of equal liberty, mandates that every person has an equal right to the most extensive system of equal basic liberties compatible with a like system of liberty for all.[33] These basic liberties consist in the liberties of equal citizenship, including political liberty, freedom of speech and assembly, liberty of conscience and freedom of thought, freedom of person along with the right to hold personal property, and freedom from arbitrary arrest and seizure as defined by the concept of the rule of law.[34] The second principle, the so-called difference principle, stipulates that social and economic inequalities be arranged to the greatest benefit of all, subject to the proviso of accruing to posts to which all have equal access. In order to remove ambiguity from the notions of the benefit of all and equal access,[35] Rawls sees fit to reformulate the difference principle so that it mandates that social and economic inequalities be ordered to the greatest benefit of the least advantaged, consistent with a just savings principle taking into account the welfare of the least advantaged in future generations, while being attached to offices and positions open to all under conditions of fair equal opportunity.[36]

Although Rawls derives these principles from the choice procedure of the original position, which is to determine how institutions should be ordered in abstraction from given institutional forms, he grants that they presuppose and reflect a division of basic social structure into political institutions that define and secure the equal liberties of citizenship and social institutions that specify and establish social and economic inequalities.[37] Thus, although Rawls grants the first principle of equal liberty a priority over the difference principle, he conceives economic justice to hinge primarily upon the second principle of justice. Hence, when Rawls endeavors to illustrate how the principles of justice are able to determine institutions as they should be, he begins by applying the first principle to political arrangements, on whose basis he then turns to social institutions to which he applies the difference principle, granting priority to its component of equal opportunity.

The institutional order that results from these applications is a constitutional democracy with a regulated market economy. Although this signifies that such a regime comprises a well-ordered just society, Rawls refrains from maintaining that it is the only social and political arrangement conforming to the two principles of justice. He is rather content to have its example demonstrate that his principles of justice are not formal, but define a workable institutional model that reasonably approximates and extends our independently given considered judgments.[38] However, if his theory of justice is to escape the charge of formalism, it is not sufficient that there be a plurality of workable political and social orders that can conform to the principles of justice, let alone that at least one of these happens to accord with commonly held opinions. It must be shown that the principles of justice define some institutional arrangements that any state and society must have to qualify as just, regardless of what views may currently predominate. In particular, if Rawls's theory of justice is to provide any positive notion of economic justice, the principles of justice must necessitate some particular set of economic relations, even if they leave other aspects of the economy a matter of indifference as regards justice. The question, then, is what features of Rawls's model of a well-ordered society are really required by the two principles of justice?

Given Rawls's procedural conception, this question is answered by employing further choice procedures to decide how the principles of justice are applied. Due to the lexical priority of the principle of equal liberty over the difference principle and the different institutional spheres to which each principle supposedly applies, these choice procedures follow a stage sequence whose participants face progressively more limited fields of decision, within which progressively more information must be known and applied.

In the first stage following the selection of the two principles of justice the rationally self-interested participants in the original position move to a constitutional convention where they choose a constitution determining a just political process for implementing the principles they have already agreed upon. Although the establishment of the two principles of justice would seem to supplant any need to rely upon the calculations of rational self-interest, let alone, any restraints upon its workings, Rawls maintains that here the parties involved still choose under a veil of ignorance regarding their own social positions, although now they are permitted to be cognizant of both the principles of social theory and the general facts of their society.[39] The latter knowledge is deemed necessary, insofar as the problem at hand consists in formulating an institutional scheme for applying the principles of justice.

Significantly, Rawls considers the first principle of equal liberty to be the primary standard for the constitutional convention, leaving the difference principle for application at the legislative stage that follows.[40] Hence, he conceives the chosen constitution to require in its statutes the political institutions for realizing the principle of equal liberty, but not the political and social institutions for ensuring implementation of the difference principle. Although Rawls emphasizes how no political order can provide a pure procedural justice preventing unjust laws from being enacted, this is no reason for leaving application of the difference principle to legislative prerogative, unconstrained by any constitutional commitment. Nor is the lexical priority of the principle of equal liberty any reason for leaving the difference principle out of constitutional law, since that priority could be specified by constitutional statute. If the difference principle warrants selection in the original position, then a just constitution should enshrine its provisos in its statutes on pain of leaving social justice at the mercy of the private deliberations of conscience. Of course, taking such steps is only possible if the difference principle requires some specific social and economic arrangements that could be formulated by statute and politically enforced.

Since it is at the legislative stage that Rawls first brings in the difference principle, it is there that we must turn. Given the priority of the principle of liberty, institutionally enshrined in its exclusive hold upon constitutional law, the legislative application of the difference principle will consist in legally dictating that social and economic policies aim at maximizing the long-term expectations of the least advantaged in present and future generations, while ensuring fair equality of opportunity and equal liberties.[41] Rawls maintains that in order to carry out this application, the veil of ignorance must be relaxed to allow access to the full range of general economic and social facts.[42]

By treating such facts as something given and apprehended independently of justice, Rawls's construction of the legislative stage seems to relegate social and economic structure to normatively neutral factors of the human condition while leaving justice a set of formal principles incapable of entailing any particular institutional arrangements on their own. General economic and social facts only warrant consideration in applying the principles of justice when those principles and the constitution they determmine do not independently mandate a specific social order and economy, and when the legal prescription of social and economic institutions is restrained by some given nature of economy and society which no conventional arrangement can countermand. On both counts, a set of social and economic relations are presupposed that provide a normatively neutral material without which social and economic justice is empty. Admittedly, this does not guarantee that Rawls's principles of justice are so formal that no economic arrangement can have any indwelling normativity. However, it does raise suspicion that the difference principle leaves economic affairs with no more inherent justice than any other practice involving the distribution of "benefits."

Be this as it may, Rawls maintains that the choice of economic institutions is of special significance for the human good because an economic system not only provides a device for satisfying existing needs, but creates future wants that affect what kind of person its members will be.[43]

On Rawls's own terms, what decides the issue is whether rational legislators, constrained by a just constitution determining proper political procedures and conscientiously following the principles of justice, would agree upon any particular economic order.[44] Since an economic system regulates what is produced and by what means, as well as how these products are distributed and how much wealth is devoted to saving and the provision of public goods, what is at stake is determining how all these matters should be arranged to conform to the principles of justice.[45]

Although Rawls devotes most of his discussion to investigating how a private market economy should be ordered, he is more broadly concerned with showing how it and a socialist economy can both be organized in accord with justice. In doing so, he argues that their defining differences do not preclude either one from satisfying the principles of justice, nor, for that matter, guarantee that either one is just without being subject to external restraints.

Rawls points to two fundamental factors that distinguish private enterprise and socialist economies: the degree of public ownership of the means of production and the role of markets in allocating resources and distributing income. Under socialism, a larger proportion of the means of production are publicly owned,[46] whereas markets have a more restricted scope, with the prices of goods produced by public enterprises accruing to the state and hence playing no direct role in distributing personal income.[47]

Rawls is quick to point out that the greater public ownership of the means of production under socialism has no necessary connection to the proportion of social resources devoted to public goods. Public goods, such as defense of the nation, are marked by an indivisibility and publicness lacking in goods for personal consumption. For this reason, public goods cannot be provided for through the market, which is limited to satisfying the differing particular needs of its participants. Although production for market need may on occasion provide infrastructures to everyone's advantage, there is a divergence between private and social accounting that market forces do not remedy by themselves. Hence, political legislation is necessary to insure that public goods are sufficiently furnished.[48] This is true, regardless of whether socialism or free enterprise prevails. Predominant public ownership of the means of production does not guarantee that public enterprises direct their resources to finance adequate public goods, nor need the political legislation required to mandate their financing rely on the public rather than the private sector for producing those public goods.[49]

Given these common liabilities of free enterprise and socialism, why not eliminate all independent economic order and subject production and consumption to direct legislative control without any intervening market institutions, be they privately or publicly owned? And why not do so without any inequality of income? For if the economy has no autonomous normative value so that production and distribution can be handled entirely by legislative fiat, why would inequalities be required to maximize the position of the most disadvantaged? In other words, does the difference principle's legitimation of social inequality presuppose markets as a condition for differences in income being necessary for the benefit of the most disadvantaged,[50] and if so, are markets themselves dispensable as far as justice is concerned?

The difference principle is only applicable if society is so arranged as to allow incentives to channel resources and employment. Yet, for incentives to play that role, members of society must enjoy the freedom to choose their occupation and employ their other assets through voluntarily entered exchange agreements, as well as be in need of payment in exchange for their labor and other assets. A market provides precisely the institutional framework necessary for meeting these requirements. However, if markets are a precondition for the viability of the difference principle, the choice procedure of the original position becomes relative to a particular institutional arrangement and loses its Archimedean status as the privileged determiner of the principles of a just society. Instead of reigning over the contingent circumstances of a market economy, Rawls's distributive principle becomes a captive instrument of market inequity.[51] Indeed, Rawls admits that his two principles of justice already reflect an institutional division in the basic structure of society, namely that between social and political institutions. However, Rawls maintains that this institutional division is so general as to apply to all social formations, leaving the original position unbiased toward any particular institutional circumstance. Although it might be questioned whether the division of social and political spheres is as universal a feature of the human condition as Rawls maintains, markets can hardly count as indispensable for every possible society. Hence, the ethical value of markets must be established, and if the difference principle presupposes markets, then the justification of markets must lie in more than their possible conformity to that principle. Given the primacy of Rawls's two principles of justice, it would seem that Rawls must turn to his principle of equal liberty to support his acceptance of markets, and by extention, to buttress his advocacy of the difference principle. Although this line of argument would seem to recast the reckoning of the original position, it would at least conform to the lexical priority of the principle of liberty by having the difference principle depend upon an institutional consequence of the former.

As we have already noted, Rawls condones markets as institutions that can be arranged to conform to the principles of justice under either predominantly private or public ownership of the means of production. Given the privileged role of rational self-interest and formal equality in the original position, a private market economy might seem particularly suited for adoption at the legislative stage. Rawls does grant that an ideal market embodying the classical assumptions for perfect competition represents a perfect procedure with regard to efficiency, in that its free play of rational self-interest ends up securing the maximum satisfaction of all.[52] Nevertheless, this cannot alone justify market relations from the point of view of procedural justice. The members of an ideal market may stand in a formal equality and produce wealth more efficiently than under any other arrangement, but this does not mean that it ensures the stability of just institutions and fair equal opportunity, or that its prevailing inequalities of earnings maximize the position of the least well off. Perfect competition may channel resources so as to achieve optimum productivity and growth throughout the economy, but wealth may still be distributed among individuals to the increasing disadvantage of some and the privileged betterment of others, as well as to the detriment of future generations and the neglect of current public needs. Hence, even if conditions of perfect competition could be sustained, which would require continual public intervention to restrict the monopoly tendencies endemic to market activity, the ideal market would not warrant choosing by Rawls's ideal legislators.

What Rawls claims they would instead select is a largely market economy organized on either private enterprise or socialist lines, wherein private and/or public enterprises are subject to a public regulation channeling investment and redistributing income to finance necessary public institutions, provide for fair equal opportunity, maximize the economic position of the poor, and leave a fair material heritage for future generations. Still, the question remains, why should markets be selected at all?

One reason Rawls offers is that all regimes employ markets to distribute consumption goods because any other procedure is administratively cumbersome.[53] Rawls proceeds to point out that in a free market system, market demand also guides the output of commodities in respect to both kind and quantity, whereas under socialism, the direction of production tends to be more often determined by planning decisions, either autocratically or collectively made.[54] Why it is any less cumbersome to determine production without markets is something Rawls fails to explain. More importantly, he fails to show why the greater ease in using markets to regulate consumption is a sufficient reason from the point of view of justice for organizing distribution in this way.

Rawls goes on to observe that both private property and socialist systems normally maintain a labor market, where free choice of occupation and place of work is exercised.[55] Together with the ubiquitous role of markets in distributing consumption goods, this demonstrates that there is no essential tie between private ownership of the instruments of production and the presence of free markets. Hence, Rawls points out, the superiority of a private market economy cannot be argued by maintaining that competitive prices under normal conditions are just.[56] Nor, it might be added, can market arrangements of any sort be justified by appeal to the fairness of competitive prices, when, as Rawls himself has suggested, perfect or imperfect competition cannot be counted on to provide for public goods, fair investment for future generations, fair equal opportunity, or maximization of the welfare of the least fortunate members of society.

Nevertheless, Rawls's mention of labor markets is of special significance, for it brings to the fore what Rawls identifies as the basic advantage of a market system. This advantage lies in the market's consistency with equal liberties and fair equality of opportunity, given proper regulation by the requisite background institutions.[57] That is, markets are normatively valid social institutions because they conform to the first principle of justice, the principle of equal liberty. Although every market transaction might be said to involve an exercise of equal liberty and equal opportunity by the parties to exchange, Rawls mentions two specific ways in which a market system realizes equal liberty and fair equal opportunity. First, in virtue of labor markets, individuals have free choice of careers and occupations. Second, a market system, however its firms be owned and managed, decentralizes economic power.[58]

That these features of market interaction accord with the first principle of justice depends on whether the prerogatives they involve correspond to the liberty that principle advances. On the other hand, that such accordance makes preservation of markets a normative requirement depends on whether an economy lacking markets automatically provides its members a lesser field of that same liberty.

As we have seen, Rawls identifies the freedom prescribed by the principle of equal liberty, he describes it in terms of a set of basic liberties, consisting in the liberties of equal citizenship, including political liberty, freedom of speech and assembly, liberty of conscience and freedom of thought, freedom of person and the prerogatives of property ownership, and freedom from arbitrary arrest and seizure in accord with rule by law.[59] These liberties are all specific to political and property relations, even though Rawls introduces them well before the stage of constitution making where political rights and duties are to be determined. Hence, it is questionable whether market freedom accords with any one of them, with the possible exception of the rights of ownership. Property entitlements do operate within commodity relations, but they do not prescribe any norms regarding how wealth and occupations should be distributed over and beyond respect for each commodity owner's freedom to dispose of their property through freely entered exchanges. Although this entails ensuring that each person have sufficient means to survive, it does not involve altering the inequalities of wealth separating rich and poor that go beyond means of subsistence, nor does it mandate how economic functions should be performed or how centralized management decisions should be. Further, if property entitlements are subject to restriction in order to allow other, lexically prior freedoms to be exercised, such as political freedom, it is by no means self-evident that the economy need be organized in terms of markets where labor is freely bought and sold and economic decisions are independently made by each competing firm.

The privileged legitimacy of markets is no more evident if, on the other hand, the liberty properly at stake in the first principle of justice is not institutionally specific, but simply the liberty of choice at hand in the original position. If every exercise of choice stands on a par from a normative point of view, it might well be questioned whether markets provide more liberty than a nonmarket economy where democratic assemblies determine production and consumption. Rawls himself calls for a democratically decided government regulation of the market economy as a necessary remedy to the injustice of unshackled free enterprise. Yet when he questions whether a comprehensive direct planning of economic affairs is admissible, he merely acknowledges that there is no necessity for it[60] and that it is improbable that bureaucratic control of economic activity would be more just on balance than control involving prices.[61] Why a democratically supervised bureaucratic management of the economy would likely be more unjust than a regulated market system is something Rawls simply does not address. That there ought to be space for market freedom remains a claim in need of further argument.

As for fair equal opportunity, Rawls distinguishes it from formal equal opportunity to the extent that it involves affording all individuals the actual means they need for exercising their liberties on an equal footing. Rawls characterizes this in terms of furnishing individuals equal access to education and culture, equal chances in economic activities and free choice of occupation.[62] Leaving aside whether fair as opposed to formal equal opportunity is required by the contractual argument, it bears asking whether equal chances in economic activities depend upon markets or whether fair equal opportunity requires free choice of occupation, let alone a system where individuals choose their vocation by selling their labor power. An arrangement where centralized or decentralized democratic assemblies collectively assign jobs and manage production and consumption is but one example of how individuals could actually have equal opportunity to determine the economic order without markets and without deciding their employment by personal choice. Promoting fair equal opportunity in general is one thing, advancing the personal autonomy specific to market participation is another.

By the same token, there is room to doubt Rawls's claim that only market arrangements permit the problem of distribution to be handled as a case of pure procedural justice.[63] In terms of his own procedural framework, the question of ordering the economy is a matter for the legislative stage, where it is the difference principle rather than the simple claims of liberty that presumably determines economic and social policy. Although, as we have seen, the difference principle can hardly be applied without markets, for just this very reason, their legitimation must depend upon the principle of liberty, whose exclusive tie to market activity is not above suspicion.

Rawls does obliquely acknowledge this dependence. In noting how labor markets are consistent with the principle of liberty, he observes that without differences in income as arise in a competitive market, a command system of labor inconsistent with liberty is unavoidable.[64] Although this remark might suggest that the need for a command system of labor under conditions of equal incomes derives from utilitarian considerations of efficient allocation of labor, the important point is that the command system violates the freedom of vocation and that exercise of that freedom in labor markets entails unequal incomes. If assignment of occupation without the consent of individuals is at odds with the principle of liberty and a labor market realizing freedom of occupation carries with it inequalities of income, then the priority of liberty mandates both the maintenance of a free labor market and some toleration of unequal incomes. Since incentives require labor markets and income inequalities for their full operation, the condition for applying, if not prescribing the terms of the difference principle lies in the normative validity of labor markets as based upon the principle of liberty. However, if that grounding is suspect, so is the introduction of the difference principle.

These reflections suggest that the application of Rawls's principles of justice to the basic structure of society leaves largely indeterminate what order the economy should have. Nevertheless, Rawls's subsequent discussion of how society must be ordered to achieve distributive justice presupposes the validity and applicability of the two principles of justice, the normativity of markets, and the ability of market systems with either private or public ownership of the means of production to satisfy justice provided they are subject to the proper public regulation. As we shall see in our final chapter, many of Rawls's suggestions for public regulation are, with certain modifications, eminently defensible independently of the contractual argument. Yet, however correct they may be, Rawls ultimately fails to justify them due to the basic problems afflicting his procedural approach. The dilemmas underlying his move to the original position have already been indicated. What remains to be discussed are the problems besetting his derivation of the two principles of justice. It is here in this derivation that one most clearly sees how Rawls must go beyond his own contractual scruples to arrive at the principles by which he seeks to order economic justice.

The ad hoc foundation of Rawls's principles of justice

Rawls has been frequently criticized for deriving his principles of justice from the original position in an illicitly ad hoc fashion. Among the most prominent proponents of such criticism is Robert Nozick, who is of particular note for our discussion since Nozick both embraces the basic strategy of contract theory and directs the brunt of his critique upon Rawls's derivation of the difference principle.[65] Nozick's objection is twofold. On the one hand, he argues that Rawls, despite his claims of generality, slants the original position such that alternate principles are excluded from the outset. On the other hand, Nozick argues that even if one accepts Rawls's description of the original position, there is no necessity for choosing the difference principle. Indeed, Nozick maintains that a consistent contract theory must reject the difference principle as well as any principle of distributive justice that goes beyond insuring the minimum security of person and property. In this respect, Nozick follows the traditional social contract theorists, who all, Hobbes, Locke, Rousseau, and Kant included, restricted distributive justice to guaranteeing that every citizen have the means for subsisting as an autonomous property owner, but not that they enjoy any further social minimum. The philosophical crux of Nozick's critique lies in the claim that the entitled liberty which contract theory champions mandates that the rights of property owners ought to be curtailed only when necessary to secure the very conditions of their respective personhoods. So long as individuals are guaranteed the means of survival and security allowing them to exercise their will, property entitlements are sacrosanct, even if honoring them entails tolerating inequalities in the distribution of property. Any introduction of further principles of distributive justice must therefore rest upon ad hoc assumptions alien to the social contract scheme.

This is the consistent sense of Nozick's formulation of the Lockean proviso, according to which an original acquisition establishes no property entitlement if it worsens the position of others no longer at liberty to use what has been appropriated.[66] As Nozick emphasizes, the "worsening" at issue does not involve more limited opportunities to appropriate or a weakened competitive position. It has a more stringent character, which Nozick rather loosely defines in terms of a deterioration in the base-line situation of others.[67] If Nozick's formulation of the proviso is to cohere with his commitment to the exclusive priority of liberty, "worsening" must refer solely to an undermining of the pre-conditions for the exercise of liberty by others. Otherwise Nozick opens himself to the charge of ad hoc argumentation that he directs against Rawls.

MacIntyre's misinterpretation of the Rawls–Nozick controversy

Before examining whether Nozick's line of argument undermines Rawls's derivation of the difference principle and his derivative approach to economic justice, it is necessary to consider Alasdair Mac-Intyre's claim that Nozick's objections cannot possibly impugn Rawls's theory because Nozick and Rawls argue from entirely incommensurate principles.[68] MacIntyre maintains that Nozick makes primary equality with respect to entitlement whereas Rawls gives precedence to equality with respect to need. Because the difference principle seeks to benefit a worst-off sector defined in terms of present neediness in respect of income, wealth, and other goods, Rawlsian justice addresses current patterns of distribution irrespective of past occurrences. By contrast, Nozick's emphasis upon entitlement lays all importance upon past orig-inal appropriations and subsequent transfers while rendering justice indifferent to current distributions of property.[69] Hence, MacIntyre argues, if Nozick objects to Rawls's difference principle on the grounds that it violates the freedom of property, his objection only begs the question insofar as it takes for granted the primacy of equality with respect to entitlements. By the same token, if Rawls were to object to Nozick's position by claiming that someone in the original position would choose the difference principle over a principle respecting en-titlements, he would be begging the question by assuming the au-thority of the veil of ignorance to the exclusion of Nozick's presumption of inalienable rights. Lacking any common principles of adjudication, neither critique can succeed. Because Rawls's claim for the priority of equality of needs is simply incompatible with Nozick's claim for the priority of equality of entitlements, MacIntyre concludes, there is no way to rationally determine which is more valid.[70]

MacIntyre's conclusion holds true only if Rawls's difference prin-ciple is based upon an appeal to needs that is not derivative of the appeal to liberty that underlies Nozick's principle of entitlement. If, on the contrary, the needs to which Rawls directs distributive justice are themselves introduced in function of the liberty commonly pro-moted by social contract theory, then Nozick's line of critique is not so easily dismissed. In that case, Rawls and Nozick will no longer be making incommensurable arguments and it will be possible to judge whether Rawls's difference principle is consistent with the social contract framework within which he operates.

MacIntyre himself draws attention to a central feature shared by the theories of Rawls and Nozick: Both conceive the just society as if it were entered through the voluntary act of individuals who come together to formulate common laws of justice on the basis of personal interests given prior to and independently of the construction of any moral or social bonds between them.[71] This feature is fundamental both in identifying the common ground on which Rawls and Nozick argue and in singling out the particular commitments that place them within the social contract tradition.

The key presuppositions of pure procedural justice

It might appear that Rawls's guiding notion of pure procedural justice is not a reinterpretation of a particular viewpoint in ethics, but rather a rigorous attempt to exclude particular assumptions and capture the most general features of any attempt to do ethics. In defining the original position and its veil of ignorance, Rawls limits his choice procedure solely by what appear to be the constraints facing any theorist of justice.[72] On the one hand, the parties to the original position are presumed to be rational individuals who will decide the principles of justice without regard for any particular features of themselves or their given society that would make their choice relative to contingent circumstances irrelevant to ethics. On the other hand, the principles they are to choose are presumed to be general, universal in application, publicly recognized, capable of ordering the conflicting claims of moral persons, and final,[73] as would be required for any objective norms that are to govern the conduct of men in society. As Rawls himself maintains,[74] all these features are hardly specific to social contract theory, but seem basic to any engagement in ethical reasoning.

However, this is not all that defines the original position. Rawls adds three key features: 1) that the parties make their choice without any prior knowledge of what they or others may take to be good,[75] 2) that their choice is governed simply by a rational prudence that aims at constructing principles of justice furthering whatever ends they prefer,[76] and 3) that they desire so-called primary goods, which consist in those resources that are necessary to carry out personal ends of any kind.[77] All these assumptions seem innocent enough, for if ethical reasoning is not to take for granted the principles it is to establish, it cannot rely upon any given norms. Hence, the parties to the original position seem to have little else to guide their choice than a concern to forward their ends, whatever they may be. Again, Rawls appears to have identified features basic to any ethical argumentation.

Yet these three constraints upon the original position are not as general as that. Rather, they are assumptions specific to social contract theory, assumptions that rest on a prior ethical commitment that plays a deciding role without ever being coherently justified in its own right. The exclusion of prior reference to particular conceptions of the good is one thing. Reliance on rational prudence is another. The methodological truism that ethical theory cannot presuppose its norms does not mean that calculations of rational self-interest, however constrained, be granted a deciding role in determining principles of justice. Rational prudence only deserves the privileged role Rawls gives it if no ends of conduct can be rationally justified. Then alone can the problem of justice revolve around adjudicating conflicting interpretations of the good, that is, around adjudicating conflicting interests, all of which warrant equal consideration.

The turn to rational prudence is thus based upon the fundamental starting point of liberal theory: The rejection of the teleological approach to justice that presumes that ethics can and must begin by rationally establishing a highest good from which all laws and duties derive. Only if ethical argument is not in a position to consider what ends conduct should aim at, can pure procedural justice make sense. For, given its mandate of specifying a procedure that is just no matter what outcome it has, pure procedural justice enters in solely when there is no independent criterion for the correct outcome of a fair course of action.[78]

Nonetheless, as much as the rejection of teleological ethics makes room for the appeal to rational prudence and its promotion of conciliated interests, it does not make that appeal compelling for ethical inquiry unless a further commitment be made. Namely, liberty must be granted normative validity. Unless the freedom to choose and pursue personal interests has special standing, there is no reason to turn away from teleological values to pure procedural justice, even if the teleological approach be arbitrary. Lacking an accepted justification, the turn to liberty would be just as groundless as obedience to any prescribed end. Hence, Rawls's strategy of allowing the parties in the original position to choose principles of justice on the basis of rational self-interest depends upon both a prior rejection of teleological ends and a prior embrace of liberty as what has sovereign value.

Significantly, this applies equally to Rawls's assumption that the parties to the initial position desire primary goods and choose the principles of justice in line with that desire. If the hold of teleological ends were not already rejected and liberty did not already enjoy primacy, the desire for primary goods would be irrelevant. That desire only makes sense as a guiding motivational factor if the ends of conduct are matters of choice rather than of reason and the equal opportunity of choosing as one wills is what justice aims to promote. In that particular case, where no ends are either prescribed or proscribed and free sway is granted the realization of personal interests, the means for achieving aims of any character is desirable for every agent. Otherwise, those who inquire into the principles of ethics would bracket out their desires until after reason had determined which ends are good, which resources are necessary to realize those aims, and which needs are accordingly rational and deserving of satisfaction.

Consequently, the whole notion of pure procedural justice turns out to be anything but pure. Far from being free of normative assumptions regarding the good, the idea of determining justice through a choice procedure grounded in rational prudence takes for granted the unjustifiability of teleological ends and the equal right to liberty. Needless to say, this has fateful consequences for Rawls's derivation of his principles of justice.

To the extent that the description of the original position is predicated on the two above-mentioned assumptions, any procedural argument for the first principle of equal liberty, on which Rawls's acceptance of markets depends, becomes utterly circular. When, for example, Rawls suggests that the parties in the original situation opt for equal liberty as the best means of insuring that they can fulfill their interests and enjoy the self-respect psychologically needed to achieve ends of any kind, their decision is guided by considerations of rational prudence that only deserve to be heeded if liberty already be acknowledged as the primary value.

Rawls's enlargement of the extension of primary goods

Admittedly, the difference principle does not suffer from the same circularity since it involves more than an assertion of the right to liberty. Still, it too is fundamentally predicated upon the dual assumptions underlying the social contract move to pure procedural justice. This is primarily due to the definition of primary goods, to whose distribution the difference principle refers. As already mentioned, Rawls describes primary goods as the resources necessary for achieving ends of any sort. What makes the distribution of primary goods a concern for justice is the assumed legitimacy of every individual's liberty to realize interests of their own choosing. If the authority of teleological ends is denied and the right to liberty is acknowledged, then the primacy of liberty does entail, as every social contract theorist has acknowledged, that individuals be guaranteed the preconditions for exercising their liberty. Strictly speaking, the right to a fair distribution of primary goods is equivalent to this right to the preconditions of liberty. Given how Rawls has defined primary goods and the role of rational prudence, individuals cannot be entitled to any wider distribution of primary goods, since further adjustments would impinge upon liberty when the preconditions of everyone's liberty are already secured.

Hence, when Rawls advances claims in behalf of individuals' needs for primary goods he is not, as MacIntyre argues, promoting a principle incommensurate with Nozick's advocacy of equality of entitlement. On the contrary, fairness in the distribution of primary goods is entirely derivative of the principle of equal liberty, which essentially conforms to Nozick's appeal to inalienable natural rights. Although the details of Rawls's difference principle may conflict with the specifics of Nozick's account, the problem of justice which the difference principle addresses is common to both. Because primary goods are defined as nothing but the preconditions for exercising rational prudence, or to paraphrase Rawls, as what a rational individual wants no matter what else he wants since they advance a person's ends whatever they may be,[79] Rawls's concern for distributive justice is in principle indistinguishable from what motivates Nozick's reformulation of the Lockean proviso.

Nonetheless, when Rawls describes the fair distribution of primary goods he includes all wealth and income, as if differences in the value of private property holdings are always relevant to the exercise of liberty. This is the pivotal move in Rawls's account of distributive justice, a move that places him close to Fichte, but at odds with the traditional social contract theorists and their contemporary disciple, Nozick. Whether inequalities be arranged to maximize the wealth of the poorest group in society is a secondary issue. What is more decisive is the enlarged extension that Rawls gives primary goods. It provides the basis for Rawls's notion of a just political economy that considers all differences in wealth to be germane to distributive justice.

The question, then, boils down to whether securing the preconditions for exercising rational prudence, that is, for exercising one's liberty to act to achieve ends of one's choosing, in any way requires more than providing for security and the basic means of life. In other words, so long as all individuals have their person and property protected and are guaranteed satisfaction of their subsistence needs, are the preconditions for exercising rational prudence still wanting in any strict sense? Do further differences in the amount and type of personal property have any necessary bearing upon the ability to engage in a liberty that is defined prior to and independently of any particular institutional engagement? This is the problem on which Fichte's contractarian autarchy foundered and it remains a chief stumbling block for Rawls.

If the priority of freedom is to be the foundation for extending distributive justice beyond the requirements of rational agency to the requirements of a fair conventional standard of living, then the freedom in question must have a more determinate content than liberty of choice. This requires advancing beyond the framework of social contract theory to a conception of freedom requiring far wider "goods" for its exercise. As we shall see when we turn to Hegel's theory of justice, the required conception will supersede the naturally defined liberty of the original position with the notion of freedom as interaction. Only then will it become possible to conceive coherently how economic relations can entail entitlements of their own. Although this possibility might seem to be of merely hypothetical interest for the theory of justice, much more is at stake. This is because the conception of freedom that grants economic relations their own right will turn out to solve the problems of foundationalism that plague all other ethical theories.

By holding fast to the liberty underlying social contract theory, while extending justice to the whole of economic affairs, Rawls has left us with many an insight into the problems of inequality besetting economic systems. Yet, however valid some of his solutions may be, they remain in want of a proper justification. Hence, when we later turn to reconsider some of Rawls's proposals for publicly regulating the economy, the perspective of pure procedural justice will fall from view.

3

The Normative Confusions of Marx's Economic Theory

The Young Marx

Whereas Fichte and Rawls commit the error of saddling social contract with the extraneous concerns of conventional livelihood, the young Marx addresses the issue of economic justice with a succession of different notions, all tainted by self-defeating borrowings from praxis and liberal thought.

Alienated labor

In the *1844 Manuscripts*. Marx offers the first of these, his all too celebrated concept of alienated labor. Although this conception is intended to unmask the injustice of a specific social form of production, it takes its point of departure in an uneasy amalgam of technical and social parameters. From the start, Marx rests his analysis on the assumed duality of an act of labor defined in complete indifference to any social context and the social circumstance of the private appropriation of the product of labor. Marx addresses these anomalous features under the rubric of the factually discovered opposition of labor as objectification to labor as alienation,[1] oblivious to the dilemma of conceiving a normatively qualified production process in monological terms.

With the dimension of objectification, Marx reverts to the singular agency underlying liberal theory by advancing labor as an individual act of consciousness upon objectivity. However, instead of accordingly treating labor as a technical process indifferent to justice and the es-

tablishment of freedom, he celebrates it as the primordial self-objec-
tification whereby consciousness first attains autonomous self-awareness by contemplating itself embodied in a world created by its own
act. As Marx would have it, labor's objectification actually constitutes
self-conscious freedom, the substance of all right, by producing nature
as the recognizable work and reality of individual action.[2]

Conceiving how a single ego can posit itself is problematic enough,
as Fichte's absolute idealism can testify. Conceiving how an absolute
self-positing can occur in Marx's concrete terms, is a completely non-
sensical endeavor. To begin with, the engagement of laboring that is
supposed to constitute free self-conscious subjectivity already presumes
the worldly existence of an intentional agent able to labor as well as
an objective world to work upon. Otherwise "labor" would not be a
purposive activity of "objectification," but a purely natural happening.
Further, labor's product can no more constitute the totality of objectivity than contain the creative process of labor, as presumably required for the agent to become self-conscious through labor. Because
the laborer exists beside the product, it can neither be identified with
all objectivity nor with the objectivity of the laborer. Similarly, the
product can hardly contain the creative agency of labor when the laboring act has in fact extinguished itself with its completed work.

Yet even if Marx could viably claim that labor as objectification
is constitutive of self-conscious freedom, his complementary notion of
labor as alienation introduces the insolvable problem of conceiving how
such autonomy can be limited by the social form of appropriation and
transformed into a state of alienation. For there to be any alienated
labor, the fact of capitalist property relations must somehow negate
the worker's unlimited self-affirmation in the labor process at the very
same time that his self-awareness is there maintained. The latter cannot be eliminated, since alienation involves the laborer's recognition
of himself as alienated.

In order to incorporate these contradictory aspects, Marx reduces
the putatively social relations of capitalist production to bonds of force
and domination that somehow still leave the laborer able to reflect
self-consciously upon his alienating predicament. Wishing to tie the
self-consciousness of the individual to his estranged laboring, Marx
begins with the lame notion that the worker enters the employ of capital by selling himself off as a commodity.[3] Because Marx is yet unable
to distinguish labor power from labor, as he would later do in *Capital*,
he fails to realize that a party to an exchange can only trade his capacity to work for a restricted time. Then alone can an individual retain
the juridical status of commodity owner that is required for concluding
the exchange in the first place.[4] Otherwise, the individual is no longer

owner of a commodity and able to enter into a contract, but an object of ownership, that, as such, can only be traded by a separate will to which the individual is subject. By maintaining that the laborer sells his entire self to the capitalist, Marx falls into the absurdity of having a commodity sell itself.[5]

Of course, with such a "sale," the purchased labor can hardly have a coherent employment. As mere property of his employer, the worker has no more of a juridical relation to the capitalist than the capitalist has to him. Instead of being bound by rights and duties, the capitalist simply lords over a rightless thing, enjoying the same prerogatives that any owner has in regard to his property. Hence, what the worker performs under capital's rule is purely forced labor, expressing the unilateral will of the capitalist to use what is his.[6]

Although Marx so reduces the worker to a dependent object, wholly subject to the will of another, he nonetheless affirms that this wage slave maintains his independent perspective within the production process such that he can perceive both his product and his labor as something alien. How this self-conscious awareness can be, however, is mystery enough, for the estranged arrangement of production should exclude the objectification of labor that supposedly provides the genesis of the laborer's own reflective standpoint. After all, instead of positing the autonomy of the worker, labor here creates a product belonging to the capitalist, embodying his will to the exclusion of that of the worker.

If this is taken into consideration, then the entire construct of alienated labor succumbs to the inconsequence of presupposing the self-consciousness of the worker just when his situation should be annulling it. On the other hand, if Marx's notion of objectification is accepted at face value, the laborer is granted the intuition of himself in the immediate objectivity of the product, irrespective of any conventional arrangements such as private property. In that case, it is equally unfathomable how this intuition can be limited by any subsequent appropriation of the product.

Marx would like to dismiss these difficulties by believing that the whole construct holds itself together as a social relation existing in the form of a contradiction.[7] It is more truthful to admit that the drama of alienated labor only exhibits the contradiction of using a technical conception of labor, rooted in the singular subjectivity of liberal theory, for a normatively relevant social determination of production.

The confusion of forces and relations of production

Although the young Marx does subsequently rid himself of the particular formulations of the *1844 Manuscripts*, what follows is no more helpful in shedding light on economic justice.

Leaving behind his appeal to self-positings of consciousness, Marx next pursues the social anatomy of the economy by reverting to natural factors, in the manner of praxis theory's reliance upon privileged givens. In the *German Ideology* he ordains man the producing creature, defining labor and its satisfaction of need as anthropological phenomena.[8] Accordingly, he then declares production to be the given basis of all social formations, as if to reiterate that the labor process is an irreducibly natural condition determined independently of society.[9]

However, since Marx's intention remains one of uncovering the social reality of economic relations in their connection to justice and human liberation, he additionally distinguishes relations from forces of production in order to grant labor at least a social organization. In so doing, Marx seems to be placing production on a social footing, for he introduces his new distinction maintaining that though human beings work upon nature out of necessity, they do so entering into definite connections with one another such that only within these social relations does production actually occur.[10]

This impression gives way, however, once the heralded categories are laid out. They receive their classic formulation in Marx's 1848 writing, *Wage-Labor and Capital*. There Marx stipulates that the social relations of production are the social relations within which individuals produce, and that these are altered and transformed with the change and development of the forces of production, which constitute the material means of production utilized through the relations of production.[11]

Although the stated distinction of relations and forces of production refers to neither anthropological factors nor monological structures of self-consciousness, it leaves the means of production something separate from their social arrangement, effectively reducing labor to a technical operation of a material, objectlike equipment. As a consequence, the whole notion of forces of production determining their encompassing social relations becomes problematic in itself, let alone as a conception of the social reality of the economy. In their distinction from the relations of production, the forces are dead objects whose animating process lies outside them. They become functioning productive instruments only in and through the relations of production, just as these are themselves relations of production only by containing these forces as a given technical object subject to social arrangement. Thus, any development of these forces can only take place from outside, through none other than their animating agency, the relations of production.

If this undermines the determining role of the forces of production, it also casts in doubt their social unity with the relations of production.

Since the forces of production are a mere instrument, comprising a technique devoid of all social reality in its objectlike distinction from the relations of production, and the latter are a formal set of inter-relations somehow leaving out of account the actual production process itself, neither can alone constitute a social system of production, nor furnish a principle for uniting with one another in a determinate economic order. What alone allows them to stand as the two sides of a social whole is the subjective assurance of our deus ex machina, the young Karl Marx.

Thus, when it comes time to transform the inexplicable change in the forces of production into a determining of a new set of relations of production, Marx must reach into his own bag of tricks and pull consciousness out of a hat to effect the supposedly social development. As the *German Ideology* explains, the opposition of forces and relations of production now becomes a threesome where the productive forces, the state of society, and consciousness come into contradiction with one another.[12] Needless to say, it is only the extraneous factor of consciousness that here "solves" the problem of generating the new social form of the economy. How and why human awareness should have its designs mandated by given arrangements of production is left unanswered.

Base and superstructure

The dilemma is no different when Marx proceeds to oppose the relations of production to a legal and political superstructure that they supposedly ground. In the Preface to *A Contribution To The Critique of Political Economy,* he gives this notion its most famous expression, explaining that the totality of the relations of production, that is, the mode of production of the material conditions of life, constitutes the real foundation of society that conditions the whole process of social, political, and cultural life.[13] Accordingly, when the forces of production transform the relations of production, an entire civilization has been born.

However, since the mode of production never exists in a world deprived of all other institutions, nor contains in itself some mechanism for generating and defining the domestic, legal, political, and cultural relations that already accompany it, the relation between economic base and superstructure is an external correlation saying nothing about the necessity of their interrelation or about what they may be in themselves. Declaring every given phenomenon of convention to be the mere expression of the relations of production, provides no explanation of what is the limit of the totality of a civilization, how this whole is necessarily differentiated, or what distinguishes its various institutions. Once again, an extraneous viewpoint must introduce itself to claim that the reality of convention is a relation of base and superstructure. As a result, the derivative historical development becomes a mysterious sequence in which the relations of production commune with the superstructure in an unspeakable way, offering an enigma equal to the mode of production's own uneasy amalgam of technical forces and social organization.

Although alienated labor is no longer the specific form in which production is determined through an individual self, the distinctions of forces and relations of production and of base and superstructure have maintained the same self-defeating dependence upon a monological factor to conceive the economy in social terms. Together with the *German Ideology*'s anthropological characterization of production, these attempts all underscore the superior consistency with which praxis and contractarian theories exclude economics from the domain of justice.[14]

Nevertheless, the common failures of political economy, Fichte, Rawls, and the young Marx do not condemn to futility all efforts to conceive the just economy. Although they do testify to the dilemma of conceiving economic justice with the natural and monological terms of praxis and liberal thought, their examples do not even touch the issue of whether other principles might be adequate to the task.

The Ethical Irrelevance of Marx's Mature Theory of Capital

In ways that will become clearer in later chapters, Marx's mature systematic writings, the *Grundrisse, Contribution To The Critique of Political Economy,* and *Capital* do contribute economic analyses that transcend natural and monological formulations and bring to partial fruition Marx's striving for a strictly social theory of the economy providing essential lessons for the just society. However, whatever be the merits of these analyses, their contribution to the theory of the just economy is marred by recurring discussions that undermine any normative role they could have.

In these, his crowning works, Marx repeatedly injects his social analyses of economic relations with natural specifications. Again and again he introduces empirical examples and page after page of historical description to unveil essential connections of economic necessity that bear upon social justice. At times he characterizes his inquiry as a reconstruction of a particular historical form of production, only to later claim a categorial universality for the relations of capital. And the civil society that contains the economy under investigation is varyingly portrayed as a suprahistorical substrate, as the base of all modern political and cultural formations, and as a subordinate sphere of some categorial differentiation of social reality. Never adequately identifying his method nor consistently excluding all natural and monological conceptions, never specifying the institutions of justice nor concretely situating the sphere of capital in relation to the other structures of society and state, Marx ends up obscuring whatever relevance his concept of capital could have for the normative issues of economic justice. Before any of Marx's socially specific analyses of capital can be considered for their contribution to a prescriptive economics, the basic confusions pervading Marx's presentation must be unmasked and repudiated.

Marx's appeal to nature

Although Marx had long pilloried classical political economy for misconceiving social, historically established relations of production as given relations of man and nature, he continues till the end to litter his argument with analogous appeals to natural factors. As a result, however the *Critique of Political Economy,* the *Grundrisse,* and *Capital* may depart from the flawed problematic of his early writings remains largely hidden.

Marx's natural reduction of economic need and use value

The root instance of these residues of the natural approach is found in Marx's repeated assertion of the presocial character of need and use value. Ignoring any constitutive role of market or any other social relations, Marx describes use value as the relation of the particular natural features of a desired object to the particular natural needs of some human being.[15] Since such use value expresses merely the relation between an individual and nature,[16] it has its character prior to and independently of all social intercourse.

Consequently, Marx reasons, this use value is bound by the limits of its own natural qualities and hence cannot possess the measurelessness of a conventionally determined, multiplied, and refined value.[17] By contrast, luxury can here solely represent whatever stands in excess to the physical requirements of an individual's species being.[18] On these terms, use value figures as the naturally given content of transactions between men, a content thus lying entirely outside the specifically economic determination of exchange.[19]

This natural reduction leaves the use value basically indifferent to all social form, rendering it an object of satisfaction for any system of human need. As such, it is simply the irreducible matter common to the most disparate epochs of production.[20] Accordingly, Marx can only conclude that since use value comprises the material content of wealth, whatever be its social configuration,[21] the analysis of use value must lie outside the specific investigation of economic science.[22]

This exclusion of the basic material of wealth from economics gives Marx occasion to ponder, for now he must ask whether the content of use value can admissibly become a constitutive element of subsequent economic forms, such as the specific exchange relation of capital and labor.[23] If only exchange value should play an economic role, how is he to introduce elements such as capital that figures as a raw material, which he will later characterize in terms of use value?[24] Caught between the natural reductions of his theorizing and the inherent social character of market relations, Marx is finally forced to admit that the distinction of use value and exchange value does genuinely fall within the economy.[25] As he himself confesses, at various stages in the conceptualization of economic relations, use value and exchange value become related to one another as diverse social forms of wealth.[26]

Although Marx's further analyses of commodity relations ultimately testify to the necessity of conceiving need and its means of satisfaction independently of all natural considerations, his vestigial portrayals of use value as a presocial entity do not remain isolated cases. Due to the ubiquitous economic role of use value, Marx's natural characterization instead lays the groundwork for further natural reductions of the social reality of wealth. These reductions follow a logic already pursued by the political economists he so maligns: namely, if goods are just objects related to naturally given wants, then their production entails no necessary relation between individuals but can simply fall under the eternal metabolism between man and nature. By the same token, if use value is defined prior to all social interaction, then labor is left conditioned to an end, the product at which its act is directed, given independently of all intersubjective relations. Hence, all talk of any constitutively social determination of labor must be excluded from the start.

Marx's natural reduction of production

Marx embraces these consequences on all the numerous occasions where he pursues his analysis of capital with descriptions of the allegedly natural process of production. Reverting to the homilies of political economy, he repeatedly claims that labor is first and foremost a process between man and nature, a process where the human being achieves his metabolism with nature through his own act. Here, by dint of the human condition, the individual works as a natural power,[27] fashioning matter into the means for satisfying natural want without ever stepping beyond the necessity of natural process. Far from involving the conventions of any social relationship, this production proceeds entirely within the given confines of nature. As Marx states, adopting the paradigm of monological technique, such laboring is simply a purposive appropriation of the natural. Given the natural needs of man, this productive activity is itself the eternal natural condition of all human existence, a condition therefore prior to and independent of all social forms of economic life.[28] Reducing production to an anthropological principle, Marx is thus compelled to admit that just as the savage must deal with nature to satisfy his needs so must civilized man.[29] For if it is a physiological truth that all productive activity is a function of a human organism,[30] the defining essence of labor lies outside the social conventions in which justice resides.

With this case, Marx can only repeat the assertion of his early writings that a production process always constitutes the material basis of social formation, whether it be that of the Greeks and Romans or that of the modern world.[31] Being characterized as a natural precondition of humanity, labor will of course accept the external form of any society whatsoever just as effortlessly and indifferently as the naturally defined use value. Since the metabolism of man and nature is an eternal given, all that this social arrangement of labor can involve is a formal incorporation adding nothing essential to the predetermined nature of production. Little else can be at stake in Marx's all too classic statement that as soon as men labor for one another in any manner, their labor acquires a social form.[32] Whatever this adopted form may be, labor and means of production are always its predetermined factors,[33] always being reproduced with the constancy of natural law.[34]

As for the product, it too possesses its natural character of use value no matter what be the conventional manner of its production. Consistent with a vengeance striking at his own claims concerning the historical character of commodity relations, Marx doggedly adds that the product is always a good ready to enter commodity circulation, whether it be fashioned by a natural community, chattel slaves, petit bourgeois, peasants, or even capitalist entrepreneurs.[35] However, to follow the path of the product as it enters the sphere of exchange, Marx must now face up to the problem of relating his natural conception of production with the socially specific circulation of commodities.

He meets this dubious challenge by resurrecting the favorite fiction of Adam Smith—the community of petty producers of commodities, who trade with one another on the basis of their natural needs and their prior individual working upon nature. Just as Marx is about to launch his analysis of capital's social reality with an investigation of the sphere of commodity exchange, he falls back upon the models of political economy with incessant digressions to what he calls "private labor" (*Privatarbeit*).

The monological model of private labor

Bearing no mark specific to the social relations of market and capital, "private labor" simply denotes the technical activity of individuals who singly work directly upon nature to fashion goods and then trade them with one another. Despite the subsequent exchange, their work still proceeds exclusively in monological terms, prior to all interaction. Although the produced object may figure as an exchangeable product only when it is first alienated for another,[36] its fabrication remains a purely technical affair of the single agent imposing new form upon natural material. Hence, when the product of private labor enters commodity circulation, it is already defined as an objectification of the individual's own formative activity.[37] As Marx explains, the first necessity, grounded in the compulsion of physical want, is that of appropriating goods directly from nature by one's own labor. Only once this is accomplished does the second necessity enter in, the necessity of engaging in the social process where private producers barter their wares. Hence, private producers first enter into social contact through the exchange of what they have produced, not through their private laboring itself.[38]

However, given the natural relations upon which the ensuing exchange is predicated, its process cannot be taken for granted. If the participating individuals are to be driven to trade their own products, there must already be something to private labor that prevents immediate consumption and creates dependency upon the products of others. Furthermore, for exchange, rather than unilateral appropriation, to take place there must also be preexisting property relations and some commensurability to the traded products and the needs they address. In order to account for these requirements, Marx employs some of the standard natural reductions of political economy.

He first borrows again from Adam Smith by claiming that there is a naturally generated division of labor allotting complementary productions to different individuals.[39] This division supposedly occurs even though all the separate producers deal directly with nature in their private laborings, without any intervening relation to others. Be this as it may, Marx still maintains that use values first emerge as commodities only when they are made by these very same private producers who, despite their direct commerce with nature, are still supposed to fashion different goods corresponding to the needs of one another.[40]

The obvious weakness of this whole conception is that it must assume the interdependent neediness and the property relations that would allow for any such division of labor between private producers at the very same time that it bases this division upon socially indifferent natural relations that make those presuppositions inexplicable. Marx's further rationalizations only highlight the dilemma of his predicament. Having already characterized need and use value as natural factors defined independently of all social relations, Marx does not even attempt to account for the complementarity of individual neediness on which his division of labor must rest. With regard to property entitlements, on the other hand, he does at least suggest an explanation. Reverting to the natural right labor theory of property advocated by Locke and Rousseau, Marx baldly asserts that private labor's formation of natural material comprises a primary possession constituting the juridical title to property.[41] With this natural law of original appropriation through labor[42] Marx seeks to explain how the private producer is able to participate in the social operation of exchange where his possession of his product becomes transformed into a title to the ownership of commodities in general.[43] He even claims that the ensuing commodity circulation grounds the entire realm of bourgeois freedom and equality upon none other than the principle of private labor's establishment of ownership of its product.[44] This appeal to natural right reaches its climax with Marx's famous unmasking of capital's inversion of the fundamental law of bourgeois property, which supposedly bases the right of ownership in one's own labor.[45]

Needless to say, whatever be the impressed form of the product, its spatial proximity to its producer, or the force with which that individual keeps it in his grasp, none of these monological relations could possibly constitute the socially valid guarantee of property underlying any commodity exchange. Instead of conceiving the intersubjective recognition rendering a particular possession respected property, Marx offers little but a description of the physical grasp of an object marked by private labor. By excluding all interaction from his law of original appropriation through private labor, Marx follows his liberal theorist predecessors in reducing the intersubjective relation of property to an incomprehensible natural occurrence. Consequently, having one's *own* product to exchange remains just as inexplicable as the assumed interdependence of need.

In his following analyses, Marx simply ignores these dilemmas and takes for granted the engagement of commodity exchange between private producers. By so doing, he now faces the problem of accounting for the commensurability of goods within this first social contact between his naturally laboring individuals.

Assuming that private producers do in fact exchange their products, Marx recognizes that these goods must exhibit an equivalent exchangeability in order to be traded. Since each act of private labor is a monological fashioning with no inherent relation to the actions of others, the sought after value commensurability would seem to lie elsewhere. Accordingly, Marx leaves his Robinsonade of production behind to claim that products of private labor are first rendered exchange values in and through the social process of their exchange.[46] He then asserts that because the goods are here traded by their respective producers, the equivalent exchange value emerging in the transaction equally establishes the commensurate universality of the particular private labor to which each commodity owes its existence.[47] Thus, even though the product originates as the objectification of a single private labor, the moment it figures as an exchange value it no less becomes objectified universal labor.[48] In effect, once the private producers posit the equality of their various products by exchanging them, their different laborings stand related to one another as human labor in general.[49]

According to Marx, this equality of different private labors can only lie in an abstraction from their real inequality, bracketing their particular operations and reducing them to their common character as expenditures of the human capacity to work, that is, as abstract human labor.[50] Who legitimately makes this abstraction and how its appeal to a natural capability can account for the socially specific value of commodities are questions Marx leaves unanswered. All he acknowledges is that the reduction of particular private labors to abstract human labor says nothing about the respective exchange values of their different products. Marx therefore adds another account, claiming that private laborings, despite their independent, naturally defined operation, become steadily reduced to their valid social proportion, whereby the socially necessary labor time required for each product asserts itself as a natural law forcefully governing all exchange relations.[51]

In each of these explanations, what determines the universality of private labor is some factor given independently of the process of exchange, even though it is the exchange process that sets private labors in any socially common relationship. As Marx describes them, abstract human labor power and socially necessary labor time are characterized in technical terms completely extraneous to the transactions that supposedly first bring private producers into social contact and thereby render their labor socially universal. Hence, it is utterly mysterious how these factors can take hold of the exchange process and determine the proportions at which commodities are exchanged.

What brings this confusion to a head is Marx's attempt to make the universality of private labor the very source of the product's exchange value. His explanation rests on the bald assertion that if one abstracts from the specific utility of a commodity, all that will remain is its quality of being the product of private labor.[52] Although this claim renders inexplicable all commodities that are not products of private labor, including land, labor power, and all products of wage labor, what is even more questionable is the use to which Marx puts it. Having isolated the residual quality supposedly shared by all commodities, he then affirms that it is the one common ground permitting individual producers to exchange equivalent goods. By so allowing private labor to determine the value equivalency of commodities, Marx once again has simply assumed both the reduction of all private labors to a social communality and the privileged role played by abstract human labor in market exchange.

Of course, when Marx later analyzes the production process of capital, his whole labor theory of surplus value rests on the condition that private individuals not sell commodities where their own labor is objectified, but rather sell their labor power to owners of capital, from whom they then purchase goods.[53] Here, however, in the naturally defined world of private producers, the relation of private labor to exchange must remain a vexing dilemma. In the *Critique of Political Economy* Marx finally admits the aporia to which his argument has led. On the one hand, given the privileged role of abstract human labor, commodities must enter into the exchange process as objectified universal labor time if they are to be exchangeable in the first place. On the other hand, he confesses, the expended labor time of the private producer is itself universal only as a result of the exchange process.[54]

Marx's basic problem is that private labor's monological appropriation of nature has no social universality in itself. By virtue of its formative activity, its product is merely a physical artifact related to natural want. In attempting to construct commodity exchange from the postulation of a plurality of private producers, such that their exchange is based on their private labors, Marx must somehow account for the social commensurability exhibited by the traded goods and the privileged value determining role of private labor. This, however, simply cannot be done when labor and its product are characterized independently of all social intercourse. Once they are reduced to monological factors, neither can already contain the value relation in terms of which exchange can proceed.

As glaring as this difficulty is, Marx ignores it again and again, even while directing his critique of political economy at analogous natural reductions. Unfortunately, the further occasions where he appeals to private labor are among the most favored discussions to which subsequent philosophical appreciations have turned.

The natural reduction of Marx's "Fetishism of Commodities"

The most celebrated of these instances is Marx's analysis of the fetishism of commodities in the first volume of *Capital*. Attempting to ground a normative critique of commodity relations, he here returns to the fold of political economy and its natural division of private laborings, and once again grapples with the problem of relating the monological appropriation of nature to the social dimension of exchange.

Marx unveils the mystery of commodity fetishism as a result of observing that since private producers first enter into social contact through the exchange of their products, whatever social character their laboring acquires must first emerge within this exchange. Hence, he concludes, the social relations connecting their private laborings appear as what they are: not as social relations by which individuals interact within their respective laboring activity, but rather as external thing-like relations of individuals and social relations of things.[55] What Marx condemns as the fetishism of commodities is this relationship where the social quality of the private producer's own labor, namely, its character as value-producing abstract human labor, appears as something derivative of the object that he has produced and then exchanged.[56]

As should be evident, Marx's whole construction of commodity fetishism rests upon the questionable foundation of an exchange process built upon private labor. The adoption of this framework automatically excludes any constitutive social relation from the act of labor by reducing commodity production to a monological fashioning of a natural object. By the same token, it reduces the product to a mere artifact, whose subsequent exchange is as external to its technical being as it is to the formative activity of its producer. Because Marx here has characterized need and labor in terms as presocial as they are precapitalist, any ensuing exchange must remain an unessential barter, where private producers enjoy no inherent social bond, but relate to one another solely through the accidental meeting of the things they have separately fashioned.

The great secret of commodity fetishism thus entails no rude awakening to how things rule over the relations among autonomous individuals. It rather represents a conceptual confusion foisting the plurality of private producers, who work upon nature in response to physical and psychological want before ever interacting, upon the social terms of the market, whose participants relate to one another through their conventional needs for commodities and their complementary commodity ownerships. As we shall see, when commodity exchange is properly taken for the social process it is, the very possibility of commodity fetishism is eliminated. Needless to say, this has fatal consequences for all the talk about reification that has since sprung from Marx's analysis of commodity fetishism.[57]

*Marx's natural reduction of the basic production
process of capital*

Not surprisingly, Marx's analysis of commodity fetishism is hardly his last reversion to the natural reductions of political economy. Although Marx's appeals to private labor may well be dismissed as vestigial discussions unessential to his theory of capitalism, it is far harder to claim the same for his persistent recourse to natural relations in conceiving capital's own basic production process.

These reductions are of greatest importance, because here in his analysis of capital's production of commodities, Marx should be bringing his critique of political economy to positive fruition, depriving natural and monological relations of any irreducible hold on production. Instead, the one analysis of capital's commodity production published by the mature Marx, Chapter 7 of the first volume of *Capital,* beats the trodden path back to given relations of man and nature and monological technique.

Marx makes his turn to capital's production process by first introducing abstract labor power, which the wage laborer must sell the capitalist in order for production to get underway. Its introduction arises from what Marx conceives to be the problem of reconciling the analytic equivalence of the exchange value of traded commodities with capital's accumulation of wealth by means of the M-C-M' exchange circuit, where commodities are bought to be sold for ever increasing exchange value. Ignoring how the agreements of the parties to exchange might be all that is required to enable goods to be retraded at a profit, Marx reasons that there must be some commodity whose consumption creates additional value. No sooner said than done, Marx discovers in the market the available presence of labor power, as if no profits could ever be realized in exchange without an intervening production process involving a relation of wage labor and capitalist.[58] Conceptually speaking, this move has a troublesome circularity. In order to declare labor power the unique commodity whose consumption produces additional exchange value, Marx must presuppose the entire labor theory of value that establishes how labor generates exchange value. However, the conclusion that labor produces surplus value has yet to emerge from the analysis of the workings of the immediate production process, workings which themselves first become conceivable after labor power his been specified.

While this suggests that labor power's potential to produce surplus value through its consumption is something indeterminate when it is offered for sale by its owner, the laborer, Marx sees fit to denude labor power of all social character and describe it anthropologically as man's innate capacity to expend muscle power in general.[59] Disregarding any constitutive role of property and market relations, Marx reduces labor power to the *Inbegriff* of the mental and physical abilities that are set in motion whenever the human organism fashions useful things of any sort.[60] Since this purely natural definition leaves labor power without any social specificity, Marx can later go so far as to speak of the labor power of peasants,[61] whose subsistence agriculture involves the same direct tie to nature enshrined in the notion of private labor.

Marx maintains his appeal to natural relations when he proceeds to analyze what results once capital has absorbed this completely extrinsic factor and made it an element of capital's socially defined production process. Although the capitalist's purchase of labor power has ostensibly opened the door to the inner workings of capital, Marx conceives its labor process as that familiar metabolism of man and nature. Instead of relating labor to its raw material in some way specific to capital, Marx once again turns the productive agency into a monological formative act.[62]

This time, however, Marx does so emphasizing how the labor process operates in indifference to the social reality of capital. Because, Marx argues, the labor process is essentially a process between man and nature, and not a social relation, how the immediate production process fashions use values is something completely independent of the fact that it proceeds for and under the control of the capitalist. Accordingly, its fabrication must first be considered independently of every specific social formation.[63] That is why, Marx remarks, it is here unnecessary to depict the laborer in relation to others. In analyzing capital's production of use values it is sufficient to have the individual and his purposive activity on one side, and nature and her material on the other.[64]

Admittedly, Marx's description of the technical dimension of the capital's production process poses little problem, provided it not play any constitutive role in determining specifically social features of economic relations. For, as Marx properly emphasizes, every labor process does involve some technical relation where form is imposed upon a given material, even when the product is a performance consisting in the act of laboring itself. Problems enter in only if the socially indifferent structure of technique is treated as the determining factor of socially specific economic relations, such as those by which Marx defines capital. In his further analysis of capital's inner working, Marx falls prey to this confusion, so emblematic of the political economy he seeks to overcome.

To begin with, Marx claims that the technical activity of the labor process not only comprises the natural condition of human life,[65] but produces a use value responding to the needs of others. Within the social context of the market, the labor process may well produce an article that figures as a commodity bearing use value for market needs, provided the product is subsequently marketed. By itself, however, the labor process can no more produce a good with a socially defined utility than can any metabolism between man and nature. Without taking into account the contribution of the market relations within which laboring occurs, all technical formation can supply are things related to natural wants. Because Marx has already reduced the use value to such a thing, confusing market needs and commodities with natural wants and objects, he is driven to ascribe laboring a social significance transcending its technical definition.

This takes its most problematic form when Marx addresses the creation of exchange value, which motivated his turn to the sphere of production, and asserts that the monological action of labor produces exchange as well as use value.[66] Not surprisingly, the only way Marx accounts for labor's ability to produce exchange value is by harking back to his previous private producer "derivation" of the labor theory of value and letting it furnish the explanation that should first here be established in the analysis of production. To make his transition from use value to value production, Marx simply assumes the social universality of private labor alleged in the former analysis of private precapitalist producers. Hence, just when he would be expected to establish how exchange value production takes place in terms specific to capital, Marx bluntly announces that we already know how the value of every commodity is determined by the quantity of socially necessary labor time required to produce it. With this dismissal of any need for new argument, all that can remain at issue is the trivial exercise of tallying up the labor objectified in the product.[67]

Trivial as such computation may appear, Marx goes about it here and elsewhere by referring to the expenditures of an abstract labor defined in anything but social terms. The labor to which he points does not possess a generalized nature determined through the social relations of capital's production process. Instead, Marx repeatedly claims that the value-positing labor to be tallied owes its common character to an external abstraction from the different concrete forms of labor, analogous to the abstraction from the particular facticity of the use value that supposedly resulted in its general character of being a product of labor.[68] On these terms, there is nothing inconsistent in Marx's conclusion that when one so abstracts from the specific useful character of a laboring, what remains is the general expenditure of human labor power in its bare physiological sense.[69] As Marx admits, this leaves the abstraction of universal human labor with no real social specificity. It simply consists in the average labor of the average individual in any given society whatsoever.[70]

What follows less coherently, but all too familiarly, is Marx's accompanying conclusion that this abstract human labor is what builds the values of commodities.[71] As for what can account for the value-producing genius of such a socially indifferent abstraction, Marx's answer is a telling indictment of his own attempt to supersede the natural reductions of political economy. The value-producing talent, he says, is a gift of nature, which bestows living labor with the ability to preserve value and create it anew.[72]

Hence, the ensuing calculation of "socially" necessary labor time proceeds not through any social determination, but via Marx's own private reckoning. The universal measure of socially necessary labor time is determined by the monological reflection of an external standpoint that takes an average of the existing production times of those particular laborings of average skill and intensity which produce a certain commodity taken as the average example of its kind. Since such a tally can be made upon any given array of work situations, Marx does not give it any more social specificity than he accords abstract labor. Thus despite all his intentions to analyze the exchange value production specific to capitalism, he is compelled to remark that in all epochs of history the labor time expended in means of subsistence is of interest to men,[73] as if exchange value production and the measure of exchange value were defined by eternal technical features of the human struggle for survival.

Although Marx does not bother to question why a measure resulting from an external averaging should govern the rates at which commodities are bought and sold, he does begrudgingly admit that the conditions of such averaging make its real application a vexing problem. Since the socially necessary labor time is an empirically ascertained average, its measure cannot be expected to be confirmed in individual work situations. As Marx acknowledges, the realization of this labor law of value will only begin to make itself manifest in a particular case when a producer employs many workers simultaneously.[74] However, even in the case of such empirical corroboration, each and every expenditure of labor remains a singular effort wholly indifferent to its abstracted standard.

In order to remove this externality and give greater assurance that socially necessary labor time has real bearing upon value production, Marx finally attempts to establish it as an actually existing universality by distinguishing so-called "simple" from "complicated" labor power and labor. Simple labor power is defined in completely asocial terms as the capacity possessed by a normal individual prior to any special development of his body. Complicated labor, by contrast, is defined in correspondingly asocial terms as merely a multiplied potency of expended simple labor power. Marx maintains that this allows different types of labor to be reducible to simple labor as their unity of measure.[75] To the extent that the latter measure determines the exchange value of products, for which, as we have seen, Marx gives no satisfactory explanation, there arises a hierarchy of labor where more developed and qualified labor powers command higher prices and produce relatively greater value in an equal period of time.[76]

Even if the privileged role of simple labor were granted, it is questionable whether it supplies a workable measure for resolving the qualitative differences of individual labors into commensurate matters of degree. Choosing which work is to represent simple labor can be no less arbitrary than calculating how other types of labor comprise its higher potencies. Since Marx has differentiated simple and complicated labor in technical terms completely indifferent to any social relations, let alone to those specific to capital, he is at license to claim that the labor power of a peasant is the valid measure for simple labor power, expending itself as human labor power in general, whereas a textile cutter expends a more developed labor power.[77]

That this leaves the key to Marx's analysis of capitalism, his labor theory of value, resting upon a precapitalist subsistence work antithetical to wage labor and capitalist production, only testifies to Marx's continued characterization of production in natural and technical terms effectively removing production from the domain of social justice. Once again he has conceived the universality of labor and labor time as a result of an external reflection either abstracting from or comparing the given array of particular work situations. Instead of establishing any necessary economic connection between commensurate expenditures of labor and the exchange value of products, Marx appeals to the generalizations of an observing consciousness whose object is left technically differentiated, without regard for the market transactions in which exchange values are realized.

With this the case, it is hardly surprising that Marx crowns his reckoning of value production with a naturally defined surplus value. He here deprives what should be the emblematic fruit of capital's production process of all social as well as normative significance. Instead of treating surplus value as the specific outcome of a set of social interactions, Marx bases it upon the purely technical condition that nature be so bounteous that an expenditure of labor taking less than what is feasible during an entire day be sufficient to furnish a man's means of subsistence. This naturally determined productivity, Marx maintains, is the foundation of all surplus labor,[78] whose specific economic form can then only involve how unpaid surplus value is subsequently extracted from the immediate producer.[79] On these terms, surplus value is not an economic category rooted in a capitalist economy or any other social formation. As Marx acknowledges, such surplus value can exist anywhere where one part of society has a monopoly over the means of production, whether the expropriator be Athenian aristocrat, Etruscan theocrat, *civis romanus*, Norman baron, American slaveholder, Walatian boyar, modern landlord, or even, let us not forget, a mere capitalist.[80]

With the social specificity of surplus value thereby eliminated, the necessity of capital determining value production is also removed. As a consequence, Marx will allow capital's own identity as self-expanding value to result from the labor process only under the incidental circumstance of a sufficiently long expenditure of labor time.[81] It may well be true that a unit of capital realizes its constitutive end only when it succeeds in earning a profit, but how any naturally defined productivity of labor determines this market outcome is a mystery Marx cannot unravel.

Marx's flight from the sphere of necessity to the realm of freedom

What finally results from Marx's recurring use of natural and monological terms in specifying economic relations is the inevitable admission that production is not an objective realization of freedom in which rights and duties could figure, but an irreducible sphere of necessity, beyond the pale of good and evil. In his celebrated sketch of communism in volume 3 of *Capital,* Marx brings this acknowledgment to a telling conclusion.

He begins by pronouncing economic necessity an eternal fate, observing that just as the savage must deal with nature to satisfy his wants, so must civilized man under all social formations. Since this leaves production a natural bane of the human condition, there is one conclusion for Marx to draw: freedom can only appear within such a sphere of necessity as the technical mastery of socialized men who bring their metabolism with Nature under their common control, applying the instrumental rationality suited to subduing things in cognizance of Nature's own laws and the nonconventional, "authentic" needs given by human nature.[82] Although Marx looks to these associated producers as codeterminers of the just society, their joint subsumption of production to technique cannot eliminate the fact that the autonomy of the technical artificer is not constituted within his work, but already presupposed by it. Hence even if the associated producers democratically determine the master plan for dominating nature and distributing the fruits of applied technique, their engagement in production can only remain an instrumental, formative action for material ends indifferent to the relation of free selves to one another.

Marx effectively realizes this, and admits that communism's rational domination of nature does not remove the necessity of man's satisfaction of natural need. Since he has relegated economic activity to a natural metabolism, the economy must always remain the arena of constraint beyond which the true realm of freedom first comprises itself.[83] This mandates the task of communism. As Marx consistently concludes, the basic condition for the further development of freedom can only reside in progressively limiting production's claim upon human activity by shortening the working day, while eliminating the conventional toils of the market in favor of an increasingly automated system of production and distribution.[84] In this way the leisure of the polis citizen becomes the free time of the emancipated proletarian, shorn of the chains of family, market, and state, and left with nothing but his species being, for which no history remains but human evolution. Instead of providing an overcoming of bourgeois society rooted in the dynamic of market relations, Marx has here fled capital's social reality for a natural utopia.

Marx's appeal to history

Marx's recurrent use of natural and monological terms is not the only factor undermining the normative relevance of his theory of capital. What equally compromises his contribution to a theory of the just economy is his recourse to history. Although Marx turns to history as if that were the remedy for political economy's reduction of social arrangements of production to ahistorical relations of man and nature, it actually undercuts the critical import of his theory of capital.

This is so despite the fact that Marx develops his theory of the capitalist economy as the theory of a specific historical formation largely due to his normative judgment that the capitalist economy is not a timeless paragon of economic justice. Capitalism's status as a merely historical economic order fit for analysis within a theory of historical social development does not derive simply from Marx's recognition that market relations are conventional structures whose existence is not eternally mandated by any natural necessity of the human condition. One may grant that capitalism is but one of many possible economic orders that men may erect, and that hence the categories of capital are not universally descriptive, as political economy wrongly tended to think. However, even if the capitalist economy is not the only possible form of economic organization, it might still enjoy a normative universality rendering the theory of capital a theory of economic justice indifferent to history. Because Marx judges capital to be inherently unjust, due to its exploitation of labor and its subjection of society and state to the iron wheel of capitalist accumulation in the particular interest of the capitalist class, he cannot treat the relations of capital apart from history as if they were universally valid structures of justice.

While Marx can be said to conceive capital in historical terms due to this normative consideration, it is a notorious fact of Marxist theory that Marx provides no independently argued concept of justice that could be used to determine either the illegitimacy of capitalism or the legitimacy of communism. Instead, Marx presents his theory of capital as if its description of the historical reality of capitalism can both confirm the injustice of capital and shed light on the character of the just economy. Although Marx never methodically reflects upon how his descriptive theory of capital could have prescriptive ramifications, his normative judgments follow two alternate strategies. On the one hand, he attempts to certify the injustice of capitalism by showing how the market economy contradicts its own principles of freedom and equality by fostering class distinctions involving inequalities of wealth and opportunity. On the other hand, he purports to show that the dynamic of capitalist accumulation leads to the breakdown of the capitalist system and its substitution by a socialist and ultimately communist society consistently realizing the same bourgeois ideals of freedom and equality. At first glance, each of these argumentative strategies enjoys the virtue of relying on an immanent critique requiring no externally given criteria of justice. Capitalism seems to condemn itself, by both contradicting its own norms and by undermining itself and giving rise to a new society conforming to those norms.

This would be a conclusive condemnation of capitalism and justification of communism if, and only if, the ideals of justice of capitalist society are normatively valid. If they are not, the inconsistency of capitalism is no more a mark against it than the consistency of communism is a mark in the latter's favor. Even if capitalist society necessarily gives rise to a communist order, the latter need not be normatively superior unless its principles can be justified in their own right. However, no descriptive theory of economic development can prescribe which principles of justice have validity. The most such a theory can determine is what lies in the existence of a certain order and where its dynamic may lead. These are both matters of fact which of themselves tell nothing of how just an economic system is. Hence, Marx's two strategies of immanent critique fail to provide any normative lessons unless they are supplemented by an independent theory of economic justice, which Marx never undertakes in any meaningful way.

Lacking such an account of economic justice, Marx's theory of capital seems to be no more than an empirical model of a particular historical economy. If this is so, it is as incapable of establishing universally necessary laws of economic development as of prescribing the principles of economic justice. In the second Afterword to the first volume of *Capital* and the introduction to the *Grundrisse* Marx himself asserts as his methodological guide the idea that genuine science consists in ideally reconstructing what is concretely given.[85] In confirmation of this embrace of ideal-typical model building, Marx accompanies his unfolding argument with comments upon the successive abstractions that we must make in order to recapture faithfully the phenomena at issue, free from disturbing influences. So it is necessary, Marx maintains, to begin by treating the total world of trade as one nation where capitalist production has conquered all areas of industry.[86] Then one can consider the total average of the average compositions of all branches of production in a country, which is supposedly the matter of the last instance.[87] Marx even suggests that the succession of categories duplicates the historical order of the relations they describe. In this vein he remarks that the whole value discussion of volume 1 of *Capital* is theoretically prior to the price discussion of volume 3, just as commodity exchange at rates of value historically precedes commerce at prices of production.[88]

Whether the categories of capital be presented as generalizations from one given historical formation or successive mirrors of economic development, they involve an empirical reduction of the theory of capital carrying with it the reduction of capital to an individual historical formation, lacking any descriptive or prescriptive universality. Instead of addressing economic relations per se or the just economy, they have as their object the capitalist form of production and its corresponding exchange relations.[89] Accordingly, Marx announces in the opening pages of *Capital* that the categories of bourgeois economy are only the objective forms of this particular historical mode of production.[90] The commodity economy in which capital dwells is thus just another production process with no more privileged status than that of Greece or Rome.[91] Hence, the positing of exchange value by labor is no more definitive of production than the commodity is definitive of the use value.[92]

If this empirical approach is the fate of economics, then the categories of production per se can only be empty fictions in search of a real counterpart. Hence Marx maintains, the formal categories common to all production epochs are only abstractions incapable of specifying any actual historical form of economic relations.[93] Mute to all *differentia specifica*, they are the empty scaffold left over when the particular capitalist character is extracted from the wage, necessary labor, surplus value,[94] and every other element of commodity production and exchange.[95]

Although Marx regards the formality of such universal economic categories as the counterpart of the concreteness of the historical character of his theory of capital, it equally reflects the natural reductionism at play when Marx robbed features of commodity relations of their social specificity and turned them into factors of the human condition. Either way, the concept of capital is deprived of any categorial universality by which it could figure in an a priori descriptive or prescriptive theory of economics.

Marx's admission of the categorial universality of capital

Nevertheless, Marx accompanies his natural and historical characterizations of capital with suggestions that the categories defining the social reality of capital are of universal significance and that their order has little to do with the mimesis of empirical reconstruction. Contrary to his frequent recourse to historical description, Marx remarks that it would be false to let the categories of capital follow one another as though they were historically derived.[96] For example, within the theory of capital the formation of the general rate of profit follows from the competition of industrial capital only to be later modified through the mediation of commercial capital, whereas the historical order is the exact opposite.[97]

Simply cataloguing further supporting cases would only contradict the procedures of empirical model building without conveying any persuasive alternative. Of far greater importance is Marx's further claim that the order of economic categories is determined by the relation they have to one another in modern civil society, a relation that is exactly opposite what appears either natural or corresponding to history.[98] This suggests that although the specifications of capital emerge historically, their interrelation within civil society is somehow definitive for economics. In other words, the concept of capital enjoys a categorial universality rendering it much more than a mere description of some particular economic order. If the connection between the relations of production are found preeminently within the internal ordering of civil society's economy, then the order of economic categories is no longer decided by how we most conveniently abstract from what is empirically given. With the universally valid order of economic categories established by capital's process within civil society, the ordering role of an external, generalizing observer is eliminated as is the reduction of capital to a factual datum determined in reference to an opposing empirical standpoint.

The sense of this privileged status of relations of capital is further indicated in the intermittent passages where Marx discusses the universal character of labor. In the *Grundrisse,* Marx observes that whereas earlier in history work was done only in some particular, naturally defined manner, in modern civil society labor comes to exist in its universality, socially defined as exchange value positing activity per se. Hence, all prior instances of work can first be understood in terms of the category of labor only from the vantage point of modern civil society where each particular act of work actually proceeds as socially commensurate labor in general. By the same token, it follows that the determinations of capital are the key to understanding all prior historical forms of production to the extent that all the relations of modern civil society are already socially universal and thereby already conceptually determinate in their own particular existence.[99] In ascribing the economy of civil society such categorial universality, where economic relations have come to embody a generality adequate to their concept, Marx here echoes Hegel's suggestion that modernity presents a social order that is preeminently rational.[100]

On such a basis, capital could arise historically, yet still realize relations definitive of production in general. The history to which it belongs would then no longer be a procession of social formations where every era is relative and every emergent standpoint subject to historicity. For this reason, Marx can claim that history itself emerges as universal world history only in modern times.[101] First with the advent of capitalism, economic reality becomes freed of natural determination, achieving an entirely social character whose universality makes it conceptually transparent. Hence, history can finally manifest itself as what it is, the generation of a social order that is universal in scope. Of course, if the modern economy has this preeminent actuality, then the equally modern theory of capital will be free of all timely qualification and of all relative perspectivity.

At various points, Marx draws the consequences this has for the development of the concept of capital. If the categories of capital express the structure generic to economic relations when they are socially determined, then the conceptual articulation of the social relations of the economy will begin and end with capital. Therefore, Marx maintains, all the elements of production and distribution should be conceived as moments of a whole, as differences within a pervasive unity[102] where capital is both point of departure and endpoint.[103] In this way, the economic sphere of capital can appear just as much as the result as the subject of the entire process of determination.[104] With our subject matter being the historically emergent, yet self-moving foundation of civil society,[105] all its different economic structures are but elements of the self-constituting manifestation of capital. What individuals appear within the conceptualization of the economy do so only as interrelated agents defined in terms of its social process.[106]

However evocative these remarks may be, they comprise neither an argued doctrine of method nor an argued development of the economic system of capital. Admittedly, the universality they ascribe to the categories of capital would allow the latter to bear upon the theory of the just economy, either as specifications endemic to any economic association or as privileged forms generic to an economy that has freed itself of naturally defined relations and won a social form worthy of normative stature. Still, they remain fragmentary assertions, counterbalanced by all Marx's other discussions in which the concept of capital is reduced to either a natural assumption or a model of a particular historical economy undeserving of any special place in the pantheon of economic justice. Due to the absence of any full-fledged argument establishing the universality of capital relations, Marx's claims in its behalf remain promissory notes of questionable worth.

The ill-defined social context of Marx's concept of capital

If Marx's intimations of capital's categorial universality cannot afford his theory of capital the normative relevance undermined by his appeal to nature and history, what further weakens his normative contribution is the confused way in which he situates capital with regard to other institutions. Just as Marx fails to provide any systematic discussion of justice in general, so he fails to provide any argued theory of the different spheres of institutional life among which capital is located. Neither the *Critique of Political Economy,* the *Grundrisse,* nor the three volumes of *Capital* offer anything approaching a developed theory of property relations, morality, the family, the state, international relations or world history. Even the noneconomic institutions of civil society remain wholly unanalyzed. All Marx provides is a sparse collection of conflicting assertions, none of which goes beyond the barest of outlines. As a result, it is virtually impossible to rely on Marx in assessing how economic justice stands in relation to the normative principles of other institutional spheres.

This problem is most acute at those junctures where Marx obliterates the social context altogether by characterizing capital as a naturally given suprahistorical substrate. In such passages, Marx reduces capital to a material ground standing in the same relation to the rest of modern society as economic activity in Greece and Rome is alleged to have stood with respect to their other institutions.[107] This supplants the specific difference between such divisions as *oikos*-polis and civil society-state with an indifference toward institutional distinctions expressed in the formal contrast of base–superstructure. This old chestnut from the 1848 pamphlet, *Wage-Labor and Capital* gets intoned again and again in the *Critique of Political Economy,* the *Grundrisse,* and *Capital* without ever furnishing any additional explanation than its original unargued claim that capital, like all forms of production, is the inner foundation of the entire construction of social reality.[108] Marx proclaims that all legal and political relations are rooted in the material relations of life, yet never does he develop how these noneconomic institutions are actually generated from that basis. Civil society gets identified with the entirety of the material base,[109] capital becomes one of its particular forms, and both are left alone beside the unfulfilled promise of a construction of the superstructural domain.

On the one occasion where Marx relates a feature of capital to its supposed superstructure, he claims that commodity exchange is the basis of all juridical, social, political, and ideological realizations of equality and freedom.[110] In *On The Genealogy of Morals,* Nietzsche extends the same point, arguing that the relation of buying and selling lies at the root of all guilt, obligation, and justice, supplying as it does the underlying canon of justice: "everything has its price, *all* things can be paid for."[111] Admittedly, the exchange relation does set value upon goods according to whatever terms the parties to exchange may will. In this respect, exchange, like promise making, offers Nietzsche a procedure whereby values and obligations are newly created and imposed upon individuals through nothing other than their acts of will. Given Nietzsche's conviction that all values are mere posits of a will to power, that is, that norms have no foundation in reason or nature, but are arbitrary creations of those who impose them, it is not surprising that he seizes upon promise making and exchange as fundamental to the establishment of norms. However, although commodity exchange does involve determining the measure and value of goods and services, this does not mean that it can lie at the root of all relations of justice as the privileged determiner of practical norms.

Marx's own economic analysis manifests the absurdity of such a claim. For despite Marx's suggestion that the right of property derives from exchange relations,[112] Marx's own conception of commodity exchange presupposes property entitlements and property owners' right of contract in that the commodities being traded are exchanged rather than unilaterally appropriated only insofar as their respective ownership is honored by all parties to the transaction.

Marx's reduction of capital to a material base overlooks this elementary circumstance so fundamental to commodity relations. By treating the commodity economy as a prior base, Marx thus renders its own constitution as inexplicable as its supposed generation of all other institutions. What results is a rupture between the privileged givenness of capital and the derivative differentiation of superstructural institutions, a rupture not unlike that Marx bequeathed when he contrasted the primordial metabolism of man and nature with the various social forms it supposedly acquires.

In contrast to this characterization of the system of capital as a prior material base, Marx offers an opposing view following his understanding of the path of empirical reconstruction. Here he maintains that capital's specification presupposes the state, as well as international relations and history, since conceiving capital entails abstracting from the given concrete whole of social reality so as then to construct the economy as situated within one ideal nation.[113] Further instances where Marx's analysis of capital assumes the state are found in his discussion of government intervention in factory legislation[114] and primitive accumulation.[115] In every case, however, these references to a preexisting political sphere remain on the level of empirical descriptions providing little in the way of a systematic analysis of capital's relation to the state.

The only times when Marx ventures beyond his base-superstructure schema and empirical observation to situate capital are the few instances when he outlines the full plan of his theoretical project. On these rare occasions he offers, albeit without any argument, a basic division of institutions in the order in which they should be conceived.

In the *Critique of Political Economy* he lists successively capital, landed property, wage-labor, the state, international trade, and the world market, with the first three headings comprising the economic foundations of the three great social classes of civil society.[116] In the *Grundrisse*, Marx similarly begins by stipulating capital as the inner division of civil society in which capital, landed property, and wage-labor are contained in their interrelation. He then presents the consolidation of civil society within the state, which involves the "unproductive" classes, taxes, state debt, public credit, population, colonies, and emigration. Next come international relations of production, including international divisions of labor and exchange, and finally the world market and crises.[117]

Both of these outlines situate the system of capital within civil society, which is topically followed by the state and then international relations. In each listing, Marx appears to restrict civil society to the system of capital, while transferring all other civil institutions to the state, although elsewhere he maintains that capital is not simply identical with civil society, but comprises its historically emergent foundation.[118] Of course, whether the system of capital is coextensive with civil society or is its determining base is something none of these fragmentary outlines can decide. The conflicting claims of the base-superstructure schema, the empirical references to the state, and the stipulated divisions of institutions provide no more theoretical satisfaction than Marx's unfulfilled promises that the complete system of bourgeois economy will have its own negation as its last result,[119] or that the analysis of the world market will arrive through the idea of crises at the concept of a new historical shape.[120] In each case, Marx's claims are incomplete and offered with no argument.

Marred by his appeal to natural factors and history, his failure to supply an independent theory of justice, and his inability to systematically establish the universality of economic categories or locate the economy in relation to other institutions, Marx's mature theory of capital cannot supply the tools for conceiving the just economy.

PART II

Conceiving the Just Economy

4

Hegel's Mandate for the Just Economy

Whereas the praxis and social contract conceptions of justice leave little room for a prescriptive economics, the political economists, Fichte, Rawls, and Marx undermine their own efforts to treat the economy as an ethical concern by relying upon natural and monological paradigms of economic activity. The lesson their examples together provide is not that a normative economic science is unthinkable, but that a dual revolution in thought must be carried through before the just economy can be conceived. Somehow the theory of justice must be reconstructed to make place for an ethical economy and economic theory must be purged of the natural and monological conceptions that condemn economics to ethical neutrality.

The first thinker to meet this dual challenge and establish the framework for prescriptive economics is Hegel. He draws the economy into the realm of ethics by rethinking justice as the reality of self-determination and then reconceiving the economy as a sphere of social freedom, whose character is undetermined by natural and monological factors. Admittedly, his efforts are fragmentary and often misguided, yet they do provide a viable starting point for addressing the just economy.

Hegel's attempt to work out a normative economic theory is most fully presented in his discussion of the "System of Needs" in his *Philosophy of Right*. In certain respects, Hegel's conception shares many features with political economy. Like Adam Smith, he conceives of an economy forming an independent social sphere, liberated from the confines of housekeeping and free from any direct management by secular or religious authorities. It, too, consists in a market system of commodity relations with an order of its own, situated within a civil society. Indeed, Hegel himself acknowledges the achievements of the political economists in using their understanding to discover laws of motion within the world of commerce confronting them.[1] Nevertheless, Hegel understands their success in describing the lawful motion of a given economy to be of no direct aid in pursuing the entirely different enterprise of using reason to conceive what order the economy should have. Although the political economists may have understood their theory to display the anatomy of civilized trade and industry, Hegel is adamant in rejecting their framework and conceiving a strictly social rather than political economy. This reflects his understanding that just economic relations can neither be natural, monological, nor political, but must belong within a civil society whose structures of freedom are not committed to the same ends as civil government, nor derivative of the state of nature construct of social contract theory. In contrast to the political economists, Hegel argues that if economic relations are to be matters of justice falling within a civil society, then both they and that society must consist entirely in nonnatural, intersubjective structures of freedom, distinct from the other conventional modes of freedom comprising just property, moral, household, and political relations.

Hegel's Reconstruction of the Theory of Justice

To understand the justification and consequences of this line of thought, it is necessary to examine what leads Hegel to make his decisive break with the natural and monological terms of political economy. The key lies in the dual insight informing his entire *Philosophy of Right*. By thinking through the dilemmas in traditional ethical philosophy, Hegel comes to realize that 1) justice can have no foundations, and that 2) justice possesses this foundation-free character only if it consists in the reality of freedom where freedom's own structures are determined by free willing rather than by any independent factors such as natural law or the given nature of the self.

Hegel reaches these conclusions by taking in earnest the common truism that justice involves only what lies within the power of voluntary action and not what occurs independently by nature. Although this entails that what ought to be exists only through convention rather than natural necessity, Hegel comprehends that the distinction between "ought" and "is" prohibits given convention from automatically providing the standard of justice. Operative practice may comprise the order to which action conforms, but that only signifies that that conformity has the quality of existence, and not that it possesses legitimacy. Although justice can exist only by convention, convention is just only if its own relations are such that they ought to hold irrespective of what happens to prevail. For example, if an economic order were relative to certain cultural factors that were not themselves structures of justice warranting respect, that economy would be determined by a convention that was not just and thereby lack legitimacy.

Hegel reasons that since given convention cannot prescribe what is just, the relations of justice must be in their entirety both universal and unconditioned. They must be universal insofar as they should hold for every particular situation in which ethics applies. They must be unconditioned insofar as they cannot be relative to any condition lying outside justice without sacrificing their own validity. These qualities do not deprive justice of the particularity of content that ever since Aristotle has been recognized to be basic to conduct. It rather signifies that the only particular factors that can legitimately affect a relation of justice are other relations of justice, whose own right to intervene can follow alone from justice itself. Otherwise, justice would be regulated by independently given factors, whose questionable authority would leave it no more justifiable than any other convention of ordered behavior. Accordingly, justice conditions and particularizes its own relations, which is precisely what allows them to be universal and unconditioned with respect to what lies outside them. Only by being determined through itself can justice avoid being relative to the given conditions of particular circumstances, and attain the unconditioned universality constitutive of normative validity.

The ground-breaking conclusion that Hegel draws is that justice can have no foundations, but must be its own ground and standard. Hence, the theory of justice, including any theory of the just economy, must refrain from deriving the relations of justice from prior principles, such as teleological ends given in nature, or from procedures of construction, such as social contract. In either case, it would be grounding the structure of justice upon something else, raising all the problems of relativity that must be avoided.

Further, Hegel reasons, in order for justice to be its own ground, it must consist in enacted relations of freedom among individuals. Only a thoroughly self-determined convention can owe its character to its own activity, and satisfy the foundation-free requirements of normative validity. Therefore, the theory of justice is not a theory of the Good, where conduct and institutions have validity by embodying given forms antecedently prescribed by reason. Ethics must rather be the theory of right, to the extent that right designates, as Hegel puts it, nothing but the respected reality of freedom.[2]

Admittedly, when Hegel proceeds to develop the theory of justice as a theory of the recognized reality of freedom, he does follow the lead of liberal theory, which first made the freedom of liberty the basis of justice in place of the teleologically prescribed norms of virtue. Nevertheless, Hegel radically departs from the liberal path out of recognition that the freedom of justice can neither be conceived as liberty, nor as a prior principle of justice.

Whereas just action cannot owe its legitimate character to exogenous factors, liberty is afflicted with a heteronomy, a dependence on external matters, extending not only to the content of its ends, as Kant critically observed, but also to its form. Just as its ends are chosen from among alternatives independently supplied by outer circumstance or separate inner faculties of desire and reason, liberty's own form of choice is rooted in the given nature of the self, rather than being determined by its acts of will. That all agents must possess such liberty of choice in order to engage in any conventional activity need not be denied. What must be admitted, however, is that due to its dual bondage to givenness, expressed in the given character of both its ends and its form, liberty lacks the unconditioned universality justice requires and hence warrants no unqualified right. If, nonetheless, naturally defined liberty is made the principle from which institutions of justice are derived, through such procedures as social contract, liberty becomes the determining ground of justice. This immediately destroys the necessary identity of freedom and justice by leaving the institutions of justice determined by a principle of freedom given prior to and separately from them. As a result, justice is robbed of the foundation-free, self-determined character it requires. For these reasons, the economic freedom that would constitute the just economy cannot be founded on the exercise of liberty, so dear to political economy and all natural and technical notions of economics.

By default, the normative inadequacy of liberty suggests to Hegel in what kind of freedom justice must lie. Unlike the natural capacity to choose, it must be a freedom whose form and content are both products of willing, instead of dependent upon external factors. Further, in order to maintain the identity of freedom and justice, its self-determination must be concrete enough to comprise the entire reality of justice. Although Hegel never denies that the choosing will of liberty is a capacity all individuals possess as part of the nature of their selves,[3] he strictly maintains that the freedom of justice must involve an artificial agency that acts in terms of a normative framework that its own willing brings into being. Only then can the structure of willing and all the particulars of its action be truly self-determined as well as coincide with the enacted conventions of justice.

What leads Hegel beyond these basic provisos to the positive conception of justice containing his theory of the just economy is the realization that the will can exercise the mandated freedom of justice not by acting upon nature or its own self, but only by interacting with other wills. So long as the will restricts itself to technical or any other monological activity, the parameters of its action remain defined by independently given, normatively neutral factors of nature and the self that are no more products of willing than structures of justice. If, however, individuals act toward one another so that how and what they will is determined solely in reciprocity with how and what others will, they will all exercise an autonomy whose specific character derives entirely from their freely entered relationship. In such a mutual interaction, what they will is not supplied by independently given factors, but rather by ends whose particulars are specific to the relation between individuals comprised by their concomitant actions. This relationship is not something imposed upon them, where how and what they will are ordained by a structure they have not willed into being. On the contrary, this relationship is nothing but their self-determination, for each participant wills his relation to the others through an act of his choice. This involvement of choice does not signify a reversion to monological action because the particular prerogatives open to it in this context exist only in virtue of the other parties willing that same relation through their own voluntary action.

On these terms, the enacted structure of freedom is one in which each participant wills his own end and relation to others by respecting the self-determinations that they will as part of the same relationship. For this reason, Hegel describes the interaction of freedom as a process of reciprocal recognition.[4] He further observes that such freedom is itself a relation of justice on two accounts. Not only is it self-grounded, defining its own autonomy through its activity, but the complementary self-determinations comprising it proceed in a conjunction of right and duty. The constitutive reciprocity of the interaction renders each act an exercise of right and duty, simultaneously enjoying the respect others afford through their concordant actions and showing respect for their self-determinations by not violating their respective limits. For this reason, each participant can be said to exercise an objective freedom, whose form of mutual respect provides an intersubjective validity assuring its reality.[5]

Although the right and duty endemic in objective freedom make it an existing structure of justice rather than a regulative ideal, Hegel is well aware that the unity of justice and freedom requires that freedom not consist in a single relation of interaction, incapable of containing all the different institutions of right. If freedom were to be conceived as a single mode of interaction, it would comprise but one convention of justice, beside which others independently existed. As a result, freedom and justice would no longer coincide. This discrepancy would put their common normativity in forfeiture and rule out any philosophy of right, let alone one developed as the theory of objective freedom. Consequently, the reality of freedom must comprise a system of interactions incorporating all institutions of justice.

Conceiving the reality of freedom as an all-inclusive system of justice is insufficient, however, if the unification of the various institutions is accomplished from without. That would violate the self-grounded character of justice by introducing an external agency to hold the whole together. Instead, the unity of the system of justice must be imposed from within by a particular institution whose freedom unites and orders the whole as a self-ordered system. Hegel recognizes that the freedom constitutive of a civil society cannot play this role to the extent that social action confines itself to addressing particular interests and welfare. However broad its aims may be, civil activity never involves determining the total structure of justice as the end of its action. The sphere of freedom whose function does consist in ordering the whole framework of right of which it is a part is the political association of self-government.

Hence, Hegel reasons, the system of right must be crowned by a sovereign self-governing state institutionalizing a political freedom whose exercise determines the whole by ruling over all other spheres of right so that their freedoms are secured in unity with its own self-governing activity. Only when political self-determination achieves this preeminence can the entire reality of justice be the source of its own order and unity and free itself of foundations. Then alone can the conventions of justice ground themselves and enjoy unconditioned universality. If, on the contrary, the state collapses public freedom with free enterprise, or reduces government to management of the public welfare, or champions proletarian interest so as to cause itself to wither away, politics becomes an instrument of independently given nonpolitical ends, rather than the self-ordering interaction whose rule allows right to rest on its own freedom.

Because justice, however, requires a sovereign political unity, politics must be for its own sake, as Aristotle already maintained. Politics can figure as a master end in itself only if no other institutions of right challenge its supremacy. Accordingly, no economic order can be just that acts as the determining base of a political superstructure. In this regard, the young Marx's notion of the primacy of an economic base could be said to preclude any talk of a just economy just as much as it precludes any positive affirmation of political relations. More generally, the requirement of the primacy of self-governing politics means that all nonpolitical structures of right must be conceived both in their own right as specific modes of freedom and as subordinate institutions incorporated within the free state.

These dual considerations provide the basic mandate for Hegel's theory of the just economy. Given the foundation-free character of justice uncovered by the *Philosophy of Right,* establishing what the economy should be can only be accomplished by determining both the economic order that consists entirely as a structure of freedom and the relation that economy has to the free state as well as to the other institutions of freedom. Since Hegel locates the just economy within civil society, his prescriptive economics must be evaluated by examining the following: 1) how civil society comprises the normative sphere of social freedom; 2) why the just economy involves the freedom specific to civil society; 3) to what extent Hegel has properly developed prescriptive economics; 4) how the justice of the economy relates to other civil institutions; and finally, 5) how the just economy stands under the rule of self-government.

The Justification of Civil Society

If Hegel's prescriptive economics is to have validity as a normative science of a social rather than a political economy, the justice of freedom must entail not only a civil society, but one containing economic relations. In the *Philosophy of Right* Hegel undertakes to demonstrate that this is so in the course of arguing that right has its exhaustive reality in the freedoms constitutive of property relations, morality, the just household, civil society, and the self-governed state.

As always in a systematic philosophy, the order of exposition bears upon the content of what is presented. Two essential features of civil society lead Hegel to conceive it after property relations, morality, and the family, but before the state. To begin with, although civil society cannot be determined by any natural liberty without losing its self-determined character, it comprises an association whose members already interact as property owners, moral subjects, and family members without, however, pursuing their civil relations in terms of any political involvement. Consequently, civil society can only be conceived if the concepts of personhood, morality, and household have been previously developed. By the same token, Hegel maintains that the just state cannot exist without there being civil freedom with all the social institutions that comprise its exercise. Hence civil society must be accounted for before the institutions of political freedom can be conceived. On these terms, if civil society is to have legitimacy, it must provide a type of freedom presupposed by just politics, yet left lacking by property, moral and household relations.

What satisfies this requirement and gives civil society its legitimating mandate is the respected freedom to realize particular ends of one's own choosing in reciprocity with others. This right is something unfurnished in property relations, morality, and the household, even though it can only be exercised by individuals enjoying the rights of persons, moral subjects, and adult family members.

Indeed, the personhood of an owner is a prerequisite for all further freedoms, since without ownership of one's own body, there is no way one's actions can be recognized as rightfully one's own. Nevertheless, disposing over property does not of itself realize an individual's particular ends in reciprocity with others. As Hegel points out,[6] the property-owning will of the person has no particular end in itself, but first acquires definite content by embodying itself in some external entity. All that is at stake in property relations, considered by themselves, is the establishment, use, and transfer of property. Whether or not owners relate to one another in terms of satisfying each other's interest is a matter of indifference as far as ownership is concerned.

Similarly, as much as morality may underly all ethical institutions by rendering individuals responsible for realizing right through their own actions, the end of moral action is not the mutual realization of particular interests, but whatever conscience determines to be just. Given the prerogative of conscience to decide what is moral regardless of the norms of existing institutions, there can be no guarantee that moral action will promote any of the other modes of freedom.

By contrast, the household does provide an existing association whose members enjoy the right and duty of acting for its common good. However, although the home gives them a private realm on whose basis they are free to enter society, the unity of the family is destroyed if its own members interact within the household in terms of independent interests. In that case, the household loses the common welfare and livelihood making it one.

If these points indicate that the freedom of interests requires more than property, moral and household relations for its realization, what makes a separate civil sphere devoted to its exercise an indispensable necessity is the role such freedom plays as a precondition of free politics. If the state were deprived of a separate civil society to realize the reciprocal pursuit of individual interests, political rule would stand in irreconcilable opposition to the interests of its citizens. Instead of securing the totality of freedom, the state would preside over a nation excluding a whole dimension of its members' autonomy. As this would leave the state responsible for a situation curtailing the freedoms of its citizens, government would forfeit its own legitimacy. Therefore, Hegel concludes, there ought to be a civil society to provide the institutions of freedom for the reciprocal realization of independent interests.[7]

Although this line of argument points to the legitimacy of a civil society, it tells neither what civil society actually is, nor how economic relations fall within it. Rather, it raises the question of what institutions can realize interest as a right and make "civil society" and the "just economy" more than wishful slogans.

Commodity Relations as the Elementary Structures of Civil Freedom

What Hegel discovers is that the immediate answer to this question establishes prescriptive economics as a science of a social economy. Inquiry into civil society is no sooner begun than it arrives at this result because the minimal institution of freedom in which interests are reciprocally realized is none other than the market and its system of commodity relations. Hegel comes to this insight by thinking through the basic mandate of civil society, not as naturally defined by liberal theory and political economy, nor as conditioned by some historical necessity in the manner of dialectical materialism, but in accord with the foundation-free requirements of justice.

On these normative terms, civil society has the task of providing the institutions allowing individuals to realize their interests through a just interaction of self-determinations rather than in an exercise of natural liberty, where all pursue whatever ends they choose without any mutual recognition of right. Hegel recognizes that if civil society is to save the pursuit of interest from a war of all against all, that pursuit must somehow be so fashioned that each individual can achieve his freely chosen ends only by realizing and respecting the like pursuit of others. In that case, action toward others to achieve particular ends of personal choosing will be a doing of justice since it will proceed as part of a mutual observance of right and duty. Instead of following an unconstrained atomistic egotism, each participant would be acting in view of his own interest in cooperation with others insofar as his aim could only be achieved by simultaneously honoring their concordant exercise of that same freedom. Such an arrangement would thus allow for a just community of interest in which the free realization of each member's personal ends figures as a right that all are duty-bound to respect insofar as only in so doing can they engage in their own respected pursuit of interest.

Participation in this minimal framework of civil freedom accordingly consists in seeking the satisfaction of particular ends of one's own choosing where those ends are attainable only through action toward others entailing the concomitant fulfillment of their respective ends. For this to be so, these ends must be personally pursued interests that their bearer cannot realize with either what nature directly provides, what already lies within that individual's household and private ownership, or what others may furnish without thereby realizing an interest of their own. If an interest can be fulfilled by taking what nature immediately offers, there is no question of justice, since relations to other agents do not even enter in. The same is true of ends that can be satisfied solely by using what one already owns within or without one's home. On the other hand, if the end is such that its satisfaction depends upon others without rendering them a like service, it represents a unilateral fulfillment of interest lacking the reciprocity of civil justice, no matter how voluntarily others may lend their aid. For the pursuit of interest to form a just civil activity, the interests at stake must instead require for their realization something that can only be supplied by other individuals, who can offer what is needed only by voluntarily obtaining in return what they need to satisfy their own chosen ends.

Hegel's entire theory of the just economy follows from his recognition that the particular ends meeting these requirements of civil justice consist in needs whose content is completely a matter of personal preference, yet which can only be satisfied by what someone else has to offer under the condition that the bearer of the first need own and agree to offer in return something satisfying a similarly advanced need of the latter. Hegel realizes that due to these social features, such need can be determined neither naturally, as a physical want for what the body requires, nor monologically, as a psychological yearning for what the soul may desire. It may be true, as Hegel grants in his discussion of the right of distress (Notrecht),[8] that every person has a right to satisfy his subsistence needs, insofar as the maintenance of life is a precondition for any exercise of freedom. Nonetheless, the mere maintenance of life does not comprise the specific justice of civil freedom, for the latter extends legitimacy to reciprocally realized interests free of any natural limit. The same holds true for psychological needs. Their satisfaction may be a precondition for the sanity required to exercise one's rights, and therefore should be afforded as far as possible. However, the content of psychological wants cannot prescribe what can figure as a need in civil society, since they lack the reference to the needs of others that can first give need a specifically civil legitimacy.

Accordingly discarding all natural and monological definitions of civil need, Hegel understands that what does characterize it is its direction upon means of satisfaction that can only be obtained from correlatively needy individuals. In line with the freedom of interest, the particular content of such need is a matter of personal preference, and hence may well coincide with some physical or psychological wants. However, what gives a need the normative status of an object of civil right is that its satisfaction is sought in reciprocity with the analogous needs of others. Only this social dimension, consisting in the complementary pursuit of interest of a plurality of individuals, can mandate what figures as a rightful need within the normative relations of civil freedom. Any attempt to limit what can count as a legitimate need by appeal to some "rational" distinction between "natural" versus "artificial," "essential" versus "nonessential" or "authentic" versus "inauthentic" human needs, would only violate the freedom of civil justice, and hence vitiate itself. Conversely, nothing other than the conventions of civil freedom can determine what needs do not enjoy social legitimacy. If, for example, individuals are able to satisfy certain physical or psychological needs, such as for air or water or for affection or counseling, without interacting as proprietors of what the other needs, these needs play no role in the social relations of the community of interest.

Consequently, what comprise the exclusive objects satisfying need that is neither simply natural, psychological nor conventional, but specifically civil, are commodities, goods owned by other individuals who are willing to exchange them to satisfy their own correlatively determined wants. Only within a market, a context where a plurality of commodity owners can freely enter into exchange, can need enjoy the legitimacy of being the particular end pursued within the reciprocal relation of civil freedom. Conversely, only within the market interaction of individuals who need what others own and own what others need, can property function as a commodity, related to not just the will of its owner but the civil need of others with commodities of their own. Hence, the needs at play in the minimal interaction satisfying the mandate for civil society are economic needs in the specific normative sense of needs for commodities, needs that by that very character can only be satisfied in reciprocity with the analogous needs of others.

Hegel therefore concludes that civil society immediately entails a system of needs building a market economy of commodity relations. This nonnatural, nonpolitical, social economy is the institution providing the freedom of interest with its basic reality. Due to the identity of freedom and justice, nothing more is needed for its market order to command the normative validity making it the subject matter of prescriptive economics. Other economic arrangements may be topics of descriptive analyses, but it alone offers a field for developing an independent economic justice.

By repudiating the foundationalism underlying praxis and liberal philosophies of justice, and following out the logic of the philosophy of right, Hegel paves the way for a systematic investigation of what the economy ought to be. His basic line of reasoning has revealed why prescriptive economics can be pursued by conceiving a social economy of commodity relations building the basic institution of civil society. However, what remains to be seen is whether Hegel has properly developed the system of needs as the elementary structure of civil freedom or adequately determined the relation of the market to the other social and political institutions of justice.

The Focal Controversies in Hegel's Theory of the Just Economy

Hegel's account of the anatomy of the system of needs is marked by four overriding features that are as crucial for determining social and political justice as a whole, as for prescribing the just economy.

To begin with, Hegel conceives commodity relations as legitimate structures of freedom proper to civil society. This basic move involves several important considerations. It signifies, first of all, that, contrary to political economy, the market economy is not to be conceived as a natural outgrowth of the human condition that will always arise so long as conventional institutions do not stand in the way. It instead comprises a conventional institution in its own right, presenting just one form in which economic affairs may be ordered. Hence, an analysis of commodity relations does not provide a descriptively universal economic science. It may have descriptive power when a given economy happens to contain commodity relations to greater or lesser extent. However, there is no necessity that such a situation persist or even be encountered in any particular place at any point in time. Needless to say, history and modern anthropology have confirmed this by providing innumerable examples of societies in which markets play little role.[9]

Intimately tied to the nonnatural, conventional contingency of the market economy is the character of whatever laws might define its inner movement. Insofar as Hegel conceives the market economy to be an institution of freedom rather than a product of nature, whatever laws it has are not laws of necessity, conceivable in the manner of a natural science, but laws of freedom, expressing the conventional necessity of a certain enacted social formation. However, to the extent that commodity relations have normative legitimacy as basic features of civil society, the theory of the market economy does not present a model of just any conventional order. It rather has prescriptive universality as a section of the philosophy of justice.

By locating just economic relations within civil society, Hegel by no means precludes a normative consideration of these aspects of economic activity that depend for their determination upon other social and political institutions or upon the relations between nations. Such factors as taxation, public benefits and commercial regulations, tariffs, national currencies and balance of payments can still all be considered, but only after an account is provided of the noneconomic institutions they involve. In this respect, the theory of the just state and proper international relations will incorporate a further determination of the just economy in light of the additional institutional involvements that bear upon it. However, if commodity relations have a character of their own that underlies and shapes any further economic influence of public regulation and international boundaries, the theory of justice must still first conceive the market in its own right regarding the normative features that are already at hand, however incompletely.

The second salient feature of Hegel's prescriptive economics is that he works out the total structure of commodity relations without subsuming them under a system of capitals whose profit derives from wage labor commodity production. Although Hegel does make brief mention of the relationship of capital and labor, he treats it as a subordinate element within the market economy. In contrast to Marx, he does not view it as a privileged determining structure that envelops and orders all commodity relations within its process of capital accumulation.

Third, while Hegel grants legitimacy to commodity relations, he nonetheless argues that they cannot insure that everyone can actually exercise the very right they alone make possible, namely, the respected freedom to satisfy needs of one's own choosing in reciprocity with others. The market economy may provide a framework in which civil freedom can operate, but by itself, it cannot offer its members an equal opportunity to practice their economic rights.

Fourth, Hegel conceives classes as necessary elements of the just economy, but characterizes them in terms more appropriate to estates. As a result, two of his three classes, the so-called "substantial" and "universal" ones, have identities entirely unrelated to commodity relations, whereas the remaining class, the so-called "reflective" one, pursues all the types of earning specific to the market economy.

The significance of the first two features of Hegel's account is set in relief by Marx's mature critique of commodity relations and of the civil society that rests upon them. In contrast to Hegel, Marx rejects the legitimacy of commodity relations, and with them, civil society, because he considers both to be bound up with capitalism. That connection robs them of normativity because, in Marx's view, capitalism is an unjust historical formation resting on the exploitation of labor and subjecting society and state to bourgeois rule in the interest of capital's unlimited and ultimately pernicious accumulation of wealth. Marx does not analyze commodity relations in a prescriptive theory of the just economy, but in a descriptive theory of capital. There he determines commodity relations to be swallowed up within the accumulation process of capital, which comprises not the elementary structure of a normative civil society, but the determining base of a historically given bourgeois society whose overthrow is a necessary prelude to the realization of justice.

If Hegel's prescriptive economics is to provide any contribution to conceiving the just economy, Marx's critique of commodity relations must be countered by showing that the market economy is a structure of freedom, not only irreducible to capital, but containing none of the bonds of domination that Marx ascribes to it. Such a demonstration will equally establish that civil society is not a bourgeois society in Marx's perjorative sense.

Freeing commodity relations from the taint of "capitalist exploitation" will not, however, exonerate the unbridled free enterprise of the market if the third feature of Hegel's account is justified. Hegel's idea that commodity relations cannot automatically realize the freedom in whose exercise they consist contradicts the classic view of political economy that the market orders itself with an invisible hand insuring the welfare of all. If Hegel's argument can be shown to be valid, it will mandate the addition of further institutions of freedom to resolve the problem of social justice that the market introduces. In that case, the theory of the just economy will necessarily transcend the concept of market economy and address the problem of how and to what extent commodity relations should be publicly regulated. This turn will naturally have decisive importance for the competing claims of laissez-faire capitalism, social democracy, syndicalism, and communism.

Finally, Hegel's justification and depiction of a class society rooted in a market economy has crucial bearing upon his own conception of the just society and state, as well as upon the general problems of economic justice. If it can be shown that Hegel's estate characterization of social classes does not result from the economic dynamic of commodity relations, his class division will require major reworkings that will equally affect his conceptions of the corporations and the state, conceptions that rest heavily upon estate relations.

All these issues can only be resolved by turning to Hegel's analysis of the internal structure of the market economy, certifying its achievements, unmasking its failings, and pointing out where rethinking must be undertaken to give justice its due.

5

The Elementary Structure of Market Freedom

Logically enough, Hegel opens his account of the just economy by conceiving the most basic relationship of civil need that incorporates no further commodity relations, yet is presupposed by all other facets of the market economy. If he were to begin with anything less elementary, he would be begging the question by taking for granted certain economic relations when what is at stake is conceiving the just economy in its entirety. The most rudimentary relation of need whereby the reciprocal realization of interest can occur is the market situation where a plurality of individuals face one another both as bearers of personally chosen needs for the commodities of others and as proprietors of some commodity that others similarly need. All further normative market relations follow from this interaction for the simple reason that no one can join in the civil community of interest unless he both chooses to need a commodity belonging to someone else and owns a good that that other individual seeks to acquire. As Hegel's own further treatment indicates, any considerations of commodity production, the total circuit of wealth in the market, or class relations already incorporate the basic opposition of reciprocally needy commodity owners and thus must be treated subsequently to this, their fundamental presupposition.

Hence, Hegel's theory of the just economy must proceed from this starting point to establish the structure and legitimacy of commodity relations. Hegel takes his first steps in this direction in the opening paragraphs of the discussion entitled, "The Kind of Need and Its Satisfaction," which forms the initial section of "The System of Needs" in the *Philosophy of Right*. There he analyzes the character of civil need and commodities as they stand determined within the basic framework of market interaction.

The Civil Characteristics of Market Need and Commodities

From the outset, each of these correlative elements of market activity has its character defined in terms of the civil reciprocity by which their bearers are related. What Hegel recognizes is that this places both needs and commodities in an artificial multitude and diversity where they are marked by constitutive social qualities barring any natural principle from prescribing what they should be. Although civil need and the means of its satisfaction must still conform to the possibilities of physical reality and may indeed incorporate certain naturally given wants and objects, it is the just convention of the reciprocal realization of interest that ultimately decides what may enter in as factors of commodity relations. Since the only utilities that can figure in the market are those both owned by individuals in need of someone else's goods and answering the need of another commodity owner, what defines the variety and plenitude of commodities are not the natural requirements of human survival or the psychological desires of an individual, but the concomitant choices market participants make in deciding what to need and own. By the same token, since the only wants that can figure in the civil reciprocity of the market are those commodity owners have for the commodities of one another, the content of civil need is no more biologically than psychologically defined, but equally socially determined in reference to the needs and commodities of other civilians. How this marks each need and commodity, while rendering their possible refinement and multiplication utterly measureless and capricious are the prime topics of Hegel's opening argument.

What lies immediately at hand in the minimal market situation is the relation of individuals in terms of the correlative poles of civil needs and the commodities providing the means to their satisfaction. Although other contexts may allow these same persons to exercise the specific freedoms of ownership, morality, the household, legal personality, and politics, here in the market place they specifically relate to one another in virtue of these economic factors. It is worth noting that throughout Hegel's discussion, the agency exercised in civil society is identified as that of the bourgeois so as to distinguish it from the political agency of the citizen. To avoid the perjorative connotation of "bourgeois" reflected in Marx's dismissal of civil society as a bourgeois society, it will do to identify the participants in the market simply as civilians.

It should be understood, however, that insofar as property relations allow for the establishment of an artificial person, whose ownership rests on the contractual agreement of a plurality of individuals, the "civilian" participating in the market can just as easily be an artificial agent, such as a private or public corporation, which interacts with other "natural" or artificial agents on the same basis of independently determined needs for the commodities of one another. Although Hegel does not explicitly make this point at the outset of his discussion, and sometimes speaks as if the civilian were the individual in all the particularity of his concrete human being,[1] it is implicit in his theory and taken for granted by much of his subsequent analysis.

Granted these clarifications, Hegel's starting point offers us on one side the independently chosen, yet other-directed need of the civilian who faces in the other participants in the market the patrons of the means to his personal satisfaction. As a freely chosen personal aim that nonetheless relates its bearer to the goods and needs of others, the civil need of the market participant comprises a self-determined factor individuating the market participant in respect to others. Together with the agent's personal commodity ownership it provides the willed basis in terms of which that agent figures in market relations.

In this way civil need provides not a natural desire nor an invitation to a natural subsistence, but the conventional want on which market engagement is predicated. Although it enjoys the normative quality of standing in a complementary relation to the civil needs of others, it has no necessary determination within itself. Civil need is simply self-interest as a relation to other without any further precision as to its content. It embraces all and any commodities that the market participant chooses as the object of his personal, yet other-directed want. Since its content is mediated by both the choice of that market participant and the choices of others to own and want commodities for themselves, what need is to be satisfied through the market defies essential prescription just as does what goods are to constitute means of conventional satisfaction. As Hegel points out in his *Lectures On the Philosophy of Right,* civil need can have any content so long as what satisfies it is owned by someone else with need for commodities, just as a commodity can be anything so long as it is property needed by some commodity owner other than its proprietor.[2] Hence, the only restrictions that apply are those limiting what can or cannot qualify as legitimate objects of property. In his discussion of property relations, Hegel has already argued that only rightless entities can become objects of ownership, provided that they are such that an owner can set its will in them in a recognizable fashion.

If this leaves civil need with a virtually infinite scope, it also renders civil need infinitely insatiable. No matter what commodity may be obtained, it can only provide a particular satisfaction to a market participant. Because civil need has no fixed limit, but is a free product of personal preferences, which can always alter as matters of choice, market demand can never satisfy itself in a truly universal, everlasting fashion. Instead of satiated peace once and for all, there is momentary satisfaction, taking place in some particular manner, ready to be supplanted by newly chosen conventional wants no matter how completely natural needs may have been met. Consequently, the need for commodities just as much reproduces itself as the consequence of consumption.[3]

Although civil need thereby places its bearer in a boundless indigence and dependence upon others that no commodity acquisition can ever entirely eliminate, it equally represents a liberation of need from the natural bonds of physical necessity and given desires. Instead of being burdened by needs for whose necessity no one is responsible, the market agent gives himself artificial social wants within a framework where their satisfaction has become a matter of justice.[4] In this sense, the independent need of market agents is not only freed of natural limits, but granted an affirmative civil value. Through their complementarity, the civil needs of commodity owners allow personal preference to figure in a normatively valid pursuit of self-interest, valid insofar as it is predicated upon the social necessity of advancing the interests of others.

As Hegel observes, the incipient interconnection of needs and commodities is not something external to their character. Rather, the market situation impresses both with universal social features expressing their relation to the needs and commodities of other agents. Civil need, as a need for a certain commodity, only exists in reference to possible objects of satisfaction owned by agents having a need for some different object belonging to someone else. Hence, each market need is related through its own particular content to the needs of other commodity owners. In this sense, every market need distinguishes itself as a civil need in general, inherently related to others possessing the same social interdependence, while differentiating itself from those not sharing its reference to the specific commodity satisfying its want. It is this intrinsic commonality with other market needs that Hegel points to in describing how the need of market participants figures as an "abstract need," setting them on a par as bearers of commensurable interests whose pursuit can be a matter of right.[5]

Of course, as Hegel takes pains to point out, the equation and differentiation of market needs can only occur in tandem with the analogous social determination of the commodities to which they refer. By being an object for market need, a commodity is automatically comparable both to all other objects belonging to its owner and to all commodities that can also serve the same need addressed to it. Further, insofar as the relation of a specific market need to a specific article of property is an instance of market need and ownership per se, any object of market need and will is just as comparable to objects of market need and will in general. Hence the particular existence of a commodity equally involves the universal qualities of being an object not just of this need and that will, but of market need and will per se.[6] Just as market need could be called an abstract need, standing in a social identity and difference to the needs of other commodity owners, so the commodity is a good bearing what can be termed use value and possession value, that is, the reference to both a particular want and proprietorship and to market need and ownership in general. These correlative social qualities give expression to the commensurability and difference commodities inherently possess in regard to one another in function of the complementary needs of their owners.

They also underly the conventional multiplication and refinement of needs and commodities implicit in the basic market situation. Insofar as market needs and commodities are defined solely by the interrelated free decisions of individuals, specific needs can be endlessly duplicated by whoever chooses to want the commodities that others seek, just as specific commodities can be brought to market in any conventional amount so long as their owners are ready to relinquish them in pursuit of different means to satisfy their own needs. Similarly, since the variety of market need and commodities depends on nothing but the arbitrary decisions of commodity owners to seek different goods from one another, needs and goods are subject to an artificial variegation as measureless as the caprice on which it rests. Although this does not prevent natural needs and naturally scarce objects from figuring as market needs and commodities, it does signify that economic need and use value cannot be viewed as anthropological factors of the human condition, as political economists and Marx have suggested. Hegel's argument has rather shown how the market entails an artificial framework in which what counts as a utility is as much a matter of social convention as what counts as a need. Precisely because both the quality and quantity of needs and use values are here determined through the concomitant independent choices of market agents, the satisfaction of market need can comprise an act of self-determination, involving not just the free choice of natural liberty, but the conventional autonomy where agents determine their own agency as market participants by allowing others to exercise the same civil right.

In this light, the market's conventional multiplication and refinement of needs and commodities has crucial ramifications for economic justice and the normative status of commodity relations. By redefining the content of need in virtue of the free interaction of commodity owners, the market establishes an economic domain liberated from rule by the physical requirements of individuals and the natural scarcity of objects meeting bodily wants. Through the conventions of the market, the natural necessity of want is superseded by the artificial necessity of civil needs rooted in the conventional autonomy of market agents. By multiplying and differentiating them in as unlimited a manner as it does the commodities to which they refer, the market renders the need for commodities a factor of freedom, providing a medium for agents to determine themselves in mutual respect for the conventional autonomy they therein exercise. Given the normativity common to self-determination, justice must extend to the interdependent satisfaction of these civil needs. Although the freedom of commodity relations neither establishes nor curtails the right of agents to satisfy those natural and psychological needs that are requirements for existing and acting autonomously toward others, it widens the entitled satisfaction of need to include the conventional, unnecessary wants of the market. Because satisfying the need for commodities consists in exercising the freedom of interest in conjunction with that of others, the justice of that freedom must apply to whatever needs figure within it. However "unnatural," "inauthentic," "irrational," and "excessive" they may seem, their role as factors of market self-determination makes their satisfaction a matter of economic, civil right to which all members of the market are entitled.

Hegel is well aware that this ethical imperative of the market makes social justice a problem much more formidable than the liberal task of protecting the person and property of each individual. Due to the market's multiplication and differentiation of needs and commodities beyond all natural limit, what must be treated as a civil right of every commodity owner is the interdependent satisfaction of an interminably multifarious and refined need that can only be satisfied by commodities already owned by others in an equally artificial plenitude and diversity. Although the market gives each member of society the opportunity to select from a wealth of luxury exceeding all physical requirement, it places them all in a dependent penury just as endless. As Hegel observes, not only is each market participant's need for commodities as unlimited as the conventions of personal preference, but it can only be legitimately satisfied by goods that others own and voluntarily yield for different commodities addressing their comparably arbitrary wants.[7] Since sating the market need for commodities depends not upon a metabolism with nature, but upon freely entered social relations of commodity owners, the barrier to satisfaction does not consist in the malleable resistance of natural scarcity, which technical mastery can overcome. Realizing everyone's civil right to satisfy their independently chosen needs in reciprocity with others rather requires coping with the normative barrier of entitled commodity ownership. It can be violated by theft, but it may only be undone in accord with civil justice through the free consent of the owner.[8]

Hence, the unsatisfied need for commodities comprises a conventional poverty specific to the market. It need not involve any deprivation of the means of subsistence, for commodity owners can have all their survival needs met while yet lacking marketed goods required by their artificial wants. The problem confronting each market participant is not one of answering natural necessity with what is given in natural scarcity. What each faces is the problem of escaping the social poverty of an endless want for a conventional cornucopia of goods, where none can be legitimately acquired from their proprietors without trading a different commodity of one's own that they need.

What makes the persistence of such poverty a civil wrong is that it represents an infringement upon the economic freedom of the poor. By failing to earn the conventional livelihood to which all market participants are entitled, the victims of poverty are deprived not just of goods, but of the opportunity to exercise their autonomy as a rightful member of the community of interest. Although this poses problems of economic justice that can only be satisfactorily resolved in relation to the concrete workings of the entire market economy, it already mandates the basic manner by which the civil wrong of poverty should be made right. As participants in the market, there is only one way for commodity owners to acquire the goods they need in a mutual exercise of freedom. This is by freely exchanging the commodities they seek. Through the reciprocal deed of their exchange, each party engages in the self-determination establishing his identity as the entitled bearer of an autonomously chosen civil need who justly satisfies it in a free act duly honoring the commodity ownership and civil need of the other party. By freely entering into commodity exchange, acquiring from one another different goods satisfying their complementary needs, commodity owners confirm their membership in the community of interest by giving it that most elementary realization presupposed by all further market relations.

Commodity Exchange

Having laid bare these ramifications of the conventional character of market needs and commodities, Hegel next raises the decisive point that follows from the logic of the basic market situation. Thinking through the process of market freedom, Hegel observes that within the reciprocal relationship of exchange the traded commodities acquire a further social quality consisting in the equivalence in exchangeability of one good for another as realized in their actual exchange.[9] Although Hegel never gives this quality a name of its own, distinguishing it from the market utility or use value that each commodity possesses as the object of some market need, what he is addressing is exchange value, the equivalent exchangeability of commodities determined and exhibited in their exchange.

Hegel recognizes that commodity exchange is such that the exchangeability of goods ultimately rests on the complementary acts of will by which commodity owners choose to need and trade what each other owns. To be exchangeable, goods must already share the conventional qualities of being objects of property and objects of different market needs born by commodity owners other than their proprietors. However, commodities do not become actually exchangeable until their respective owners freely choose to trade them. Only when that occurs do they figure within a market transaction in which they obtain a determinate exchangeability. What then gives the traded commodities both the common quality of exchangeability in general and a specific exchange value are nothing but the mutual acts by which their owners render them equivalently exchangeable. Neither the natural scarcity nor psychological attraction of a good can mandate its exchange value, for the freedom of exchange leaves it up to the bilateral agreement of commodity owners to decide what goods are exchangeable against one another and in what proportions. Because the exchangeability of commodities is determined in and through a reciprocal relation of independent market agents, no natural or monological factor can dictate the exchange value of any good.

Therefore, exchange value is neither intrinsic to the natural qualities of the exchanged goods, nor rooted in a psychological evaluation of them, nor determined by anything preceding the freely entered exchange act setting them in their actual relation of equivalence. Although commodities are not exchanged unless they have use value, Hegel has already established that market utility does not refer to natural or psychological wants, but only to the socially specific want of commodity owners for the goods of one another. His analysis of exchange now reveals that there is no necessary relation between use value and exchange value, since the exchangeability of a commodity depends not just on its reference to the needs of others, but on the mutual decision of the traders involved. Hence, the conventional use value of a commodity leaves entirely undetermined what its actual exchange value shall be. The voluntary bilateral character of commodity exchange renders the determination of exchange value entirely independent of any factor other than the reciprocal acts of freedom by which exchange takes place. What makes commodities exchangeable are the concurring decisions of their respective owners, who are independent market agents, free to decide what they need and how they will dispose over their own commodities. In entering the transactions through which exchange value is determined, they need not be swayed by any particular external consideration, nor follow any putative model of "economic rationality." Although certain exchanges may have foreseeable consequences that are beneficial or injurious according to a certain standard, the constitutive freedom of commodity owners leaves them the prerogative to decide as they will. The only constraint they face is the conventional necessity of arriving at agreement with other commodity owners, who themselves act under the same civil compulsion of having to provide for the commodity needs of others in order to satisfy their own.

This is true even when one considers more concrete market relations, where consumers face a situation in which goods are sold at set prices. Even here, the exchange value of goods exhibited in price gets realized only insofar as buyers choose to accept the terms of exchange. Because exchange remains a bilateral act, the most monopolistic sellers are still under constraint to change their prices to meet the demand of buyers, or else face the prospect of a rising inventory of unsold items. As much as commodity exchange gets further qualified within the market structures that incorporate it, its constitutive bilateral freedom continues to operate with an effect that can never be ignored without falsifying the reality of commodity relations.

To what extent Hegel uncovers the working of exchange as it is embedded in further market structures remains to be seen. What his analysis of exchange already suggests is that the economic freedom of commodity owners would be infringed upon by any state of affairs where the exchange values of goods are fixed independently of the choices of the parties to exchange. This would represent an economic wrong unless it occurred for overriding considerations of justice, such as imperatives of political sovereignty or public welfare requiring limitations of market freedom, but not its complete elimination.

The freedom of exchange versus the labor theory of value

Hence, any labor theory of value that determines the proportions at which commodities are exchanged by the expenditure of labor in their production fails either as a descriptive theory of the reality of market relations or as a prescriptive doctrine of how commodity exchange should be regulated. As a normative conception of how exchange value should be determined, a labor theory of value automatically violates the economic rights of commodity owners to choose their market needs and trade their property as they see fit. As a descriptive model of how exchange values are set in the market, labor theories of value automatically falsify the reality of commodity exchange by ignoring the free mutual agreement of the parties to exchange that first determines what commodities are exchangeable and at what proportions. It makes no difference whether commodity owners find themselves in a predicament where the going market prices are such that trading below them leads to losses in personal wealth. They are still at liberty to make whatever offer they will, just as sellers holding to given market prices must contend with the independent decisions of others that engender fluctuations in demand. On all sides, what creates the constraints and restricted opportunities in a given market are preceding exchange decisions, which then as now, only take place insofar as both parties finally agree to mutually acceptable terms of trade. Although this ubiquitous element of market freedom does not preclude the working of definite laws governing the individual and global consequences of exchange transactions, its constitutive presence is always felt, so long as market institutions are retained.

Unless the determining role of reciprocal agreement is acknowledged, the very range of exchange value becomes an imponderable mystery. The conundrum posed for labor theories of value by the exchangeability of nonproduced goods, such as land and labor power,[10] disappears once the fruits of Hegel's analysis of exchange are employed. Since what makes commodities exchangeable are the mutual decisions of their owners, the origin of a good has no determinate effect on what exchange value it may bear. Be it a gift of nature or a manufactured article, a commodity can have exchange value so long as its owner offers it in trade and some other market agent agrees to give another commodity for it. Hence when it comes to exchange value, nonproduced items are on the exact same footing as products of labor. Both acquire their specific exchange values in virtue of the exchange agreement setting their equivalencies with other goods.

Accordingly, when prescriptive economics advances from the basic opposition of commodity owners to analyze exchange value as it is constituted in commodity exchange, it is addressing a social quality applying to all commodities. Exchange value is not something rooted in an antecedent production process and hence limited to the particular class of commodities qualifying as products. Hegel, unlike Marx, understands this, and therefore properly treats commodity exchange before and independently of conceiving the production of commodities. To do otherwise would be tantamount to taking for granted the constitutive features of commodities that must already be determined in order for the production of commodities for exchange to be an object of thought or reality. This is the fatal dilemma of any labor theory of value. By deriving exchange value from the labor process, it is compelled to conceive commodity production before conceiving the exchange of commodities. Then, however, it cannot allow any of the elements of production to already be commodities without falling into self-contradiction. For if it grants that commodities play a role in the production of commodities, as must be done to conceive a capitalist production process where factors of production are purchased in the market, it makes production dependent upon independently given commodities while affirming that all goods bearing exchange values are products. In this regard, it is telling that when Marx first derives his labor theory of value, he does not refer to a context of capitalists producing commodities with previously purchased factors of production, but to a collection of private producers, who first enter exchange after producing utilities they do not need.[11]

Admittedly, when Hegel subsequently examines the labor process specific to the market economy, he does claim that labor impresses its product with value.[12] However, Hegel does not thereby fall into the trap of the labor theory of value, for he refrains from claiming that labor's act sets the exchange value at which its products are actually bought and sold, or, for that matter, that labor furnishes surplus value that appears in transformed shape as realized profit. Hegel's mention of a production of value by labor instead correctly refers to how the labor expended in the manufacture of a commodity gives the material it works upon a new form providing it with a new utility. This allows the finished product to have an exchangeability different from that of the materials from which it was manufactured, although the actual measure of its exchange value will still depend upon the subsequent market agreement setting the terms of its actual sale, rather than upon what earlier transpired in its production. Hence, labor's production of a new use value may result in a product whose exchange value just as well falls short as exceeds that of the factors of its production.

What Hegel here uncovers in conceiving commodity exchange

bears directly upon the legitimacy of market relations for it disarms some of the chief objections to them that Marx has raised in *Capital*. There Marx begins calling into question the justice of the market by maintaining that commodity exchange gives rise to a fetishism of commodities where the transactions of individuals take the form of relations between things governing their conduct.[13] However, Hegel's examination of the interaction underlying exchange value has uncovered how commodity exchange involves reciprocal self-determinations by the parties to the transaction that run totally counter to the domination by objects that Marx describes. In the first place, the goods exchanged in the market do not figure simply as things defined in terms of their natural features. They rather operate as commodities characterized by the conventional market qualities of use and exchange values that they bear, not in virtue of natural or psychological necessity, but as freely determined by the complementary choices of their owners. Far from lording over those who exchange them, these goods can only be traded, instead of being appropriated by force, through their owners' voluntary agreement. This is an agreement in which they recognize each other both as autonomous property owners, entitled to freely dispose of their respective commodities, and as independent market agents, enjoying the civil economic right to satisfy commodity needs of their own election in reciprocity with other commodity owners. Therefore, whenever market agents enter into an exchange, the last thing they can do is interact as subjects under the dominion of things whose blind movements order their lives. No matter how fetishistic they may feel, market agents have no choice upon entering commodity exchange but to play the role of masters of commodities, freely using them as means to satisfy civil wants and as vehicles for exercising their right to fulfill particular interests of their own that promote those of others.

If this removes the challenge of "commodity fetishism," it does not defuse Marx's further objections to the market. Marx himself will grant that exchange relations do proceed in a reciprocally recognized and recognizing freedom and equality according them the justice of an exercise in civil right. However, their freedom and equality would be reduced to a purely formal justice if, as Marx famously maintains, expended labor creates and determines exchange value, and commodity production rests on a relation of capital and labor where labor is exploited. These intertwined claims lie at the root of Marx's repudiation of commodity relations, as well as of most critiques of market economy that have followed in his wake. Influential as these claims have been, they follow "commodity fetishism" in having their untenability unmasked by Hegel's analysis of exchange.

Accepting the natural and monological terms of political economy,

Marx is compelled to introduce his labor theory of value to remove the dilemma exchange represents so long as the constitutive role of interaction is ignored. Convinced that the exchangeability of goods must reside in something prior to the bilateral agreement of the parties to exchange, Marx follows Smith and Ricardo in reasoning that the possibility of commodity exchange must depend upon some given factor providing all goods with a commensurable exchange value. This privileged factor cannot be sought in the natural features or utility of traded goods, for their physical properties and use values are different, and indeed must be different for their exchange to take place. With reference to the exchange agreement excluded, Marx has little else to turn to than the labor commonly embodied in every produced commodity. Admittedly, this offers no solution if the labor in question be regarded in its concrete expenditure, for then every laboring is different rather than equivalent. However, if labor be regarded in terms of some aspect by which all work can be compared in a measured fashion, then this common feature of labor can serve as the basis of commensurable commodity exchange. Hence, Marx turns to the quantitative measure of labor, the abstract labor time of its expenditure, and trumpets it as the commensurable basis for the exchange equivalence of traded goods.[14]

Like all labor theories of value, Marx's conception takes for granted that commodities are all produced. By making this assumption, he commits the fundamental category mistake of conflating the genus commodity with the particular class of commodities that are products, while treating features germane to the latter as if they were constitutive of qualities common to commodities in general. As we have seen, this not only renders incomprehensible the exchange value of nonproduced goods, including that of labor power, which figures so prominently in Marx's theory of surplus value, but the production of commodities by commodities, without which Marx's own conception of capitalist production is unthinkable.

The root difficulty is that Marx's labor theory of value contradicts the bilateral voluntary character of commodity exchange that he must otherwise acknowledge to speak of any market relations whatsoever. As Hegel has shown, the sole enabling condition of exchange is the free agreement of the owners of the traded commodities. Hence, what actually determines the equivalent exchange value of traded goods is the concord of their owners to exchange them in whatever proportion they may have chosen. Since they are free to trade any alienable property that can satisfy the complementary needs of other commodity owners, exchanged commodities need not be produced. Similarly, since the independence of commodity owners gives every market agent the ability to reject offered terms of exchange, the sale of products at any given price is never automatic or unilaterally secured. In other words, the production process of traded products cannot have any binding hold upon the prices at which they are bought and sold, which is why competitive price cutting is both possible and at times a market necessity. All that the factors of production do determine is the minimum price at which the product must be sold to cover the costs of its manufacture. They do this, however, not in virtue of how they figure within the production process, but in terms of the prices at which they were purchased by the producer. As with any other commodity, their prices are determined not by any antecedent expenditure of labor, but by the bilateral agreement defining their own exchange.

Money and further forms of commodity exchange

Hegel accordingly recognizes that exchange relations involving money and the earning of profit can be considered after the elementary exchange of two commodities without making reference to commodity production and expended labor, whereas production of commodities for sale can only be conceived after the exchange relations on which it is predicated. Because money is itself a commodity whose special character is defined in terms of how it relates to the exchange values of other goods, any conception of monetary exchange incorporates and hence presupposes the account of the exchange of different commodities. By contrast, as Hegel indicates, the analysis of money and the expenditure of money for the sake of gaining more money need not incorporate and presuppose relations of commodity production.

Admittedly, Hegel only begins to bear this out by providing an incomplete and sketchy account of money and the different forms of commodity exchange. Nevertheless, he does list three principle forms: 1) the exchange of particular commodities, 2) the exchange of commodities for money, and 3) the exchange of money for more money, significantly leaving totally unspecified whether the commodities involved be products or not.[15] Hegel is able to analyze money without bringing in commodity production because he understands that all that is needed for a commodity to function as money is for commodity owners to honor it in their exchanges as the universal equivalent and standard of measure of the exchange value of all other commodities.[16] Although state fiat may be required to make the money commodity legal tender, this is not a necessary condition for a commodity to occupy the privileged position that money enjoys. For monetary exchange to occur, it is enough that market agents choose to treat a certain commodity as the exclusive medium in which the exchangeability of every good is expressed. It is through these multilateral acts of market freedom that the money commodity is enabled to stand apart from other goods as the independently existing representation of their exchangeability.[17] In this conventional role, the money commodity acquires a utility divorced from its own natural features, such as what it is to be the metal gold, and lying instead in its very exchange value.[18] Instead of responding to a specific market need, money figures as the owned and needed mediator of exchangeability.[19]

In playing this role as a means of exchange where one commodity is sold and the money received is used to purchase another, money is, as Hegel suggests, still ruled by the specific exchange value that it expresses in facilitating the trade of one good for another.[20] Because it here represents the particular commensurability established within a given exchange, money has a bound measure. However, once money operates as a means of exchange, market agents are in a position to advance money in order to receive more in return. This pursuit of exchange value for its own sake requires no more than that a market agent with money find another willing to sell a commodity that the former can then resell at a higher price to some other willing party. The free reciprocity of exchange makes this all possible, first by establishing exchange value in the exchange of two different commodities, and then by establishing money through the exchange of some commodity as an acknowledged means of exchange or means of payment for other goods. Hegel may not have analyzed all the essential aspects of these three forms of exchange, nor explained their constitutive relationship, but he has pointed out their basic features and listed them in the order in which they must be treated.[21] In so doing, he has revealed how the freedom of exchange enables market agents to advance money in order to receive more money in return. This gives market need a new object, namely, capital understood as money needed not to obtain particular use values, but to be advanced in exchange so as to acquire an ever increasing exchange value. By showing how the bilateral agreements of exchange themselves make possible this purely conventional form of wealth, Hegel has uncovered why profit can be earned through speculative trade without any intervening engagement in production, as well as why the acquisition of "surplus value" can and must be first conceived without reference to commodity production.

The breakdown of Marx's concept of the exploitation of labor

By contrast, Marx rests his entire theory of the exploitation of labor on the conviction that exchange cannot engender a profit by itself. Again ignoring the capacity of market interaction to determine exchange values, he instead treats traded commodities as if they had invariable exchange values given independently of the wills of their owners. On these terms, the exchange sequence, defined by the schema M-C-M', where one market agent purchases a commodity from another (M-C) and next sells it at a greater price than he paid (C-M'), presents Marx with a puzzle. If the exchange value of the purchased goods is not determined through the agreement of the parties to exchange, but remains constant from one exchange to the other, then the added exchange value received at the end of the second transaction is a mystery contradicting the constitutive equivalence of every commodity exchange. This mystery can only be solved, Marx reasons, if the surplus exchange value obtained originates somewhere outside the acts of exchange. His answer is that the market agent who advances money to receive more in return obtains his increment by engaging in an intervening production of commodities. This supplies him with a surplus value that can be realized through sale of the product provided its sale price exceeds the costs of its manufacture. What makes this possible, Marx claims, is that labor produces exchange value and the hired laborer is paid less for his labor power than the exchange value his labor creates.[22]

The "exploitation" of labor, so central to Marx's condemnation of capitalism, consists in this inequality between the payment the laborer receives and the exchange value his labor produces. Marx does admit that this exploitation entails no juridical wrong on two accounts. First, since every commodity exchange equates the exchange values of the goods it involves, it makes little sense to deny that the laborer is paid the equivalent exchange value of his labor power. Second, the laborer is not robbed of the surplus value created by labor because the laborer does not own his labor. Unlike the labor power he sells, the labor he performs is not a commodity with exchange value, but only the form in which the labor power already bought by his employer gets consumed.[23] Nevertheless, Marx can still maintain that the exploitation of labor condemns civil freedom to an empty formality if the rate of this exploitation does determine the rate of surplus value upon which profit and capital investment ultimately depend. In that case, the juridical equality between laborer and employer would not prevent commodity relations from being subject to a factor independent of the reciprocal willing of market agents, namely the rate of exploitation antecedently determined in the production process. The economic autonomy of commodity owners would then be a hollow shell.

What completely undermines these consequences is that Marx's whole notion of the exploitation of labor stands or falls with the basic claim of his labor theory of value: that the exchange values of commodities are determined by the quantity of abstract labor time expended in their production. Once, however, due note is given to Hegel's insight that commodities have their exchange values ultimately determined by the mutual agreement of the parties to exchange, the pillars of Marx's theory fall to the ground. It now becomes evident that no intervening commodity production need take place for market agents to engage in a M-C-M' exchange sequence and earn a profit. Furthermore, it now becomes impossible for there to be any exploitation of labor as Marx understands it.

Such exploitation is ruled out because the exchange value of a product has no necessary connection to the quantity of labor time embodied in its production. Like any nonproduced commodity, the exchange value of any product depends instead upon the wills of both its seller and prospective buyers. Since they are independent commodity owners, at liberty to reject each other's offer, capital's realization of profit is anything but an automatic consequence of its internal organization of production. Because the owner of capital cannot unilaterally dictate that and how his products be sold, but must return to the market to try to sell his products above their costs of production, making a profit becomes a contingent endeavor of successful competition, subject to all the variation in sales volumes and price levels that market dependence entails. Since this leaves exchange value neither created nor measured by the expenditure of abstract labor time, the very terms are absent that are needed to define the exploitation of labor and allow surplus value to be determined by what antecedently occurs in production.

For this very reason, there can be neither exploitation nor unequal exchange between laborer and capitalist. Insofar as the owner of capital does not unilaterally appropriate the worker's labor power, but acquires it in a bilateral exchange, the actual exchange value of the purchased labor power is determined by their agreement, which alone finalizes the terms of sale. On the basis of market relations, the exchange value of labor power cannot be determined by any independently given standard. Since this leaves no "true" value to refer to other than that generated in the exchange agreement, there can be nothing unequal in the buying and selling of labor power. This purely conventional character of the market determination of the wage is precisely what makes the transaction between workers and employers subject to the various individual and joint bargaining measures that either side may employ to cajole an acceptable agreement.

Although this does leave open the possibility of wage settlements leaving either workers or employers in positions of relative social disadvantage, it does not entail the automatic impoverishment of either party, or any automatic enrichment of one side at the expense of the other. What can be said with certainty, however, is that the labor used by an employer cannot unilaterally determine the price at which its products are eventually sold. All labor can take credit for contributing is the creation of a new utility that might help make the product saleable at a profit. Because only the wills of producers and consumers can decide what sales volume and realized price will be, labor can no more create an exchange value exceeding the purchase price of labor than produce any determinate exchange value at all.

If this brings Marx's theory of exploitation to the brink of collapse, it also bears upon capital and its relation to the market in ways that Hegel's concept of the just economy must, and largely does, take into account.

6

The Place of Capital in the Market Economy

Although Hegel's argument makes comprehensible how commodity exchange is a legitimate structure of civil freedom, whose authority cannot be challenged by any labor theory of value, the significance of capital for the just economy is still undecided. Hegel's analysis of exchange has already established that the earning of profit constitutive of capital can proceed within the boundaries of commodity relations. The question remains as to whether capital's role within the market economy has legitimacy as a consonant expression of the freedom of interest or illegitimacy as a fatal impediment to economic autonomy. Does capital's quest for ever more wealth infect the market with an uncontrollable force fostering economic disadvantage and shackling the freedom of interest to the blind wheel of capital accumulation? And if so, can capital be excised from commodity relations as a tumorous perversion, or is it a necessary, irremovable organ of the market, undermining its legitimacy and condemning civil association to the ignominy of a bourgeois society?

These questions cannot be answered by turning to the historical record of capitalism and examining the social consequences of the particular forms that capital has so far taken. Reliance on this evidence can provide no assurance that what lies observed either exhausts the possible reality of capital or offers capital's intrinsic nature rather than contingent features of only historical interest. To determine whether capital can belong within the just economy, one must instead conceive the universal structure essential to capital and consider what is necessarily entailed.

Admittedly, Hegel's analysis of capital is pitifully scanty. Nevertheless, his conception of commodity relations does provide enough resources for some preliminary conclusions.

Rethinking the Essential Nature of Capital

Naturally, any investigation of capital must begin with its constitutive M-C-M' circuit of exchange, which builds capital's most elementary reality and which all further relations of capital incorporate and presuppose. Hegel's analysis of exchange value has shown that this defining exchange sequence can be accounted for in virtue of commodity exchange, independently of commodity production or any other external factor. As we have seen, the only thing needed to enable a market agent to buy a commodity and sell it at a profit is that someone agrees to sell him that good at a price lower than someone else agrees to pay for it when it is subsequently resold. Since both exchanges involve equivalencies founded on nothing more than the market agents' agreement to trade their goods and money, these commodities need not be products. Hence, the basic interaction of capital need not rest upon any intervening production process, but may simply involve speculative buying and selling.

Furthermore, as Hegel's argument has revealed, the free agreements by which capital's sequential transactions proceed preclude anything else from governing capital's gain of profit. Far from being automatic, each exchange depends upon the prospective parties reaching a mutually acceptable bargain that decides the price at which the commodity is bought and sold. As a result each prospective owner of capital faces four possibilities, none of which can be unilaterally guaranteed: he may resell the commodity purchased with his first advance of money at a profit, at a break-even price, or at a loss, or he may completely fail to find any buyer. It is completely senseless to maintain that any prior expenditure of labor could ensure the creation of a surplus value and determine its measure independently of the arbitrary decisions of consumers. Any such predetermination of capital's accumulation of exchange value would contradict the free reciprocity constitutive of commodity exchange, thereby destroying the basis of the M-C-M' transactions that give capital its defining minimal structure.

Indeed, the whole dynamic of capital accumulation becomes incomprehensible unless the nonautomatic character of profit realization is taken into account. The contingency and variability in the sale of commodities that makes competition a possible and compelling fate for every owner of capital is entirely rooted in the mutual freedom of exchange. This interdependent market autonomy not only gives consumers and suppliers the prerogative to reject any price offering, but permits every owner of capital to make any market decision they choose, no matter what the "rational" strictures of cost efficiency and profit maximization may command. Producers may find themselves compelled to cut prices, advertise to attract consumers and differentiate their product from others, or even change their entire line to meet consumer demand. Yet they still have the liberty to refuse to change their market strategy, whereas if they do, their decisions may just as well lead to success as to financial ruin no matter what their actual intentions may be. In every case, so long as capital must reenter the market to earn a profit, the ultimate arbiter of realized exchange value remains the elusive unpredictable siren of mutual agreement.

Hence no matter what figures result from calculations of expended labor time, the owner of capital must perennially contend with a realization problem transcending the workings of production. The costs of production may indeed set the break-even point for sales, but they leave undetermined whether any sales will be achieved as well as what magnitude they and the resulting gains or losses may attain. Further, although these profits and losses may largely determine what funds an owner of capital has available to reinvest and market new commodities, they cannot mandate whether or how the capitalist will choose to reinvest, nor whether other commodity owners will offer for sale on acceptable terms the goods and services needed for any new investment to be made. And finally, even if a strategy of reinvestment is chosen and the means be purchased for a new round of production and marketing, any ensuing capital accumulation is subject to the same contingencies afflicting all prior profit realizations.

The myth of perfect competition

For all these reasons, market freedom actually precludes the ideal of perfect competition, by whose invisible hand capital gets automatically shifted from one line of business to another in quest of the greatest return, leading to a continual approximation of an average rate of profit in all branches of commerce. Falsifying the market conditions of capital accumulation, this conception presupposes that capital can be withdrawn and reinvested with an unrestricted mobility, that investors will automatically be guided by correct considerations of profit maximization, that they will find agreeable buyers and sellers to permit them to alter their investments accordingly, and that investors will automatically realize a profit in function of the cost advantages of their enterprises. Each of these assumptions ignores the constitutive willfulness of capital investment and consumer demand, whose contingency creates its own barriers to entry, compounding the limits to the mobility of capital already inherent in the fixed elements of investment that cannot be removed or divested without loss. Although Hegel's sketchy treatment of capital hardly touches upon the workings of these barriers, his analysis of exchange has provided enough to indicate how their presence is not an extraneous contortion of market relations. It rather represents an essential feature of capital accumulation that renders competition intrinsically imperfect, fostering developments of monopoly that further impede the mobility of capital and the convergence of rates of profit in different fields of investment. Admittedly, any analysis of imperfect competition requires an account of capital going far beyond the bare remarks that Hegel offers. Nonetheless, the rudimentary market predicament of capital already belies the prevalent views that competition is antithetical to monopolization or that capitalism necessarily develops from a stage of perfect competition to a stage of monopoly capital. The conditions of market freedom provide a very different lesson, confirmed whenever commodity relations are left to themselves: free competition always allows for monopolization as part and parcel of its own dynamic.

The open identity of capital

Once Hegel's analysis of exchange value is given its due and the determining role of market interaction is properly acknowledged, the identity of the bearer of capital takes on a universality ignored by Marx as well as by most of his followers and opponents alike. As defined by the M-C-M' exchange sequence giving capital its ubiquitous form, the bearer of capital is simply an owner of money needing to purchase commodities in order to resell them for a profit. Although other relations may intervene to differentiate one type of capitalist from another, a market agent qualifies as an owner of capital solely in virtue of buying commodities and reentering exchange so as to earn a gain in line with the M-C-M' circuit. To accomplish this, the capitalist has no choice but to engage in the civilities of commodity exchange, honoring the property entitlements and market need of the other commodity owners on whose exchange agreements profit depends. Because the M-C-M' sequence of capital can proceed on the basis of nothing but acts of commodity exchange, the bearer of capital faces no other restriction than accommodating these terms of market freedom. Hence, individuals, households, private corporations, public enterprises, and worker cooperatives can all adopt the economic role of capitalist so long as they engage in the requisite acts of exchange.

The impossibility of restricting the identity of the bearer of capital to any one of these market participants has fundamental normative ramifications, especially in light of how capital realizes its constitutive M-C-M' circuit of exchange with neither any exploitation of labor, nor any necessary engagement in commodity production. It makes clear that if the justice of capital is to be evaluated, capital must be conceived in its proper universality, instead of being judged in terms of one of its particular, contingent forms. This requires avoiding Marx's fateful reduction of capital to an economic structure defined by the capital-labor relation specific to privately owned industrial capital employing wage laborers, a reduction rooted in Marx's labor theory of value, which erroneously tied the creation of surplus value to the exploitation of labor. Certainly, capital can assume that specific form, as history has shown. However, the reality of capital is falsified if it is conflated with this one shape, to the exclusion of the other manifold forms that capital can take. Although Marx maintains that privately owned industrial capital employing wage labor necessarily arises from the dynamic of commodity relations as the defining form of capital, ample testimony to the contrary is provided by his own account of "primitive accumulation," where he examines the historical rise of modern capitalism. Over and over again, Marx's historical analysis brings home how the predominance of private industrial capital and wage labor in modern England resulted not from any economic logic, but from a systematic intervention of political power that separated peasants from their land, concentrated wealth in private hands, and used all its legal resources to force the pauperized masses to earn their keep in the employ of an emerging bourgeoisie.[1] If anything, the subsequent history made by Marx's keenest followers has only reemphasized the contingency and alterability of that predominance. By demonstrating how economic nationalizations following a revolutionary takeover of government can enable state-owned capital to overshadow private enterprises as the ruling force in the economy, they have underscored the essential latitude in the identity of capital and inadvertently revealed how erroneous it is to define capital in terms of privately owned wage labor commodity production.

If capital's role in the just economy is to be determined, particular economic circumstances arising from noneconomic factors must not be confused with those features that are necessary and universal to capital. Only what is inherent in capital can count when it comes to judging its legitimacy. Hegel's analysis of commodity relations may provide little delineation of capital's role in the market, but it does help draw the veil from capital's universal structure. By bringing into focus the determining role of market freedom, Hegel makes comprehensible how capital cannot only be individually, corporately, cooperatively or publicly owned, but can just as well involve no commodity production as manufacture goods and sell them at a profit without employing wage labor.

How all these possibilities are intrinsic to capital should already be apparent. Although capital must traverse the M-C-M' exchange sequence to be worthy of the name, it need not engage in commodity production because, as Hegel's analysis of exchange value has shown, profit can be earned through a speculative buying and selling of commodities without ever leaving the sphere of exchange. If, however, capital does produce commodities, this must occur in conformity with the civil relations of its defining M-C-M' circuit. Insofar as the constitutive freedom of these exchanges precludes the operation of any labor theory of value, and hence precludes the exploitation of labor Marx laments, there is no inherent reason for the production of commodities by capital to proceed solely with private employment of wage labor. Indeed, the internal arrangement of production has no bearing upon the identity of commodity producing capital. Since whatever profit capital earns by selling its products depends not upon what occurs in production, but upon what exchange agreements are subsequently concluded between the owner of capital and consumers, the organization of production is as open as the identity of the owner of capital. Just as commodity relations permit any market agent, from individual to state, to play the role of "capitalist," so they enable commodity producing capital to take any form the market permits, be it a private business whose owner is the sole employee, a worker cooperative whose members draw dividends rather than wages, a shareholding corporation whose employees receive stocks as well as wages, or a state enterprise employing wage labor.

Admittedly, commodities can be produced for profit under conditions that violate the economic rights of market agents. Although the M-C-M' exchanges require respect for the market autonomy of the capitalist's suppliers and consumers, private as well as publicly owned capital can still realize a gain using slave labor or other types of servitude to manufacture commodities. Ample testimony of this possibility is provided by the history of plantation slavery and indentured labor in the New World and the Nazi and Soviet forced labor camps that produced commodities for sale in domestic and international markets. Nevertheless, the structure of capital does not entail any such arrangements, any more than it necessitates the predominance of any particular form of wage labor commodity production. Hence, their specific evils do not derive from the dynamic of capital accumulation, but from forces outside the market that create forms of oppression that are then allowed to operate within the economy. Just as property, domestic, legal, and political relations can take unjust forms without necessarily eliminating the legitimacy of ownership, the family, legality or the state, so capital can exist in an oppressive form without condemning its essential structure to perfidy.

No matter what distortions it may suffer, capital can function perfectly well without abrogating anyone's market autonomy. Neither capital's realization of profit in the sphere of exchange nor its internal process of production need involve any curtailment of the legitimate freedom of commodity interaction. Insofar as capital does not subject exchange value to a law of value rooted in the exploitation of labor, the transactions by which capital is defined involve the same exercise of market freedom in which all commodity exchange consists. By the same token, there is nothing in capital's quest for profit that prevents its production of commodities from being organized in terms of the same market freedom through which capital accumulation is realized. Whether production for profit be undertaken by a worker self-managed cooperative, a state enterprise, or a private firm, the participants in production can all play their roles on the basis of a freely entered reciprocal satisfaction of their personally chosen wants. The members of a workers cooperative can engage in production under an agreement to receive dividends just as the laborers of a publicly owned factory or a private corporation can work for wages on the basis of a mutually accepted contract suiting the needs of employer and employee alike. In each case, capital produces goods and realizes a profit entirely in terms of the market autonomy of everyone to which it relates. Hence, whatever be the limits of market freedom, commodity-producing capital can hardly undermine it. On the contrary, the production of commodities for a profit shares in whatever justice commodity relations possess, for capital can carry on its generic functions relying on their exercise alone.

If this leaves capital entirely conformable to the civil relations of the market, the circuit of exchange defining capital accumulation subjects each and every unit of capital to the same market necessity of accommodating the needs of other commodity owners. Whether capital utilizes relations of servitude or respects every economic right of individuals, whether it earns its profit without ever leaving the sphere of exchange or by engaging in production, whether it produces commodities with or without wage labor, and whether capital operates under individual, family, corporate, cooperative, municipal, provincial, national or even international ownership, its need to buy and sell from other market agents confronts it with the same irrepressible realization problem that makes competitive pressures an inescapable fate. Once one follows Hegel in taking due account of the reciprocal freedom of commodity exchange, the sober truth is all too apparent that no alteration of the form of ownership or internal organization of capital can free it from the dynamic of accumulation defined by capital's constitutive market predicament.

A reluctant capitalist like Friedrich Engels may seek a profit by setting the price of his product above the aggregate purchase price of the factors consumed in its production, and, convinced Marxist that he is, measure the increment of surplus value in terms of the difference between the price of labor power and the value "created" by the expended labor time. However scrupulously he tries to unite theory and praxis, he will only succeed in corroborating the labor theory of value if consumers come forward and agree to buy the product at the appropriate price. If no purchaser acquiesces, our capitalist may be compelled to make no sale at all, or to lower the price to an accepted level, which will then comprise the product's actual exchange value. If, alternately, the bearer of capital intends to be a benevolent producer, setting prices so low as to reap uncommonly low profits, he will face the predicament of lacking investment funds to reduce production costs, develop new products, and advertise at levels which do not allow other producers to drive him out of business, or, if the capitalist be a worker's cooperative or public body, to carry on with ever growing subsidies from other sources. These realization problems afflict every form capital takes simply because capital's relation to its suppliers and consumers consists in commodity exchange, whose form of mutual agreement is incompatible with any unilateral command.

Contrary to Adam Smith, Ricardo, Marx, and all other purveyors of labor theories of value, capital's production of commodities is inherently governed by the principle that neither the price at which its products are sold nor the profit it thereby reaps are determined by expended labor time or any other factor entering into their production. It makes no difference whether a factory be privately run, worker self-managed, or state owned, or whether it employ wage earners, dividend receiving partners, indentured workers, forced labor or slaves. In every case of production for a profit, what goes on in the labor process determines only one thing relevant to capital accumulation: the cost of production that sets the break-even price of the product. Even here, however, what enables the factors of production to determine that cost is not how they variously function in the manufacture of the commodity, but their own purchase prices or depreciation, which are determined by prior or current market transactions, respectively.

Hence, production for a profit no more subjects the exchange value of commodities to forces independent of the wills of market agents than does the basic M-C-M' circuit of exchange, which may or may not incorporate an intervening production process. Although no commodity owner can have his way in the market unilaterally, what constrains the economic opportunities of each and every one is the civil necessity of acting in reciprocity with the market autonomy of others. This necessity may well make the exercise of economic freedom a perennial problem, but the possibilities of success are not ruled out by any barriers peculiar to capital.

Common misunderstandings of capital's limits

The failure to distinguish what is universal to capital from particular contingencies has led to fateful misunderstandings of the problems of justice that are inherent in a market economy. One of the more prevalent confusions is the equation of state ownership of the means of production with the abolition of capital, an equation made just as frequently by the defenders of free enterprise as by the avatars of the communist millenium. By laying exclusive emphasis on the question of state versus private ownership, both sides have ignored how capital can be either publicly or privately owned without affect upon the market modalities of its constitutive pursuit of profit. As we have seen, not only does capital's defining M-C-M' exchange sequence allow it to be owned by an individual, a family, a corporation, a worker's cooperative, or a state, to engage or not engage in commodity production, and to pay or not pay wages, but it confronts each and every form of capital with the same realization problem. Because no unit of capital can make a profit without completing its M-C-M' circuit of exchanges, there can be no escaping the logic of accumulation rooted in this market predicament.

Hence, the "evils" of capital can hardly be remedied simply by relying on worker self-management, nationalization of the means of production, or any other alteration in the internal organization of economic enterprise. However such a project be attempted, it cannot help foundering before a Scylla and Charybdis already well defined by Hegel's analysis of commodity relations.

If, to take one extreme, an economic revolution replaces the market with a unilateral ordering of production and distribution, it will make no difference whether the imposed plans are decided nationally or locally, or by all citizens, just the proletariat, or unconsulted official decree. In every case, a radical injustice will be perpetrated consisting in the deprivation of individuals' civil right to decide personally what commodities they need and what occupations they will pursue to satisfy their chosen wants in reciprocity with other market agents. This wrong is not avoided by an economic "democratization," be it limited to a particular commune or extended to the entire economy, that lets the free vote of its members decide how employment and goods will be allotted. Such a "democratization" may give each participant an equal say in managing the economy of the community, but it does so only by taking away their personal freedom to select their own occupation or the goods they want. By "democratizing" their economy and making the will of the majority the unique arbiter of vocation and need, individuals relinquish their autonomy of interest in both regards. Although they might qualify as authors of this majority will, its economic management cannot retrieve the civil freedom of interest it obliterates.

This problem is precisely what sets worker self-management in conflict with the imposition of a planned economy. So long as the market is supplanted by any unilateral administration of the economy, the workers of an enterprise lose their prerogative to determine either the conditions of their employment, the goods they will manufacture, or the terms under which their products will be distributed. Only if their enterprise retains some market autonomy for itself, in opposition to unilateral economic planning, can these matters begin to be "worker self-managed". For this reason, the Solidarity movement in Poland found it necessary to call for a widening of the market economy in order to give worker self-management minimal reality.

Of course, if worker self-management or nationalization be instituted without eliminating the market, any hopes of escaping the dynamic of capital accumulation cannot help but be frustrated. The avatars of worker self-management may offer it as the true overthrow of capital, but nothing could be farther from the truth. If worker self-managed enterprises are to have independent control over their own economic affairs, they must be able to throw off the reins of central planning and operate as autonomous market agents. However, by achieving this independence, worker self-managed enterprises put themselves in the same predicament as any private firm that trades and/or produces for a market. Since they now must buy and sell from other independent commodity owners, who can always refuse their terms of exchange, worker self-managed firms cannot escape the ubiquitous realization problem of capital, which confronts them with all the competitive pressures that a workers' economy was intended to suppress. Even if its members forswear the pursuit of profit and embrace the catatonics of "zero growth," a worker self-managed enterprise will still face the market imperatives of having to reinvest and expand simply to survive in face of advancing competition.

The same dilemma faces all nationalized enterprises that buy and sell commodities on either domestic or international markets. Whether they produce commodities or not, or seek to break even or gain a profit, state-owned firms subject themselves to the dynamic of capital accumulation the moment they set into the marketplace. Political measures can be taken to blunt the pressures of competition upon public enterprises, such as by erecting nonmarket barriers to entry or subsidizing unprofitable undertakings. However, so long as state firms engage in market relations, trading money and other commodities with exchange partners who are at liberty to refuse each and every offer, no unilateral plan can prevent the public economy from falling prey to the logic of commodity relations.

These ever more familiar truths only serve to emphasize how the generic workings of capital are constitutively pervaded by the interaction of market freedom in which commodity relations consist. Consequently, capital is not a deplorable deformation of market activity, but rather an essential structure of the civil economy, involving the same exercise of right at hand in every commodity relation. Although which forms capital will take is a contingent matter, decided on economic terms by the pattern of transactions market agents pursue, the presence of capital in the market economy is a ubiquitous possibility rooted in the simple fact that capital requires no more than commodity relations for its reality. For this reason, capital must share their justice as well as their failings.

Hence, it would be wrong to develop the theory of capital as if it were merely a descriptive examination of an historical economic formation, having no part in the conception of the just economy. Because capital is an essential structure of market freedom, conceiving capital is a task for prescriptive economics. The theory of the just economy must incorporate capital into its conception of commodity relations, conceiving it as a structural element whose tendencies cannot be dismissed as disposable annoyances. There is no denying that capital can take forms directly impeding the market autonomy of individuals, just as every other institution of justice can exist in distorted ways that violate the very freedoms they make possible. Indeed, capital may be endemically unable to insure equal economic opportunity and may thus require the addition of other institutions to extend the exercise of market freedom by which capital operates to all members of society. Be this as it may, the very fact that capital can carry out its defining accumulation of wealth entirely in conformity with market freedom signifies that barring it from the economy would be tantamount to violating the economic rights of civilians.

This juridical right to capital, which applies to any of its forms that do not involve infringements of civil freedom, might seem to be only a negative prescription, prohibiting the abolition of capital, but leaving its pursuit an option that need not be exercised in the just economy. What makes capital's quest for ever increasing wealth juridically indispensable is the conventional character of market need, which entails all the limitless multiplication and refinement of wants pointed out by Hegel. The market economy's self-determined pursuit of a conventional standard of living, where the choice of vocation, personal needs, and commodities is determined not by natural scarcity or psychological necessity, but by the concomitant willing of autonomous market agents, can only be realized if its economic institutions provide for a correspondingly free expansion of wealth. For this reason, capital, be it private, worker self-managed, or public, plays an essential role in enabling civilians to satisfy their freely chosen interests in reciprocity, even if no form of capital can alone insure that all market agents have an equal opportunity to do so.

Of course, it could be argued, following the Club of Rome's advocacy of a zero-growth economy, that capital's quest for ever increasing wealth should be prohibited precisely to establish an economic order that freezes the variety and number of commodities and employments. This would allow a given arrangement of production and distribution to be perennially reproduced, much like many a precapitalist economy. Although a certain security and stability would thereby be achieved, it would be at the expense of the self-determination of individuals. Given the normative validity of freedom, any such scheme would therefore be inherently unjust. Whatever be its authors' intentions, it would curtail economic freedom by confining the interests of individuals within bounds that no action of theirs could alter.

Hegel, by contrast, acknowledges the juridical claim of capital, and accordingly introduces traces of its profit-earning activity into his concept of the just economy. On various occasions he points to the M-C-M' circuit of exchange and to production for profit.[2] Certainly Hegel's intermittent treatment is far too scanty to provide the required conception of capital's involvement in the sphere's of exchange and production, and of the competitive dynamic of accumulation that results. Nevertheless, Hegel's brevity does reflect a crucial and much misunderstood feature of capital's place in the market economy: that capital is but a component rather than the unifying structure of commodity relations.

Capital's Subordinate Place in the Market

Two complementary reductions have obscured the reality of commodity relations from friend and foe alike: the conflation of capital's universal structure with the particular form of private capital producing commodities with wage labor and the reduction of the market to a function of capital accumulation. Both owe their origin to the mistaken notions of the labor theory of value and both are readily corrected once due account is taken of the determining role of market interaction, exposed in Hegel's analysis of exchange.

It should come as little surprise that advocates of the labor theory of value, such as Marx, find themselves compelled to conceive commodity relations to be incorporated without any remain by the system of competing capitals and therefore to develop the theory of the commodity economy as a theory of capital. Once exchange value is derived from labor expended in the production of commodities for profit, the market cannot help but be subordinated to the circuit of capital. If the exchangeability of goods is first created by labor operating under capital's employ, all commodities would have to emanate from productive capital. On this basis, all commodity exchange could only consist in sales and purchases of these products by the owners and employees of capital. Their own buying and selling would not only depend entirely on earnings resulting from their participation in relations of capital, but would comprise the very realization process by which capital would perennially complete and reengage its own circuit. Hence, on all sides, commodity relations would resolve themselves into the accumulation process of capital.

What precludes any such reduction of commodity relations to relations of capital is the analytic market truth that exchange value is ultimately determined by the concordant choices of the parties to exchange. As we have seen, because exchange value cannot derive from labor exploited by capital, let alone from expended labor of any description, commodity relations involve nonproduced just as well as produced goods whose purchase and sale may or may not fall within an M-C-M' exchange sequence. By the same token, since market freedom always allows for transactions whose participants no more seek than realize profit, the capital circuit cannot encompass all commodity exchange. Although capital may be particularly suited to the conventional multiplication and refinement of market need and may well unleash a competitive dynamic through which ever more wealth gets absorbed in its accumulation process, the M-C-M' scheme of capital still comprises just one form among others that commodity exchange may follow.

Hence, even if capital accumulation does tend to generate a growth of markets wherein more and more exchanges are made in pursuit of profit, that cannot automatically ensure that the commodity economy becomes dominated by transactions realizing the circulation of capital. So long as market autonomy persists, which after all is a precondition

of every form of capital, commodity owners may well choose to buy and
sell such that commodity circulation takes a predominantly nonprof-
itable form, leading even to a disaccumulation of capital beyond the
ken of any historically recorded depression. Such an outcome might
indeed curtail the satisfaction of the market's artificially multiplied
and differentiated wants, as, of course, might the predominance of capital circulation. Nonetheless, there is nothing in commodity relations
that can preclude market agents from freely conforming to such limits
over the short- or long term, provided they so choose, be it in ignorance
of cost-efficiency considerations, indifference to accumulating wealth,
religious, civic or nationalist conviction, or any other reason. That
commodity relations leave room for all these possibilities is precisely
what allows nonprofit enterprises to function in the market, be they
self-sustaining or not. Although Hegel barely treats the structure and
dynamic of capital circulation, his conception of exchange properly
takes into account the irreducibility of commodity circulation by leaving open all its possibilities without giving any one privileged
hegemony.

The Open Character of Commodity
Production

Given the fundamental role of exchange in market relations, it can
come as little surprise that the same factors that make the circuit of
capital a subordinate feature of commodity circulation also render commodity production irreducible to capital accumulation. Once again, the
key point is that products bear exchange value in virtue of the collat-
eral decisions of market agents to buy and sell them, not in virtue of
issuing from capital (which, as we have seen, may use wage labor or
not) or from some other employment of wage labor. Consequently, all
who tie commodity production to "free enterprise" capitalism labor
under an illusion, ignoring that commodities can be produced just as
well with or without profit as with or without wage labor, or under
private or public ownership. In moving from the sphere of exchange
to the sphere of production, prescriptive economics must avoid their
reductions and instead conceive commodity production in its full universality, grasping its essential forms, which, as such, must underly
and allow for every option that conforms to market freedom.

Hegel accomplishes this by distinguishing the fundamental modes
of commodity fabrication without restricting them to any of the various
forms of capital or to any specific nonprofit arrangements. In the *Phi-
losphy of Right* under the rubric of the "Kind of Labor" he instead

introduces in succession three types of commodity production: the immediate labor process, factory mass production, and mechanized manufacturing.

The immediate labor process

What comes first, as the most elementary form of commodity production, is the immediate labor process, where an individual act of labor produces a whole new commodity, transforming a given material so as to endow it with a different market utility and the potential to exhibit a certain exchange value whose magnitude will be determined by subsequent purchase agreements.[3] In characterizing this form of production, Hegel speaks as though the material of labor were automatically distinguishable from the act of labor and suggests that the material of labor may not only be a commodity, but a product of previous laboring.[4] Certainly, labor may produce its commodity by working upon an object that is both a physical thing, whose natural constitution must be taken into account in order to give it the desired utility, and a produced commodity already bearing its own use and exchange values. Nonetheless, it is equally true that the product of labor may be equivalent to the act of labor itself, as in a marketed performance by a free person, in which case, the "material" of labor is neither a commodity nor a product, but rather the very being of the performer. In any event, since the laboring in question produces commodities in response to artificially multiplied and refined market needs, its own activity will not be limited to any natural array of operations. As Hegel suggests in his analysis of the technical cultivation of the laborer,[5] commodity-producing labor will instead be subject to a proliferation of skills and techniques in as arbitrary a diversity and number as the commodites and needs they address. Whatever craft be employed, such labor will figure in full conformity with civil freedom by producing commodities for the market while providing some form of earning for the laborer in question. Commodity relations make possible any variety of ways for the latter to be achieved. As Hegel mentions, without making any claim to exclusivity, the laborer can be paid for his labor by an employer.[6] This can occur, of course, equally where commodities are produced on a profit or on a nonprofit basis, under private or public ownership. However, the laborer can just as well satisfy his needs in reciprocity with others through commodity fabrication by drawing dividends as a partner in a worker cooperative or as the operator of his own workshop.

Factory mass production

Whatever be its arrangement, the immediate labor process provides the prerequisite element for a further form of commodity manufacture where mass production is achieved by simply grouping together in one factory a plurality of individual laborings, each of which produces a whole commodity by itself. As Hegel points out, this arrangement subjects laboring to a multiplication and abstraction wholly analogous to that which commodities and market needs themselves undergo.[7] Through the duplication of a certain laboring under a common unit of production, the particular fabrication of a specific commodity proceeds as a laboring common to others. As with the immediate labor process, this can occur under all the various arrangements that commodity arrangements make possible: with or without profit, with or without wage labor, with or without private ownership. However it proceeds, what characterizes this rudimentary mass production is that each of the common acts of labor duplicates what the others perform without undergoing any alteration in its individual character. It retains the exact same form it had as an independent, uncombined act of labor.

As Hegel points out, this form of mass production can just as well be supplemented or supplanted by a factory division of labor where different laborings do not produce an entire commodity by themselves, but rather accomplish different stages in the manufacture of the same commodity. In this case, each act of labor contributes just a partial manufacture that results in a marketable product only in combination with other different operations. Here, laboring becomes refined into endlessly fragmentary and differentiated acts whose ability to produce a commodity is entirely dependent upon being integrated with correlatively refined detail labors within a common production process. Due to its very own one-sidedness, such detail labor actually participates in the manufacture of a commodity only in and through a cooperation among commonly employed workers, where each laboring act is defined in terms of its interconnection with the others.[8]

Accordingly, the formation of the detail laborer involves a habituation to working in conjunction with others that is not an external imposition, indifferent to the laboring act, as is the case in a mass production achieved by merely duplicating immediate labor processes within a single factory.[9] With the division of labor internal to factory cooperation, each act of labor is essentially interdependent, entailing a productive relation between laborers. Although Hegel tends to mention this cooperative aspect of formation within his analysis of the immediate labor process, it first pertains where manufacturing involves the factory production of a commodity through an internal division of labor.[10]

This practical facility with the mutuality of cooperation reflects just one side of the transformation the labor process undergoes through the factory division of labor. What equally occurs through the differentiation of detail operations is a systematic abstraction whereby each of the distinct yet complementary acts of labor gets fixed into a uniform type, whose regularized performance is defined not by the idiosyncrasies of the laborer, but by the objective demands of the existing system of conjoint and successive operations. Through this regularization, detail labor sheds the unique individuality characteristic of handicraft, leaving the laborer with a rote skill unconditionally dependent upon the social setup of manufacturing.[11]

Anticipating Marx, Hegel concludes that the refinement and differentiation of skills inherent in the factory division of labor necessarily results in an increase in the number of commodities produced by the same expenditure of labor.[12] Although an increase in productivity measured in terms of use values may well result, there is nothing in the arrangement of mass production and factory cooperation that guarantees such an outcome. Even if the precepts of cost efficiency do dictate that divisions of labor be introduced only when they result in higher productivity, the prerogatives of market freedom allow commodity producers to ignore, misunderstand, and ineptly apply the codes of "economic rationality," no matter how ownership or labor be handled. Furthermore, if by chance or design more commodities are produced with the same amount of labor, this still leaves utterly undetermined whether the more numerous products will be sold at a higher aggregate price than their scarcer predecessors.

Nevertheless, conceiving how certain factory divisions of labor can be introduced in order to increase the productivity of individual enterprises is something that not only presupposes the basic specification of manufacturing, but may further involve consideration of the competitive relations between various commodity producers with differing levels of efficiency. For this reason, any systematic treatment of the effects of the substitution of particular techniques of production requires a prior conception of not only the different forms of commodity production, but the competitive pressures to which commodity producers of all types are subject.

Mechanized production

What the conception of manufacturing does directly pave way for is the determination of a mechanized production process. As Hegel points out, once the factory division of labor has transformed commodity manufacture into an abstractly specifiable system of operations, the production process has in fact become a law-governed mechanism, whose motions can be captured in blueprint.[13] With the uniform regularization of detail labor replacing the unique virtuosity of craftmanship with a rote operation devoid of any independent agency, the labor process has come to better befit an automaton than an imprecise factory hand.

This sets the stage for machines to step in in place of living labor. By definition, a machine operates according to the blueprint of its construction, following the causal necessity of an external law.[14] For activity to be carried out by machinery, it must already be reduced to the formal simplicity of a regular motion, determined from without. This is precisely what factory cooperation has done to labor by bringing the concrete activity of the immedate labor process to an abstractly differentiated lifelessness, captured in the machinelike operations of detail labor. In this sense, Hegel is quite right in claiming that the factory division of labor provides the veritable prerequisite for the mechanization of commodity production.[15] Although automation may supplement, replace, or even give way to an immediate labor process or a factory division of labor, it always involves a process where the manufacture of the product is broken down into detail operations whose interconnected working is incorporated within the repetitions of an integrated machine process. What the factory division of labor performed by grouping complementary detail laborings is here the unified movement of a plurality of machine functions.

Although automation can be considered a substitution of machine movements for the rote labors of factory hands, it need not simply replicate the actions of detail laborers. A machine system incorporating its own division of operations places at the disposal of commodity production the wholly unnatural strength and mastery of mechanical technique. Just as the conventions of the market liberated need from the confines of human biology and psychology, so mechanized production frees the manufacture of commodities from the physical limitations of human agency.

This does not mean that automation can free individuals from either the natural or conventional necessity to labor, and put an end to the working day. Mechanized production cannot attain the self-sufficiency of a self-generating and self-renewing process precisely because the mechanical is in principle externally informed rather than self-determining. Automated manufacturing thus depends both upon an antecedent technological intelligence to give it its governing blueprint and upon labor to activate the machinery and then maintain its regulated movement. Hence, no matter how far automation may go in making detail labor superfluous, it cannot dispense with a labor that plans and oversees its automated process. As Hegel points out, mechanized production thus brings with it a type of labor specifically defined in terms of supervising and maintaining machinery. Hegel may not have given this productive agency a name of its own, but what it comprises is the generic toil of the technician, who no longer effects particular transformations of the material of labor, but instead activates an objective mechanism producing commodities with a completely artificial speed, power, and skill.[16]

The differentiation between the immediate labor process, manufacturing, and automated production could appear to be a purely technical matter of no bearing upon economic justice. Indeed, abstracting from the particulars of commodity production, they can be technically distinguished as different forms for producing objects irrespective of what economic institutions hold sway. What allows them to figure as just forms of production are two constitutive features that mark their role in a civil commodity economy: that they are each arrangements for producing commodities for the market, and that those engaged in their production processes do so on the basis of thereby satisfying their own chosen needs in reciprocity with others.

In line with their civil character, these forms cannot be otherwise restricted in regard to either their internal organization or their relation to one another. Given their normative status and the role of market freedom in their constitution, it would be a mistake to view them as successive historical forms, as Marx and many others have done. Although it may so happen that factory production factually supplants handicraft industry, only to be superseded by automation, there is nothing in commodity relations that necessitates such an ordering. Even though the artificial proficiency of automated production may be most in keeping with the conventional multiplication and discrimination of market needs, the commodity economy leaves room for all three forms to coexist, just as it allows for substitution of one form by another in any sequence imaginable. This is true with respect to not only different enterprises within the market, but the production process of the same economic unit. Although the market availability of instruments of production and competitive pressures may impose their own restraints, it cannot be precluded that a private concern, a workers cooperative, or a nationalized enterprise will combine craft, factory, and automated production processes, or eliminate or add one or the other with profitable or unprofitable results. Precisely because these arrangements of commodity production can all be instituted as structures of economic freedom, they are not bound to time and place, but remain normative options wherever agents interact.

By the same token, it would be wrong to tie any of these forms of production to some particular type of enterprise. However else craft, factory, and mechanized commodity production may differ, they all share in the basic latitude inherent in commodity relations. As history amply confirms, the logic of market freedom permits each and every one to be pursued on a privately or publicly owned, profit or nonprofit basis with or without wage labor.

By conceiving the fundamental forms of commodity production without excluding the full diversity of their possible market realizations, Hegel underlies once again how capital is not the all-encompassing master of the market, but a subordinate structure to whose accumulation process neither commodity exchange nor commodity production can be reduced. Any consideration of economic justice will go awry unless it keeps in mind that capital cannot escape the influence of factors exogenous to its own dynamic of accumulation, yet endogenous to the market economy in which each and every form of capital plays a component role.

The Confusion in Hegel's Discussion of Capital

Despite Hegel's nonreductive treatment of commodity exchange and production, his subsequent discussion seems to have failed to maintain the subordinate position of capital in the market economy. When, after analyzing the forms of commodity production, he proceeds to conceive the total process of commodity relations in its inclusive unity of all commodity exchange and production, he introduces his analysis under the heading of "Capital" (*das Vermogen*) and then outlines how the workings of the "capital" of society involve the acquisition of particular "capitals" by its members.[17] Nonetheless, Hegel does not thereby reduce the market system to a system of capitals, exhaustively governed by the dynamics of profit maximization. Under the title of "capital," he refers simply in general to the wealth of the civil economy as it is composed of all the particular commodity ownerships and earning activities figuring within its network of exchange and production. Although profit-making enterprise certainly has its place within this economy, the total capital of society here addressed does not represent an ever accumulating aggregate exchange value consisting in the competitive system of profit-seeking firms. It instead designates the whole amalgam of all commodity relations, in whose market system of interdependence economic agents acquire and dispose of particular "capitals" comprising whatever commodities they own that enable them to satisfy their needs in exchange through any of the earning activities that they are at liberty to choose among. For this reason, T. M. Knox, the English translator of the *Philosophy of Right* would have better conveyed the concept at issue by translating "Vermogen" as "wealth." By choosing "capital" as his translation, Knox inadvertently suggests that Hegel conflates wealth with capital. Such a conflation only makes sense if commodity relations are inextricably relations of capital, an equation that Hegel's entire analysis of exchange fully refutes.

It cannot be overemphasized how crucial the distinction between wealth and capital is for both diagnosing and coping with economic injustice in a market economy. If commodity relations were entirely absorbed and governed by the dynamic of capital accumulation and that dynamic imposed economic inequalities preventing certain market agents from exercising their freedom to satisfy their chosen needs in reciprocity with others, there would be no way to right that wrong. With commodity relations identical to oppressive relations of capital, not only would the market economy be irrevocably tainted, but the economic right whose infringement comprises the injustice at issue would be utterly unenforceable. It could no longer be realized in any way since its exercise consists in participation of the disadvantaged in commodity relations, whereas this participation would be precluded so long as a market economy exists, given its complete subordination to an exploitative capital accumulation. Economic justice would then remain a mirage, whose fulfillment would require curtailing the very relations by which its reality is defined.

What eliminates this dilemma is the irreducibility of commodity relations, which places capital in its subordinate role and allows for the full variety of market arrangements. In giving play to the right to a personally chosen conventional livelihood, the commodity economy may well foster accumulations of wealth that impede the economic freedom of the less advantaged. Yet commodity relations still leave room for private and public nonprofit undertakings that may be driven by other considerations. Hence, the very nature of the market is such as to permit countering disadvantage without eliminating commodity relations and the freedom they realize. Hegel, for one, does not neglect these issues. However brief his treatment may be, he does investigate to what extent market relations carry within them infringements upon the very freedoms they make possible, and to what extent commodity relations impose limits upon the righting of these wrongs. In dealing with these questions, Hegel recognizes the need to first uncover the entire structure of the commodity economy. To this end, he turns his attention to what results from the total network of exchange and production. This, he recognizes, is not the hegemony of capital, but the formation of economic classes whose character and justice must be considered.

7

Classes, Estates, and Economic Justice

If Hegel's analysis of commodity relations has not lent support to a necessary hegemony of capital over the market, it has uncovered how the commodity economy automatically generates class divisions. In conceiving the different forms of commodity relations, Hegel has effectively indicated how the reciprocal satisfaction of market needs proceeds through a variety of participations in exchange and production where different types of earning are pursued in conjunction with different types of commodity ownership and need. For instance, whoever seeks to earn a profit by completing the M-C-M' exchange sequence needs capital to advance in the market. Those, on the other hand, who earn rent as their form of income need landed property or some other rentable commodity, whereas wage earners need a marketable labor power and whatever other conveyances may be necessary to enter someone else's employ. Hence, no matter how a commodity owner participates in the market, the moment he enters its chain of interdependence through some self-chosen transaction, he engages in one, or perhaps several distinct modes of earning common to whomever else has undertaken to satisfy their market wants in like manner. Although the choice of commodity needs and market activity remain matters of personal preference, the very fact that commodity relations allow for certain types of earning involving certain needs and goods joins individuals into different groups according to the common market role they have chosen to fill. Consequently, the market necessarily gives rise to a class division the moment its members exercise their economic freedom by choosing their commodity needs and occupation and interacting on that basis.

For Marx and his followers this outcome condemns the commodity economy, since in their view, the just society requires the elimination of all class divisions. Hegel's account offers a completely contrary verdict, provided the universality of commodity relations is properly observed. In that case, Hegel's analysis serves to demonstrate how economic classes need not be instruments of oppression, as well as why a classless society cannot solve the true problems of economic injustice.

Classes and Economic Inequality

By paying due attention to the role of interaction within exchange, Hegel has already established that commodity relations do not entail any exploitation of their own, whereby certain individuals are subject to the unilateral will of others by dint of market forces alone. To the extent that class divisions arise in and through commodity relations, independently of any outside intervention, the economic relation between classes cannot consist in bonds of domination, but must rather involve the same structures of market freedom by which all commodity owners interact in the commodity economy. Participants in the market may well rely upon relations of servitude, such as serfdom and slavery, to pursue their trade, as history has shown. However, when the relation between classes is at stake, and these classes are defined in terms of their members' engagement in common modes of market activity, the agents in question all fill their class roles by exercising the same interdependent autonomy at work in every commodity relation.

To earn their characteristic profit, the owners of capital must enter into the commodity exchanges comprising the M-C-M' circuit. In doing so, they necessarily interact with members of other classes on the basis of allowing them to satisfy their own chosen needs through the buying and selling of commodities. Whether capital be owned by private individuals, members of a workers' cooperative, or the state, the relation is the same: instead of lording over supplier and consumer, the bearer of capital stands in an economic relation to the members of other classes only by accommodating their market autonomy. As Hegel's discussion of exchange and production has shown, this will apply just as well when owners of capital use wage labor to produce commodities for a profit. Because the relation between employer and employee is consummated through an exchange agreement, it also involves a mutual exercise of market freedom, and not any unilateral mastery and subjugation. Although private as well as public employers may otherwise impose conditions upon their hired hands that violate their market autonomy, there is nothing in the economic relation between employee and employer that necessitates such domination. On the contrary, the very terms by which profit can be earned require that the reciprocal satisfaction of need be observed in every relation between owners of capital and other market agents.

The case is no different with the class relations between earners of rent and those with whom they must interact in order to receive their characteristic form of revenue. Given their defining economic role, owners of a rentable commodity can only obtain their rent when other autonomous market agents choose to enter a rental exchange, obtaining some specified use of the commodity in return for an agreed payment. Consequently, rentees and renters are economically related through the same voluntarily enjoined reciprocal satisfaction of need that underlies not just the form but the very content of every market interaction.

Of course, it may still be suspected that the autonomy realized in every class relation is systematically undercut by differences in earnings that automatically befall separate classes in virtue of their defining economic activity. For if, as Marx maintains and recent historical experience seems to confirm, the owners of capital amass an ever growing share of the economy's wealth, leaving their wage laborers with an ever diminishing portion, the mutual agreements between capitalists and wage labors would merely mask a widening social disadvantage, progressively stripping workers of their equal opportunity to exercise their economic freedom.

Although there can be no denying that external factors can well contribute to pervasive class inequalities that may take on a logic of their own, Hegel's analysis of commodity relations reveals two fundamental features that mitigate against any class automatically receiving privileged wealth due solely to market forces. These are the endemic contingency afflicting all commodity transactions, resulting from the willful interdependence of market activity, and the corresponding latitude in the forms of exchange, commodity production, ownership of capital, and class membership.

The situation of the owners of capital is particularly illustrative, since they have been presumed to be the commodity economy's gilded class. Even if competitive pressures were to make the accumulation of ever greater wealth a principle of survival for every owner of capital and one were to reduce commodity relations to relations of capital and then conflate the general structure of capital with that of private capital producing commodities with wage labor, the capitalist class could still have no assurance that its profits would outstrip wages and rents, let alone increase at a higher rate than either of these forms of revenue. Since profit margins, wage rates, and rental fees all ultimately depend upon the multilateral decisions of independent commodity owners, no matter what efforts owners of capital undertake to cut costs of production and improve their marketing, there can be no guarantee that members of other classes, or for that matter, other capitalists will agree to transactions enabling aggregate profits to be in any specific proportion to different types of earnings. Even if revolutions in production techniques reduce the employment of wage labor and allow prices to be lowered while increasing profit margins, buyers may well decide to ignore these enticements, whereas the remaining wage laborers and owners of goods for rent may demand wages and rent so high as to diminish the share of profits in the wealth of the economy.

Of course, once capital is properly considered as a subordinate element within market relations, the absence of an automatic relative enrichment of the capitalist class becomes even more patent. Insofar as commodity exchange and commodity production can be undertaken on a nonprofit basis and consumers, laborers, anad landlords are at liberty to be partial to nonprofit enterprises even when profitable firms have a cost or marketing advantage, capital need not incorporate a growing share of wealth at all. Since each class relates to the others through mutually agreeable transactions, these contingencies do not just apply to owners of capital but to every other class.

What further precludes the inevitability of class advantage is the absence of any necessary connection between the relative aggregate earnings of the difference classes and the relative affluence of their individual members. Although the revenues of a particular class may well exceed those of the others, its members may still have smaller individual earnings if their numbers are disproportionately great. Hence, the relative wealth of a certain class need not reflect higher individual earnings. Marx could reckon on capitalists having much greater personal incomes than their wage laborers since he assumed that workers would far outnumber their employers. However, once capital is conceived in its proper universality with due recognition of the open identity of the capitalist, the contingency of such inequality is evident. It is not hard to see how the owners of capital could far outnumber the members of all other classes if capital is predominantly cooperatively or publicly owned. Indeed, even if capital is primarily privately owned, capitalists could still outnumber wage- and rent earners if there were sufficient private enterprises and they refrained from employing wage labor, which they are at liberty to do, as Hegel's account of exchange value underscores. In each of these cases, owners of capital could actually be personally disadvantaged despite a market conjuncture where investment in capital exceeded all other forms of wealth and profits exceeded all other types of revenue.

What provides the final coup de grace to any automatic connection between economic disadvantage and class divisions is the open, non-exclusive character class membership possesses in virtue of the conditions of market freedom under which commodity owners engage in common types of earning. Although Hegel provides the conceptual tools for understanding this key nonexclusivity, he joins most other theorists of class, notably including Marx, in assuming that the members of a market economy each belong at any moment to one and only one class. Hegel fails to recognize that the market leaves its members at liberty to join several classes at once. All this requires is that a commodity owner choose to engage in more than one mode of earning and that other market participants accommodate this decision by entering the transactions that make this possible. Since what counts in determining the class affiliations specific to commodity relations is not "social background" or "Weltanschauung," but freely chosen economic function, any combination of multiple class memberships is possible. An individual who elects to work for wages and simultaneously draws income from renting some commodity will be both proletarian and landlord, just as someone who earns interest from share holdings in a profit-making enterprise while renting out property and drawing salary will simultaneously belong to all three classes of wage earners, owners of capital, and landlords. Indeed, triple class membership could even be held by everyone in the same firm, if, for instance, they were all partners in a profitable worker cooperative who not only draw wages for their labor, but receive dividends tied to their joint ownership as well as shares of whatever rent their firm receives from leasing some of its property. Given all the possible forms of nonprofit and profit-earning enterprise, it should be evident that the class relations endemic to the commodity economy are far more fluid and complex than normally supposed. The same is true of all institutions, such as economic interest groups, in which class interests may play a determining role.

Although extraneous historical factors can always limit these possibilities and transform class divisions into instruments of inequality, the logic of commodity relations does not make class the source of economic advantage and disadvantage. The market may well leave individuals in comparative wealth or poverty, but this will not be an automatic result of their class memberships. Only when commodity relations are conceived in their full universality, with due account of all the varieties of capital and class affiliation, can the real roots of economic injustice be identified and meaningful remedies be proposed. If instead blame is laid upon contingent forms of market arrangements, which do not exhaust the possibilities of commodity relations and whose tainted existence may well depend upon noneconomic forces, the problems endemic to the market will be misdiagnosed and the wagered cure may turn out worse than the affliction.

The Injustice of a Classless Society

This is precisely the case with the Marxist call for a classless society to remedy the inequalities of the market economy. As Hegel's argument makes manifest, Marx and his followers have misconceived class relations, conflating them with particular historical forms, whose own character has been misunderstood in virtue of the mistaken notions of exploitation and the labor theory of value. Far from entailing domination and subjugation, belonging to a class is an act of civil freedom tied through bonds of reciprocal recognition to the same exercise on the part of others. In contrast to caste, tribe, estate or other groupings where membership is determined by factors given independently of the wills of their members, the classes generic to the market can only be joined by voluntarily undertaking to satisfy personally chosen needs for commodities in reciprocity with others. Although the constitutive autonomy of market agents gives all the formal opportunity to exercise any mode of earning, the options of particular agents may well be restricted by market factors including the relative commodity ownerships and needs of different parties to exchange and the economic decisions that are made on that basis. Nevertheless, no matter how few opportunitites a market participant may have, whatever mode of earning he ends up practicing is still undertaken through an act of choice predicated upon a like decision by other commodity owners. Because individuals can perform their class roles only in an interdependence mediated by commodity exchange, their mutual acknowledgement of others' market autonomy cannot be merely a disguise for a unilateral domination. The very structure of commodity relations gives its participants little choice but to recognize and respect the market autonomy of the members of other classes with whom they must freely interact in order to engage in those modes of earning making them class members in their own right.

Extra-market forces may well distort the independent relations between classes, as can occur with another structure of justice. Nevertheless, taken by itself as it issues from commodity relations, the class division represents a realization of economic freedom, just as class membership represents not a burden but a right to which all members of the market are entitled. Since, as we have seen, class divisions do not disrupt the exercise of market autonomy, but are rather necessary instruments of economic freedom, classes have a legitimate role in the just economy. It may well be true that commodity relations cannot secure equal economic opportunity for all without being supplemented by other institutions, whose own legitimacy will depend on their being structures of freedom. If, however, the class division is a necessary outcome of satisfying self-chosen needs in reciprocity with others, the just society must be a class society.

What condemns the Marxist endeavor to establish a society without class divisions is not that it is hopelessly unrealizable but rather that it automatically violates the strictures of social justice. A classless society cannot be established without depriving everyone of their personal economic freedom to choose their own needs and to decide independently what activity they will engage in to satisfy them in conjunction with others. Both these freedoms would have to give way simply because it is the exercise of this market autonomy that creates and sustains class divisions. This very fact makes the foundation of a classless society an entirely clear and practicable enterprise. All it requires is eliminating the market in favor of a universal compulsory administration of benefits and occupations, where the differentia of class, the needs and modes of earning of individuals, are all strictly limited to one and the same type.

Although various options are possible, a most familiar one is to prohibit individuals from seeking capital or rentable property as objects of need and to restrict their wants to consumer goods, while requiring that they undertake wage labor as their sole form of earning. These measures would indeed establish a classless society whose members would be subject to a universal proletarization in whose collective administration they might take greater or lesser part. All could well enjoy a perfect economic equality and security, and perhaps an equal say in managing the social enterprise. However, what would be totally suppressed would be each individual's freedom of interest, whose impeded realization comprises the economic wrong that the elimination of classes is supposed to rectify. The inability to earn a conventional livelihood through self-chosen activity is the socially specific injustice at stake in the economic disadvantage rooted in inequalities of wealth. By eliminating all exercise of market freedom, the classless society generalizes the very wrong it should remedy. In place of the failings of an unregulated market, it imposes a secure equality of servitude that cannot be mitigated by any participation in a collective management of associated producers. No matter how much influence individuals may wield in determining the common benefits and occupations to which all are subject, this does not give them back the freedom to choose independently their own wants or the activities they will personally undertake to satisfy those needs in reciprocity with others. This is why the exclusive rule of collective interest requires the annulment of the market. A classless society cannot survive if room is given the freedom of interest, for once individuals exercise this right, the door is open to the formation of class divisions.

Closing that door is all too real a possibility. The classless society cannot be dismissed as a fictitious utopia, beckoning from beyond history's end because neither human nature nor human convention can support it. On the contrary, it is a very real social alternative, whose implementation is both technically feasible and potentially durable. Just the support the notion of a classless society has attracted in our time should be evidence enough of how great a danger it poses to the just economy's institutions of freedom.

Hegel's Misconception of the Class Division

When Hegel turns to analyze the classes of the commodity economy, he duly enumerates the essential features that endow them with civil legitimacy. To begin with, he points out that inasmuch as market activity involves a variety of engagements in commodity exchange and production, the moment individuals participate in the web of commodity relations, they fall into groups each pursuing a different common mode of earning tied to a certain type of need and commodity ownership. Thus, although the market places commodity owners in no other relation than a general interdependence defined by their concomitant self-chosen wants, the workings of commodity relations automatically give rise to class divisions that no market participant can escape.[1] Hegel proceeds to emphasize that, given how classes are established, class membership is not a fate imposed upon individuals independently of their choice. No matter how much the arbitrary contingency of the market may affect the economic options of individuals, they become members of a particular class solely on the basis of how they decide to participate in commodity relations. Although the market choices of others play a necessary part in consummating the commodity transactions by which a mode of earning operates, their decisions can only enter in conjointly with the individual's own choice of activity. Unlike social divisions rooted in unwilled factors of gender, race, or birthright, or unilaterally imposed by some social engineer, class affiliation is thus always predicated upon an element of private decision, facilitating the like prerogative in others.[2] Conversely, Hegel further argues, since classes issue from commodity relations entirely through the exercise of market freedom, what distinguishes these classes from one another can be nothing but the distinct modes of earning specific to the commodity economy.[3]

Although these observations properly set the stage for conceiving classes strictly in terms of the dynamic of commodity relations, when Hegel proceeds to characterize the particular classes of the just economy, he ignores what is generic to the market. Instead, he offers a class division incorporating conventional descriptions of estates, which, in contrast to the classes of a commodity economy, involve natural foundations and political privileges entirely at odds with the civil freedom of social justice. Letting the contingent conditions of his day distract his attention from the different types of earning endemic in market activity, Hegel anomalously introduces a "substantial" class of peasants and nobles, a "reflective" class swallowing virtually all participants in market activity, and a "universal" class primarily filled by civil servants. It takes little reflection to see how not one of these three candidates can qualify as a bona fide class of the commodity economy.

As if confessing his own confusion, Hegel begins by ascribing the substantial class a livelihood dependent upon nature that not only proceeds at total remove from the conventional interdependence of the market, but stands endangered by the spread of commodity relations. Far from pursuing a particular mode of earning commodities in reciprocity with others, the members of the substantial class live immediately off the land, satisfying the domestic needs of their own households by wresting produce from the earth without entering exchange.[4] Although the soil they work demands intelligent cultivation and has all the possible uses of private property, it figures not as a type of commodity with its own exchange value, nor as a subordinate material of commodity production, nor as an individual capital, but as a given environment posing its own natural resistance to their perennial struggle to meet the naturally recurring wants of the household.[5] Just as their needs are predicated upon natural family requirements rather than the conventions of commodity demand, so their livelihood depends upon such variable natural conditions as seasonal change and fertility rather than the artificial necessity of the market.[6] Thus, as Hegel consistently acknowledges, what the members of the substantial class consume are gifts of nature's alien power, not commodities won through free individual occupation contributing to the economic freedom of others.[7] Accordingly, this entire class subsists in a naturally bound autarchy,[8] securing its daily bread free, as Hegel admits, from the insecurity of trade, the quest for profit and the caprice of others.[9] What Hegel fails to recognize is that this leaves members of the substantial "class" free from taking any part in commodity relations and the interdependent modalities of earning by which classes are to be distinguished.

Although Hegel at one point remarks that the substantial class provides the raw material for the reflective business class,[10] the subsistence livelihood of this peasantry and nobility excludes any essential connection with the commodity economy. What Hegel has here described is the life of a naturally confined household, resting upon relations of belief, trust, and sentiment,[11] and satisfying its own restricted wants in complete indifference to the self-reliant interdependence of market agency. Submerged in their subsistence production, the members of this substantial class have neither socially specific needs for the commodities of others, nor an occupation based on reciprocity, nor a livelihood secured through commodity consumption. Consequently, they do not exercise market autonomy at all, let alone any of the common modes of earning by which classes are to be defined.

To his credit, Hegel effectively admits the complete incompatibility of a peasantry and nobility with the market economy. Repeatedly he notes how the spread of commodity relations overthrows the natural basis of the substantial class, freeing the economy of the land from the household autarchy of peasants and the privileged birthright of nobles, and allowing agriculture to be transformed into a factory industry producing for the market.[12] Significantly, Hegel explains that this takes place through the agency of the reflective class. Its pursuit of business eventually detaches the peasantry and nobility from the land giving them their substantial foundation, leaving them in want of the goods of others, and dragging them down into the ranks of factory operatives.[13] Instead of the interdependence of classes, where each realizes its own mode of earning through the others, what reigns here is a relation of one-sided annihilation. Little else could be expected, for the class embodying the spirit of commodity relations can only find the substantial class to be a barrier to market activity, representing a vestige of precivil relations whose impediments to economic freedom make it worthy of being uprooted and abolished. Hegel minces no words in underlining this antagonism, noting that the peasantry and nobility, through their own immediate bondage to the land, are necessarily subject to force and compulsion when confronted with the *introduction* of commodity relations.[14] This signifies that the substantial class not only exists on its own entirely apart from the commodity economy, but that the market leaves no room for peasants and nobles to sustain their natural ties. Hegel's own observations confirm this, for as he expressly acknowledges, the forced elimination of the substantial class has actually occurred where else but in England, the most developed civil society of his day, where land figures only as a material for a factorylike employment and production.[15]

Although Hegel's universal class does not suffer a like annihilation at the hands of commodity relations, its defining features are just as extraneous as those of the substantial class. What makes the universal class an anomaly are not natural features, such as those that exclude peasants and nobles from the roles specific to civil society, but an occupational identity based upon holding public office rather than upon pursuing a form of earning rooted in commodity relations. Instead of characterizing the universal class in terms of a certain livelihood with its own particular interests, Hegel distinguishes it in terms of its service forwarding the universal aims of government.[16] Although he variously describes the universal class as including civil servants,[17] the military,[18] or the full potpourri of soldiers, lawyers, doctors, clergymen, and scholars,[19] what invariably unites its members are their action for the universal end of the state, action that should accordingly involve political rather than market institutions. Since this class's universal interest transcends the narrow particularity of each type of market need, Hegel is forced to admit that its vocation does not directly comprise a form of earning. Hence, he concludes, its members must be provided with either some independently given private wealth or public support to relieve them of having to do what their class activity does not include, namely, attending to their own needs.[20]

However this occurs, it leaves the universal class without any economic identity of its own. If the private or public provision of independent means furnishes the members of the universal class with a livelihood as unencumbered by participation in commodity relations as their own class vocation, then they would fail to practice a distinct mode of earning, as required to qualify as an economic class. If, by contrast, their independent wealth or state subsidy involved commodities, monetary income, interest-bearing capital, or rentable property by which they are drawn into the market, and the members of the universal class were regarded in view of their resulting modes of earning, they would lose their common bond and disperse into the different groups of individuals living off wages, rent, or interest and profit. In neither case does the dynamic of commodity relations provide any unity to the universal class.

Since this renders the universal class just as alien to commodity relations as the substantial class of peasants and nobles, it is not surprising that Hegel characterizes his remaining "reflective" class as if its earning encompassed every form of market activity. Unlike the civil servants of the universal class, who practice their generic vocation only insofar as their needs are provided for independently, the members of this class consume only what they earn through their own diligence and free choice in the exercise of their characteristic occupation.[21] Further, unlike peasants and nobles, who subsist in a nature bound autarchy, the members of the reflective class premise their activity upon the needs and labor of others,[22] while treating nature as a wholly subordinate material.[23] In so doing, this reflective class seeks to satisfy its own freely chosen particular needs through relations of mutual dependency where its members engage in commerce and trade, manufacture commodities, and advance capital in search of profit.[24] In other words, the members of the reflective class do everything called for by commodity relations. Consequently, the reflective class is really no class at all, for instead of devoting itself to one mode of earning, it rather pursues the entire gamut of market activities. In effect, Hegel has conflated his reflective class with the entire commodity economy, resurrecting the conceptual confusion of his earlier social writings where the "System of Needs" had not emerged as an autonomous sphere, economic interaction was still subordinated under a particular estate, and civil society was not yet radically distinguished from the state.[25] Accordingly, if Hegel is to offer any genuine class division it must fall within the bounds of the reflective class, which embraces every role generic to the commodity economy.

Although when Hegel first distinguishes his reflective class, he tentatively limits its affairs to the production of commodities,[26] as if it pursued a particular mode of earning, he finally admits its all-encompassing character by subsequently subdividing it into three groups differentiated, as economic classes should be, by their type of participation in commodity relations.[27] In contrast to his estate division of peasants and nobles, civil servants, and men of business, these subgroups comprise a handicraft class, making individual goods to satisfy singular needs, a factory class mass producing commodities for general market demand, and a commercial class, having exchange as its business and the accumulation of exchange value as its aim.[28] Although it can be questioned whether this trinity adequately captures all the common modes of earning of the commodity economy or properly distinguishes between them in an unambiguous way, it does at least employ the purely economic differentia appropriate for determining the class division. In this connection, it is worth noting those rare moments when Hegel foregoes using the term *Stand*, with all its naturally determined and political overtones, in favor of the economically specific term, *Klasse*. This occurs on but two occasions, when Hegel employs the category of *Klasse* to describe the proletariat[29] and the "wealthier classes."[30] Since the proletariat owes its identity entirely to its role in the production of commodities and the wealthy enjoy their status on just as purely economic terms, neither group can properly be called an "estate," given the latter term's implication of natural and political distinctions.

Social and Political Ramifications of a Rational Reconstruction of Hegel's Class Theory

This terminological shift from *Stand* to *Klasse* is symptomatic of how Hegel's estate characterization of classes must be rejected and replaced by a class division genuinely rooted in the dynamic of commodity relations. In the context of Hegel's social and political theory, this revision carries with it fundamental changes in the structure of civil society and the state, bringing to completion the demarcation of social and political spheres that remains only partially realized in the *Philosophy of Right*. By default, Hegel's class analysis has revealed three prescriptions that must be implemented for there to be a just economy within a just civil society.

First, there should be no economic class of peasants and nobles, or of any other grouping resting on natural differences and natural autarchy. So long as individuals retain an economic status determined by any given factors of nature, they stand bound to economic relations structured independently of the normative exercise of their wills. Whether they endure their predicament in resignation or by express choice makes no difference in regard to economic justice. Either way, their economic engagement lacks the rightful character residing in the mutual satisfaction of freely chosen needs.

Second, civil servants must lose their social status as a separate class and be merged instead into the type of economically differentiated groups into which Hegel subsumes his reflective class. Only in this fashion will class divisions involve the modes of earning generic to economic self-determination. Then, of course, civil service will carry with it no special consideration in any relations of classes and politics.

Third, the economically differentiated groups within the reflective class must cease to be sections of a single class and obtain their due recognition as independent classes organized in terms of each and every mode of earning in accord with market freedom. As such, they should accommodate all the legitimate forms of livelihood that commodity relations allow, as well as the multiple class affiliations that market agents may enjoy.

With these redefinitions of class, the economic interest groups that Hegel introduces under the rubric of "corporations" can no longer be considered outgrowths of a single class. Although Hegel conceives his corporations to be voluntary associations created to promote the varoius shared interests vested in the common forms of earning of the market economy,[31] he singles out the reflective class as the privileged source of corporate activity.[32] This restriction is perfectly consistent with his subsumption of all commodity relations within the reflective class's internal subdivision. However, once all classes are properly identified in terms of common modes of earning, corporate activity becomes the prerogative of the members of every class, no matter how they earn their living, nor how the enterprises they participate in are structured. Whether market agents be wage laborers of private firms or nationalized industries, members of a worker cooperative, private or public capitalists, or private, cooperative or public landlords, they have equal reason and equal right to join in civil groups to advance the economic interests they share. Naturally, since individuals may belong to several classes at once, they may just as well participate in several corporations, even though their interests are liable to conflict.

These alterations in the structure of the classes and corporations of civil society necessitate a fundamental transformation of Hegel's political theory insofar as he endows his classes with different political privileges, as extrinsic to their role in the commodity economy as the other naturally determined features that give them an estate, rather than a properly class, identity. By assigning classes distinct political functions, Hegel collapses the distinction between civil society and the state in accord with the estate formations of his day. What results are government institutions consistent with his misconception of classes and corporations, but incompatible with the class structure of the commodity economy and the independence political freedom should and can only attain through the radical demarcation of civil society and state.

This dual deformation comes to a head in Hegel's conception of the estate element of the legislative power of government. By his own admission, Hegel recognizes that because the political function of the legislature consists in enacting laws to realize the constitution in face of contingent changing circumstances in society, government and foreign affairs, its office requires an assembly representing different political opinions concerning this preeminently universal aim of legislative policy.[33] If any groups were to occupy legislative seats on this basis, they would be political parties, organized in terms of shared political opinions on how to realize the universal ends of constitutional self-government, and not social bodies, organized in terms of particular interests. Nevertheless, Hegel turns to his suspect class division to determine the distribution of legislative office under the guise of reconciling the civil freedom of interest with the common concerns of political sovereignty.

To this end, Hegel calls for a bicameral estate assembly, designed to balance the particular interests of society with the universal aim of politics. He argues that two legislative chambers are necessary, a lower chamber to give direct representation to the different interests of civil society, and a countervailing upper chamber to represent the universal interest of the state, not, however, as some foreign imposition upon society, but as something immanent in civil activity.[34] Although these complementary mandates apply indifferently to the various modes of earning inherent in commodity relations, Hegel's estate characterization of class divisions does not leave each class an equal player in both chambers. Insofar as he relegates all modes of market earning to the reflective class, he makes its corporate representatives the sole delegates of the lower chamber, even though a proper representation of civil interest would require delegations from every social class.[35] With equal predictability, Hegel makes the upper chamber a house of lords, entrusting the nobility with the privileged role of legally mediating civil interests with the governing ends of state. Since their existence is completely extraneous to market affairs, the nobility enjoys a patrician aloofness from social interest that allows it to fittingly masquerade as the element "of" civil society that affords the universal ends of politics a civil foundation.[36]

However, civil society not only has no place for nobility, but defines its classes in terms of modes of earning specific to the commodity economy, all of which are directed at particular needs rather than universal ends. Consequently, the mediation between their social pursuits and the aims of politics cannot arise immanently within class activities and their corporate extensions. Because these are always relative to particular needs categorially distinct from affairs of state, the integration of social interests and political activity can only proceed from the agency of the state itself. What unites the aims of civil freedom with those of self-government is not some incipient universality underlying market affairs, but the state's independent rule over civil society so as to enforce social justice in conformity with the exercise of political freedom.

Accordingly, to fulfill its proper functions, the legislature should neither have bicameral assemblies, divided in view of civil interests, nor class representation of any kind. Because, as Hegel himself emphasizes, what the state addresses in legislating and governing are universal ends common to all members of society in their role as citizens, class affiliation can carry with it no political office. Once this is duly observed, classes lose the vestigial political marks of estates, and retain the purely social role by which they are defined.

8

Commodity Relations and the Enforcement of Economic Justice

Although Hegel's estate characterization of the class division inherent in civil society leads him astray on important social and political issues, it does not prevent him from uncovering the intrinsic inability of commodity relations to extend to every market participant the exercise of freedom in which they consist. Unlike the political economists, Hegel understands that there is no invisible hand by which the self-regulating market guarantees equal economic opportunity to all. On the contrary, he recognizes that the justice of the market economy has an endemic limit, defined by two fundamental features of commodity relations that cannot be overcome no matter how market units are owned and organized. These irrepressible problems do not, however, undermine the legitimacy of commodity relations. Instead, as Hegel shows, they call for two very different remedies, both requiring the intervention of institutions of freedom extrinsic but not antithetical to the market.

Commodity Relations and the Insecurity of Person and Property

To begin with, all market activity presupposes and involves the property relations allowing for commodity ownership, civil need and exchange, without, however, being able to enforce those relations through its own economic practices alone. The just economy cannot possibly secure the person and property of its participants by relying on the commodity relations in which it consists simply because they themselves operate only so long as commodity owners interact in terms of respecting each other's property entitlements. However, as Hegel details in his discussion of "abstract right," the property rights of persons are subject to nonmalicious wrong, fraud, and outright crime which cannot be adjudicated and punished with authority by means of the resources provided by property relations themselves.[1]

This leaves economic freedom in a double bind. On the one hand, market activity can proceed only so long as the property rights involved in commodity transactions are not violated. On the other hand, neither market forces nor the property relations they incorporate can insure respect for the person and property of market agents. As much before as after entering exchange, the market provides nothing to prevent individuals from disputing rival property claims, defrauding one another, or engaging in crime. Although commodity owners may well succeed in obtaining what they need through exchange, their earnings can always be unilaterally taken away through subsequent fraud or theft. Further, since each commodity relation operates through mutual agreement, it is structurally impossible for any to serve the unreciprocated function of punishing malfactors or duly retributing victims. Hence, market relations are as unable to guarantee the commodity ownerships comprising the precondition of every commodity exchange as to secure the altered commodity ownerships in which they result.

These limitations hold regardless of whether the market be dominated by private capitals, worker self-managed cooperatives, or nationalized enterprises. Because these alternate arrangements differ only in respect of the ownership and management of individual enterprises, none carries with them any means of their own to insure the property entitlements either within their own units or throughout the economy as a whole. Similarly, the insecurity of commodity ownership remains no matter how small or great economic disadvantage may be. Since violations of person and property need no other preconditions than the arbitrariness of individuals, the poverty or privilege of an individual has no automatic bearing upon whether they will be victim or perpetrator of nonmalicious wrongs, fraud, or crime.[2] In every case, the realization of economic rights requires some noneconomic agency to attend to enforcing the property relations that the market presupposes, but cannot guarantee.

Therefore, Hegel concludes, it is an imperative of economic justice that market institutions be supplemented by a public administration of civil law enforcing property rights with a recognized and effective authority to adjudicate entitlement disputes, punish offenders and provide victims with due retribution.[3] Accordingly, Hegel follows his conceptualization of the just economy with a detailed treatment of the administration of civil law. Although it can be questioned whether Hegel has properly conceived the institutions of civil law, what is most decisive for economic justice is his recognition that no matter how courts operate, the civil enforcement of property rights still leaves economic rights at risk.

Commodity Relations and the Insecurity of Equal Opportunity

At most, the public administration of civil law can secure what individuals own before, during, and after engaging in market activity. However, neither the adjudication of civil suits, the punishment of fraud and theft, nor the payment of civil and criminal damages can provide a direct remedy to whatever economic disadvantage may plague the market. Protecting the given property and contractual entitlements of commodity owners is one thing; altering the distribution of wealth and the organization of production so as to insure equal economic opportunity is another.

If the market were guided by an invisible hand insuring the welfare of all through the untrammeled workings of supply and demand, then the enforcement of civil law would be enough to insure economic justice. In that case, so long as every commodity owner had their person and property protected, they would be in a position to enter the market and have its self-regulating process insure the satisfaction of their needs in conjunction with those of every other member of society. Hegel, however, recognizes that the basic structure of commodity relations leaves the market constitutively unable to insure the reciprocal satisfaction of needs which its own commodity relations have established as matters of economic right. Hence, the problem of economic justice cannot be resolved through the civil protection of person and property, but requires additional measures defined by the insecurity of welfare haunting the market, no matter how secure property entitlements may be.

Hegel's analysis of commodity relations reveals two fundamental reasons why the market cannot extend to all the exercise of economic freedom it makes possible, be it through its own devices, or with the aid of an administration of civil law.

First of all, because commodity relations operate through mutual agreements of exchange, where the satisfaction of every party is dependent upon the concordant choices of their counterparts, no market participant can ever be assured of encountering others who not only have appropriately correlative needs and commodities, but the will to enter into an acceptable exchange.[4] It makes no difference what modes of earning would be effected by the respective needs and commodities. Whether the required goods are products, whether their exchange would advance the accumulation of one or several capitals, and whether whatever capital be advanced be owned by a private individual or family, a share-holding corporation, a worker cooperative or a state enterprise alters nothing. Whatever needs, goods, and form of organization market participants may have, their ability to satisfy their particular commodity needs still depends upon the autonomous, arbitrary decision of other commodity owners to market what the former need in return for the money, labor power, capital, or other goods the latter choose to offer. This most simple, irrepressible, ubiquitous feature of commodity relations renders every exercise of market freedom a contingent endeavor, with no guarantee of success. Although every participant in the market may have a formal possibility of satisfying their needs in reciprocity with others, none can rest assured of encountering consumers or producers able and willing to bring any sought exchange to conclusion.

Although this endemic contingency of market earning faces all participants alike, it does not mean that the insecurity of their economic welfare is solely a function of the subjective caprice of others. As Hegel points out, the livelihood of commodity owners may also be favored and frustrated by unequally developed natural endowments, differences in acquired skills, and accidental circumstances having nothing to do with commercial activities.[5] Admittedly, such natural factors as innate talents and capabilities, health, and chance subjection to natural disasters are as exogenous to the market as are such conventional variables as education and training and subjection to war and social upheaval. Nevertheless, by its very nature, the market is an institution of living individuals situated in an historical world involving other noneconomic institutions. Consequently, participants in the market cannot help but be subject to nature and noneconomic conventions in ways that can effect their economic welfare. To the extent that neither the workings of the market or the civil protection of person and property can be counted on to remedy the impairments to economic freedom that these factors introduce, they represent a source of economic injustice calling for some further institutional solution.

What compounds the problems arising from dependence upon the arbitrariness of others and the effects of exogenous natural and conventional factors, are differences in commodity ownerships, differences that are just as much the outcome of market activity as given conditions under which every commodity owner first engages in commerce. As Hegel points out, this diversity of wealth can readily turn the formal equal opportunity of market agents into real economic privilege and disadvantage by prejudicing not only their further opportunities to enter exchange, but the possible productive employments of their particular skills.[6] Although differences in the quantity and quality of commodities an individual owns may be the result of such noneconomic circumstances as inheritance, what makes such differences crucial to economic justice are two purely economic considerations, both suggested by Hegel's discussion. First, discrepancies in wealth can unequally impede and promote different agents' exercise of market freedom, even though all commodity owners are at liberty to enter exchange and all market transactions take the form of mutual agreements. Second, the market creates through its own workings diversities in commodity ownership that enhance the economic opportunities of some while aggravating those of others.

The source of both these principles of economic disadvantage lies in market freedom itself. By its very nature, the exercise of market autonomy is predicated upon differences in wants and goods that are not eliminated through exchange, but reproduced in altered form. Whenever market agents engage in commodity relations, they do so in function of having different needs that can be satisfied not by what they already own, but only by exchanging the different goods of one another. Hence, diversity of commodity ownership is as much a precondition as a consequence of every market transaction. However, such diversity does not automatically impede any commodity owner's economic opportunity for the simple reason that it is the very basis for market agents to be able to satisfy their needs in reciprocity with one another. Nevertheless, this same market freedom allows for differences in commodity ownership such as to leave certain market agents in a better position to conclude further exchanges than others. This may be because the goods some possess are in relatively greater demand or because the commodities they own enable them to produce and market valued goods in lucrative ways that others cannot afford.

In considering the full scope of this problem it must not be forgotten that market freedom determines the exchange value of commodities through the actual agreements effecting their exchange, irrespective of any labor expended in antecedent production processes or any qualities intrinsic to the goods themselves. Consequently, the economic advantage and disadvantage deriving from differences in commodity ownership is not limited to any particular type of wealth, such as private ownership of the means of production. On the contrary, any kind of commodity can be a source of enhanced commercial opportunities provided other commodity owners are willing and able to trade for it on terms favoring the market position of its owner. Nothing in the nature of commodity relations precludes relative enrichment arising from the possession of nonproduced goods such as money, labor power or land, nor, for that matter, relative impoverishment following from the possession of produced means of production. Naturally, once commodities of any type have realized their value in the form of price, what counts in regard to economic advantage and disadvantage is the amount of money they provide their owner. Given market freedom, there will always be market agents who succeed in amassing enough wealth by trading their labor power, land, money or products to be able to translate that wealth into a far greater range of economic opportunities than other commodity owners whose resources for investment are more limited. Although the arbitrariness of market freedom precludes any guarantee that the relatively rich will maintain their position of economic privilege, the enhanced opportunity their relative affluence provides can well fortify their position of advantage still more, while leaving the less wealthy in comparatively worsening straits.

Because the basis of such unequal economic opportunity applies to market agents in general, irrespective of how they be defined, it would be wrong to link economic advantage and disadvantage to different types of commodity ownership. Since commodity exchange is sufficient of itself to foster economic advantage and disadvantage, the resulting infringements upon the exercise of economic freedom are not a curse of certain kinds of commodity ownership, which other forms can overcome. On the contrary, no matter how market agents function, the moment they engage in commodity relations they submit themselves to an economic order in which differences of commodity ownership cannot help but be reproduced to the relative benefit of some and the relative detriment of others.

Insofar as market agents may include artificial corporate persons as well as single individuals, the barriers to equal economic opportunity created by the market do not just consist in inequalities in personal wealth. They also consist in the disparities in economic resources that render whole enterprises underprivileged, thereby jeopardizing the economic options of those whose livelihood depends upon them. Once again, this problem is not unique to a market dominated by private firms operating for profit. Worker self-managed firms and nationalized plants are just as likely to become differentiated into those that acquire the financial, productive, and marketing muscle to dominate the market and those of lesser means that are left with continually deteriorating prospects. Admittedly, the form of ownership and management of an enterprise may well affect the respective economic opportunities of its participants. However, no feature of a firm's internal structure can alter its external market predicament of having to enter into commodity exchange with other independent commodity owners, beholden to all the pressures of imperfect competition that being a market participant involves. Since it is the contingent workings of these relations that give rise to a diversity of fortune that then impinges upon the universal exercise of market freedom, economic injustice remains a problem that neither nonprofit nor profitmaking, public nor private, worker self-managed nor corporate enterprises can surmount by their own resources alone. All are incapable of preventing disparities of wealth from emerging, just as they are all incapable of preventing these inequalities from spawning competitive advantages so great as to undermine the equal opportunity of individuals to satisfy their market needs in reciprocity.

Consequently, the vision of a self-regulating market optimally satisfying the needs of all is a falsification of the reality of commodity relations. Contrary to the reveries of political economy, the market cannot govern itself with an invisible hand securing everyone's economic welfare through the blind repetitions of commodity exchange. Hegel's argument leaves little doubt on this score. While his analysis of market freedom testifies that commodity relations invariably involve reciprocal satisfactions of need enjoying the normativity of mutually respected self-determinations, it equally reveals that these particular exercises of economic rights are not equivalent to an exercise by all. Due to the insecurity of commodity entitlements, the contingency of exchange, and the formation of inequalities in wealth imposing barriers upon market participation, commodity relations are intrinsically incapable of insuring that all members of the economy actually satisfy their self-chosen commodity needs by their own free earning, renting property, finding gainful employment, or marketing goods.

The Indifference of the Market to the Natural and Conventional Preconditions of Social Justice

What further compounds these difficulties is that commodity relations do not automatically protect and sustain the natural preconditions of the well-being of market agents or furnish the resources necessary to maintain market infrastructures themselves or other institutions of justice, including those of civil law on which the security of commodity entitlements depends.[7] Even though every market transaction occurs through the mutual agreement of the parties to exchange, this formal condition does not prevent commodity owners from engaging in commercial activity, be it commodity production, renting property or simply buying and selling goods, that despoils the environment and endangers the lives and earning capacities of themselves or other market participants. Nor does the reciprocity of exchange and the conditions of competition preclude situations where market forces leave transportation, training, health, and other commercially vital facilities in decay and unequal development, exacerbating inequalities of economic opportunity by depriving whole sectors of the economy of the means to engage in commerce. Further, although the need for financing public institutions such as the various branches of government and the military, involves issues of right transcending the problems of economic justice, it bears directly upon the exercise of economic freedom to the extent that other institutions are required to enforce the property entitlements underlying market activity, as well as to secure the public welfare. Accordingly, insofar as the market makes no automatic provision for public finance, this represents one more economic wrong that must be remedied.

The fact that all these impediments to the exercise of economic freedom are imposed through the voluntary agreements of commodity owners does not in any way mitigate the injustices they represent. Certainly, the market gives consumers the prerogative to rent or buy commodities that are injurious to their health, just as it gives producers license to despoil the environment and workers the option to accept employments that endanger their lives and livelihood through unsafe working conditions, oppressively long working days, and insufficient wages. As history has shown, this can all occur whether or not market enterprises are public or private, or even worker self-managed. In every case, the contributing element of choice does not eliminate a situation in which freely entered commodity relations put in jeopardy the further market autonomy of their participants, either by striking at the natural preconditions of economic agency consisting in personal and environmental health or by contributing to conventional barriers to everyone's exercise of market freedom.

The Injustice of Free Enterprise

Taken together, these self-afflicting limitations of market freedom have crucial significance for economic justice and the relation between the market and other social institutions. Their lesson is clear: Although the market offers every commodity owner the entitled opportunity to satisfy self-chosen commodity needs through activity of their choice in reciprocity with others, this right is jeopardized by the very commodity relations in which its exercise consists. Because market activity generates its own obstacles to equal economic opportunity, no internal reorganization of the commodity economy can solve the institutional problem of having all members of society satisfy their needs in normative relations of self-determination.

Hence, any system of "free enterprise" permitting market relations to follow their own dynamic automatically condemns itself by violating its own strictures of economic justice. Due to the open identity of market participants and the open identity of capital, both of which are made conceivable by Hegel's analysis of exchange, the injustice of free enterprise is an affliction extending well beyond a market dominated by unregulated private capitals. It applies not just to this particular case, but to all economic formations where the problem of ensuring an equal exercise of market autonomy is addressed by some principle for internally organizing market enterprises. Subjecting individual enterprises to public ownership or worker self-management provides no solution so long as they still face one another as independent parties to exchange. Although these reorganizations may alter the ownership of capital, they leave each enterprise subject to the same market dynamic by which free enterprise is defined. Far from remedying the problems of "capitalism," worker self-management and nationalization of commerce thus only reproduce the same self-limitations of market freedom, albeit while adding restrictions of their own regarding which market options may be pursued.

False Remedies to Free Enterprise

The economic injustice afflicting any free enterprise system, be it dominated by private enterprises, worker self-managed firms, or nationalized industries, could suggest that a just economy can only be established through the complete abolition of commodity relations. Indeed, why not replace the market with a planned economy where the organization of production and the distribution of occupations and goods is determined by either a central public authority or decentralized communes? Admittedly, most ventures in this direction have ignored the exclusive normativity of freedom. Instead of promoting economic planning as a way of institutionalizing economic self-determination, they have advanced it as a triumph of a technically defined "economic rationality" addressing teleologically fixed "true human needs and productions." In that case, it is only proper to subordinate economic management to the exclusive control of a privileged vanguard party, whose superior grasp of economics and human potential is reason enough to leave everyone else with no say in the running of the economy. Yet, could economic planning not be liberated from prior prescription and oligarchic domination? Could it not operate strictly as an institution of economic freedom, either through democratic control of a central state planning administration or through local communes whose economic management is governed by direct democracy? Either way, would democratic collective planning not offer each member of the economy an exactly equal role in determining their own and everyone else's livelihood, solving once and for all the problem of economic disadvantage that the market introduces but cannot eliminate?

Certainly, it cannot be denied that if the market were supplanted by a collectively planned economy subject to democratic control, every participant would enjoy an equal say in its administration. However, enjoying that prerogative is not equivalent to exercising the secured equal economic opportunity whose universal attainment eludes the free enterprise of an unregulated market. Collectively furnishing jobs and goods is one thing; insuring that every commodity owner can pursue an autonomous livelihood in reciprocity with others is another. The problem of equal economic opportunity refers to exercising the right to satisfy self-chosen needs through self-chosen activity such that others can engage in the same economic self-determination. Although a collectively planned economy may leave all in identical economic straits, it thereby only generalizes the infringement of equal economic opportunity by preventing everyone from exercising mutually corroborating autonomy in respect to their own needs and occupations. This imposition upon economic self-determination holds whether individuals collectively control a centralized planning administration through representative democracy or collectively manage a local commune through direct democracy. Either way, everyone would lack all freedom to determine independently what they need and how they will earn a livelihood in conjunction with others, despite enjoying an equal voice in collectively administering the economy of their community. Even in a radical commune, where the majority decision of its members decides what goods they receive and what jobs they must fulfill, there remains an unbridgeable difference between the collective edict of the majority and the personal prerogatives of its members. So long as all economic matters are collectively determined, that is, so long as market activity is entirely abolished, the freedom of interest is totally annulled. Only if commodity relations are retained can individuals enjoy the freedom of particularity, by which they are at liberty to choose their own needs and occupations in facilitating the correlative freedom of others.

Does this leave economic justice at an impasse? Any retention of commodity relations carries with it the market dynamic that irrepressibly jeopardizes the exercise of economic freedom in which market activity consists. Nevertheless, precisely because the economic wrong afflicting commodity relations lies in their inability to insure that all commodity owners can exercise their freedom of interest, the abolition of the market through a "democratization" of the economy can offer no solution to the injustice of economic disadvantage. Instead of realizing equal economic opportunity, collective economic management only curtails the exercise of freedom in which that opportunity consists.

Further, by canceling market autonomy, the democratically planned economy does not provide an otherwise unattainable contribution to political freedom. Because its collective decision making is restricted to matters of economic management, the participation it offers members of society is not equivalent to participation in self-government. Insofar as politics involves not just a national housekeeping, but the irreducibly political concern of determining how the state should order itself, collective economic self-management cannot alone realize political self-rule. Those who turn to economic democracy as a remedy to the alleged formality of parliamentary democracy ignore this fundamental discrepancy between the limits of economic management and the extent of political governance. Hegel tends in this direction when he argues that participation in the common advocacy of corporations, economic interests groups, provides a remedy to the restricted share in public affairs that citizens have under modern political conditions.[8] Although Hegel may be right in maintaining that such social participation affords individuals a mode of activity possessing a public character above and beyond their purely private affairs, it still does not grant them any greater participation in the specifically political affairs of state rule. Nor does economic democracy give citizens a better appreciation of the connection between the public and private spheres, as Carole Pateman suggests,[9] echoing Hegel's claim that corporate activity immanently ties the pursuit of particular interests in society to the universal ends of politics.[10] To the extent that political institutions reign supreme over society, regulating civilian life on the basis of politically determined government policy, any connection between political ends and social interest is ultimately mediated by political rather than social action.

In this regard, the avatars of economic democracy also ignore that, although political participation does involve overseeing the economy to the extent that government lords over society, this supervision can operate democratically without eliminating the market. Citizens can exercise the freedom to order the economy without relinquishing their freedom of interest provided their engagement in self-government involves participating in publicly regulating commodity relations while retaining their own market autonomy within the limits they have collectively imposed upon themselves through their democratic political involvement. Hence, it makes little sense to argue that the suppression of market freedom through democratic planning provides an alternative form of self-determination for which commodity relations are worth sacrificing. Whatever freedom to manage the economy such measures offer is equally at hand when commodity owners engage in self-government and determine how the market should be regulated. Consequently, supplanting the market with democratic planning is no more an answer to the problems of political justice than to those of economic disadvantage.

Clearly, if any solution to economic injustice is to be found, it must lie somewhere between free enterprise and the abolition of commodity relations. Insofar as justice is bound to the reality of freedom, the injustice economic disadvantage represents consists in the impairment not of any collective imposition of prescribed goals or democratically decided economic plans, but of the realization of personal economic self-determination.

9

The Limits of Private Intervention in the Market

If the just society is to succeed in realizing the economic freedom of its members, it must do more than enforce the property and household rights which give market activity its formal prerequisites. Somehow, the abiding problem of economic disadvantage must be resolved, not by canceling commodity relations, but by extending to all civilians the equal exercise of market freedom whose deprivation defines economic wrong. Further, the economic autonomy of individuals must be secured so as to maintain the other freedoms to which right applies, for present as well as future generations.

Hegel provides part of the answer by calling upon a pair of institutions whose complementary interventions represent the two avenues of remedy consonant with civil society's framework of social freedom. He calls these "corporations" and the "police,"[1] referring to what essentially comprise economic interest groups and the public administration of welfare. These are the civil bodies engaging in private and public intervention upon the market, respectively, in order to provide individuals with economic opportunities they would otherwise lack. Hegel, unlike those who stand him on his head, recognizes that the solution to economic injustice lies not in overthrowing commodity relations or restructuring the ownership and management of market enterprises, but rather in supplementing economic activity proper with these two distinct civil institutions. Although Hegel's discussion of their role is both incomplete and marred by his confused estate conception, it provides the basic institutional distinctions allowing the problem to be handled.

Economic Interest Groups and the Civil
Struggle for Economic Justice

In conceptualizing how civil institutions must right economic wrong, it is logical to begin with the organs of private intervention upon the market, economic interest groups, since the limitations inherent in their activity define the need for a further public intervention. Hence, we turn first to the corporate activity of these groups instead of following Hegel's ordering, where the analysis of the "police" precedes that of "corporations."

The need as well as the legitimacy of economic interest groups lies in their function as extensions of the same freedom of interest at play in commodity relations. Economic interest groups, as Hegel defines them under the rubric of "corporations,"[2] are voluntary organizations whose members have joined together to advance particular shared economic needs through common action consonant with the civil rights of all. Insofar as such economic interest groups promote their common cause by using the economic and legal opportunities to which every member of civil society is already entitled, the right to participate in their activities is part and parcel of economic justice. By giving individuals the right to exercise their market freedom and enjoy the protection of civil law, civil society equally entitles them to unite into particular associations to forward needs they share so long as they do so by employing market freedom and civil law without depriving others of their like entitlements.

In using their economic and legal opportunity in this way, individuals consciously aim at the feature of their self-chosen needs already implicit in the class divisions of the market economy. This feature consists in the sortability of commodity needs and market activities, whereby the livelihoods of individuals fall into different common types, despite being determined by personal preference. Although class divisions group individuals according to the kind of market activity they pursue, being a class member does not involve making the common welfare of one's class the aim of one's activity. By voluntarily participating in the activities of an economic interest group, however, individuals expressly advance their own interest as part and parcel of the welfare of an economically defined group.

Admittedly, participation in an economic interest group does inject a new general dimension into the pursuit of interests at play in the market economy. Nevertheless, the common interest which any such group seeks to promote is not automatically shared by all members of the economy. It remains a particular aim specific to the economic sector from whose ranks individuals have banded together to form their economic interest group. Although its aim might coincide in special circumstances with the interest of some or even all other sectors of the economy, this coincidence is not essential to its formation or activities. An economic interest group is predicated simply upon the presence of some economic aim common to some members of the economy and upon the shared resolve of some of them to advance that aim through common intervention in the market and before the law. When promoting the satisfaction of its chosen end, an economic interest group thus aims at advancing the economic freedom of its own members and only incidentally at the economic welfare of society at large. The interest advanced by an economic interest group is thus, as Hegel suggests, restricted to something only relatively general.[3]

Nevertheless, groups having this character enjoy civil legitimacy in three respects. First, they conform to civil freedom insofar as they have a voluntary membership open to all who have the appropriate shared interest. Second, the particular interests they promote are civil in character, which is to say, that they can only be realized in reciprocity with the interests of other civilians, who may or may not have similarly organized themselves. Third, because the interests they advance are realizable only by satisfying the complementary needs of others, whenever an economic interest group pursues its common cause by participating in civil institutions, it not only allows its own members to exercise the economic freedom to which they are entitled, but facilitates at least some nonmembers doing the same. In these ways, economic interest groups operate entirely in the service of the civil freedom of interest, functioning as private instruments of economic justice, legitimately employing joint action in the market and the civil law courts to overcome barriers to their members' exercise of economic autonomy.

Given these features enabling economic interest groups to possess civil legitimacy, it is essential to clarify the identity of the common interests on which economic interest groups are formed, the just options open to economic interest groups within a civil society, and finally, how far these options can counter economic injustice.

The Open Identity of Economic Interest Groups

Insofar as economic interest groups are predicated upon particular market needs held in common by groups of individuals, the identity of these groups rests upon that of those needs. Since, as we have seen, commodity relations generate particular types of need and earning by which individuals become grouped in economic classes, economic interest groups would seem to have their primary basis in the different interests specific to each class. Accordingly, economic interest groups would consist, in the first instance, in voluntary organizations formed by the members of a particular class to forward their common class interest in the marketplace and before the law. Granted that commodity relations group individuals into classes of capitalists, wage earners, and landlords, each with its distinctive commodity needs, occupation and corresponding form of income, it would be expected that members of each of these classes would form their own economic interest groups to advance their welfare, be it at the level of an individual enterprise, a particular trade or industry, a particular locality, or on a national, or even, international basis.

Although Hegel limits corporations to one class, the reflective class of business,[4] and describes them as if they were craft guilds, organized in each trade,[5] his discussion implies a general connection between economic interest groups and class insofar as his reflective class of business actually incorporates all purely economic class divisions within itself. Accordingly, once Hegel's estate division is replaced by a purely economic differentiation of classes, economic interest groups become the prerogative of members of every class. Hence, just as owners of capital can join together in employer associations, so landlords can organize their own interest groups, just as wage laborers can organize unions and professional associations. However, it would be a mistake to limit economic interest groups to these familiar forms.

Two factors that complicate membership in class-oriented economic interest groups are the open character of commodity relations and multiple class affiliations. As we have seen, market freedom allows for varied forms of laboring and of ownership and management of rentable property and capital, as well as for the corresponding opportunity of commodity owners to engage simultaneously in several types of earning making them members of more than one class at one and the same time. Consequently, economic interest groups can include leagues of worker cooperatives or federations of public enterprises, just as well as business associations representing family-owned, corporate, worker self-managed, and public enterprises all together. Likewise, an individual can belong to several economic interest groups, whose aims may hardly be in harmony.

In addition, economic interest groups can equally be formed to advance particular economic interests that do not correspond to class divisions. Individuals whose economic opportunities are limited by physical and mental handicaps, by discrimination according to race, gender, sexual orientation or religion, by regional factors, or simply by poverty may make common cause to promote their livelihoods, bringing together into a single economic interest group individuals of varied classes. Similarly, environmentalists may band together to protect the natural preconditions of economic autonomy, just as private groups may organize themselves to promote the interests of consumers. In each case, what brings members of such groups together are economic interests that cut across class lines.

Such groups would be superfluous only if the promotion of class interest exhausts all joint private effort to advance shared economic aims whereby the exercise of economic freedom is extended. This, however, is hardly the case. The promotion of different class aims can by no means be counted on to address all the needs left unattended by individual participation in the market. Where the promotion of class aims involves conflicts of interest, the efforts of class-oriented economic interest groups may cancel one another, leaving room for joint action on a different basis. Similarly, where class aims coincide, their advance by class organizations may well jeopardize the welfare of those individuals falling into other economic groups. For instance, workers and capitalists may struggle over the division and management of the wealth their enterprise generates, with the result that they end up destroying the economic viability of their enterprise and the branch of industry or economic sector to which it belongs. On the other hand, they may recognize that they have a common interest in maximizing the success of their firm, since the greater profit it achieves, the greater will be the spoils for them to contest. However, their joint interest in benefitting their enterprise may well be to the detriment of other firms, the environment, or consumers at large, creating all the more need for joint action in defense of economic interests defined independently of class.[6]

Consequently, even though the basis for economic interest groups lies in the different shared interests that typify the common forms of earning distinguishing economic classes, the market's endless variegation of needs, commodities, and occupations provides ample incentive for individuals to make common cause in behalf of interests extending beyond the confines of a single class or focused upon some economic need more narrow than what members of any class might all share. In sum, economic interests groups may be established to advance any economic need, however narrowly or broadly shared, that its members have chosen to promote together. The problem of unsatisfied market needs gives just as much impetus for voluntarily joining labor unions, professional associations, cartels of private corporations, leagues of worker cooperatives, federations of state enterprises, and other organizations with members from the same class, as for enlisting in consumer unions, tenant associations, environmental groups, organizations of the handicapped, neighborhood associations, and other economic interest bodies whose members belong to different classes, yet work together to advance their economic freedom.

However they be defined, economic interest groups are obligated to obey two complementary edicts regarding membership. On the one hand, they cannot legitimately compel individuals to join who may share its particular aims but lack the will to participate. On the other hand, they cannot justly exclude anyone from membership who shares the appropriate interest as well as the resolve to promote it under the group's common aegis. In either case, individuals' right to advance self-chosen needs in reciprocity with others would be usurped and infringed. Whether one be compelled to join a union under a closed-shop agreement or be excluded from membership due to extraneous factors such as race, gender, sexual orientation, or religion, the injustice is the same. The individual's freedom of interest would be encroached, when the whole justification of economic interest groups lies in promoting that freedom above and beyond the limits of isolated individual effort. Hence, individuals have the right to belong to economic interest groups on a purely voluntary basis, without restriction due to any considerations other than the personal decision to join in advocating the interest in question.

The Civil Options of Economic Interest Groups

In promoting the economic welfare of their members, economic interests groups aim at a particular economic welfare that is specifically civil in character. This welfare consists not in the sating of their members' natural needs, nor in the fulfillment of some given human potential, nor in the satisfaction of rationally prescribed desires, but in the realization of their member's freedom to satisfy their self-chosen particular needs in reciprocity with others. Assuring the exercise of this economic self-determination gives economic interest groups their normatively valid mission and prescribes the two avenues of activity suitable to its achievement. Because the economic autonomy which every economic interest group aims to extend for its members can only be achieved in advancing the same freedom of others, economic interest groups must work within civil institutions. If they do not, but strike against the institutional organs of the freedom of interest, they only undermine the very conditions for realizing what they promote. Hence, economic interest groups have little choice but to take advantage of the two options civil institutions provide: joint action in the market-place and before the law. Both modes of intervention offer the possibility of particular successes, but neither can be counted on to secure the welfare of a group's members, let alone to provide any remedy to economic disadvantage at large.

Economic interest groups before the law

In a just society, economic interest groups are at liberty to go to court to take advantage of any kind of legislation that bears upon their member's welfare, including whatever law may specify how public bodies should regulate the market. Nevertheless, it is necessary to examine the option of collective legal action first solely in reference to civil law, whose statutes stipulate the entitlements and enforcement of property and household rights. To what extent economic interest groups can advantageously use laws addressing public regulation of the economy is an issue for later consideration. Not only does it presuppose an analysis of what public regulation is needed, but that analysis itself rests on a prior consideration of the market and civil law options of economic interest groups. This is because the very rationale for public regulation is predicated upon the limitations besetting private activity, either individual or collective, in the market and before the civil law courts. Hence, only after conceiving the activities of economic interest groups in the market and civil law courts can the need for a public regulation of the market be established and its principles determined, and only after that analysis can there be any discussion of how economic interest groups can employ the widened legal options created by a public administration of welfare.

To the extent that civil law is restricted to realizing property and household rights, it offers economic interest groups a very limited instrument. Their members may obtain more powerful legal representation by taking collective legal action to enforce the property rights and contractual obligations underlying their commodity ownerships and exchange relations. Legal costs can be shared and joint legal action may facilitate more frequent and extensive legal challenges with greater public impact. Nevertheless, no matter how more successful collective litigation may be, economic interest groups are no more able than individuals to use the civil courts to transcend the limits of their jurisdiction. Civil enforcement of property and household rights may secure the foundations for market activity, but it cannot provide new economic opportunities that require more than reaffirming current terms of contract and the current distribution of property. Any economic disadvantage resting upon inequalities of wealth resulting from legal market activity is simply beyond remedy by individual or collective appeal to the civil courts. Because civil law protects property and households, it cannot be employed to redistribute legally obtained wealth, prescribe types of investment and divestment, or otherwise impinge upon given property entitlements to advance the economic welfare of an individual, a group, or society at large. In bringing common suit before the civil courts, an economic interest group may forward the enforcement of its members' property and household rights, but this cannot remove the problem of unsatisfied need that individual activity in the market leaves unresolved.

To give its members greater economic opportunity, economic interest groups must go beyond their court interventions. Admittedly, they can extend their activity into the political arena and press for certain political policies whereby public intervention in the market can enhance their economic position. However, as already indicated, the rationale for such appeal to public regulation can only be understood after the limits of economic interest groups' civil options have been ascertained. Hence, what must first be considered is the only civil opportunity remaining for economic interest groups: making common cause in the market place.

Economic interest groups in the market

Given the constitutive structure of market freedom, the members of economic interest groups have one basic means for promoting their common welfare through market intervention: collectively deciding their terms of exchange so as to promote their economic welfare. This involves deciding when and where to engage in commerce, what investments to make, what to produce, what products or nonproduced goods to bring to market for sale or hire, what goods to buy or rent, as well as what prices to accept. All these market-directed decisions can be jointly made to put added pressure on those other economic agents with whom the members of an economic interest group must deal to achieve their economic ends.

Needless to say, the ways of making common cause in the market are as varied as the different types of exchange and economic roles that commodity relations allow. Given the open character of capital, class memberships, and economic interest groups themselves, market freedom provides a wide field for corporate maneuver. Labor unions can decline all offers for their members' employment until employers agree to acceptable wages and work conditions, just as professional associations can withhold the services of their members until clients consent to favorable rates. Similarly, associations of family businesses, private corporations, public enterprises, and/or worker self-managed firms can decide in common how to plan their investments, how much to pay for their means of production, what to produce, what prices to set, and how to market their goods to their best advantage. Likewise, owners of rentable property can jointly agree to acceptable levels of rent, just as consumer and environmental groups can boycott certain products and enterprises, be they private or publicly owned and managed, until their demands for product quality, price, and environmental care be met.

Every one of these joint interventions in the market operates in terms of the reciprocity of economic freedom. Although the common fronts of labor unions, producer cartels, and consumer groups give their opposing economic parties fewer options to choose among, this does not entail any unilateral appropriation of their commodities. In each case, the common action undertaken represents but a concerted effort by one economic group to persuade other commodity owners to *agree* to an exchange on terms beneficial to the former.

Admittedly, this persuasion relies upon the degree to which its common market decisions threaten disadvantageous consequences for the economic well-being of the other parties. In general, the potency of such measures depends upon how far an economic interest group succeeds in establishing a monopoly over whatever economic factor it provides. When labor unions establish cartels of labor power, when associated enterprises monopolize the manufacture of certain goods, or when consumer groups consolidate purchasing power, they are able to put those they seek to influence in an economic bind, from which an economically viable escape may be impossible. Nevertheless, this does not remove the fact that what lies at stake is the achievement of a certain commodity exchange, whose bilateral agreement remains mediated by the autonomous choice of both parties, regardless of their other economic opportunities. Even if the common front of an economic interest group is so powerful as to eliminate alternative sources of a desired commodity, there is always room for opposing economic agents to refuse the group's terms and leave their need unsatisfied. Although, as we shall see, such an outcome is not without significance for economic justice, it is important to keep in view that the formal reciprocity of market freedom remains unimpeached.

This feature is crucial, not just because it involves a respect for the economic autonomy of others that keeps the market interventions of economic interest groups within the bounds of civility. What is no less fundamental is that the reliance upon the bilateral form of exchange confronts every economic interest group with the same dependence upon the will of others that left the economic welfare of individuals insecure and gave them reason to band together to begin with. It is the contingencies inherent in this dependence that define the limitations afflicting each and every market intervention of each and every economic interest group.

First of all, it bears repeating that however an economic interest group takes joint action in the market, it cannot liberate the economic destiny of its members from the independent exchange decisions of other commodity owners. Whether an economic interest group oversees the market decisions channeling its members' labor power, products, investments, rental properties, or consumer demand no more alters its general predicament than does the degree to which its common front succeeds in cornering some part of the market. As long as an economic interest group must go to market to realize its members' economic autonomy, it cannot unilaterally dictate its terms but must still contend with the arbitrary choices of other economic agents. Although joint market intervention can wield significant force by creating a monopoly to limit the economic options of others and thereby pressure them to come to desired terms, no monopoly can automatically secure willing parties to exchange. Not only may the opposing parties be ignorant of what is most advantageous to them in their newly limited situation, but ignorant or not, they may simply balk at the one "economically rational" option they have. Labor unions and employer associations may refuse each others' "final" contract offers, leading to their collective ruin, just as landlord and tenant associations may reject their respective lease proposals, leading to the deterioration and abandonment of rental properties, just as consumer boycotts may destroy the very enterprises they seek to reform. Hence, even if an economic interest group's action leaves others with no alternative but economic ruin, they may choose privation and leave the monopoly empty-handed.

This possibility is an ineluctable feature of the structural position of economic interest groups in the market. They may frequently succeed in facilitating exchanges to the advantage of their members, exchanges that their members could not have arranged individually. Yet economic interest groups remain but particular actors in the marketplace who can only satisfy their members' needs through the agreement of other independent commodity owners. For this reason, economic interest groups can never guarantee the economic welfare of their members. It matters not how resolutely and persistently they unite, nor how effective a monopoly they create. Their market interventions may outperform their interventions in the civil courts. Still, labor unions, employer associations, leagues of worker cooperatives, consumer groups, tenant associations, landlord associations, and federation of public enterprises remain imperfect instruments for their own members' interests insofar as they advance their common cause through the bilateral freedom of commodity relations.

Even if an economic interest group were to forge so great a market power as to secure its members' interests, this would not provide any solution to the problem of economic injustice. Although the bilateral character of exchange signifies that an economic interest group fulfills its members' needs only in conjunction with satisfying some needs of certain other commodity owners, that does not mean that what is an advantageous exchange for one economic group has favorable ramifications for its partner in exchange, or for other uninvolved groups and unaffiliated individuals. A strongly organized economic interest group may obtain terms of trade that leave its exchange partners in a weakened market position, despite what they receive in return. As for other economic interest groups and unorganized individuals who do not participate in the transaction, their economic opportunities may just as well remain unchanged or worsen.

This holds true, even though different economic interest groups can have converging interests of varying scope and duration. All economic interest groups may benefit from reducing runaway inflation or insuring a stable currency. On a more local scale, employers and employees of the same enterprise share an interest in improving its competitive position. Nevertheless, group interests can equally clash. Certain groups may benefit from a moderate inflation and currency devaluation that harms others, just as the success of an enterprise may benefit its employees and employers at the expense of consumers or at the expense of other firms whose position is thereby undermined. Similarly, in fighting over the spoils of their enterprise, employees may achieve a success that translates into a defeat for their employers and vice versa, regardless of how consumers and other firms may benefit. In this respect, the market interventions of economic interest groups may only perpetuate, and indeed exacerbate, the very disparities in wealth and economic opportunity that call for their creation.

This is true no matter what identity an economic interest group may have. Because each promotes a particular interest whose realization has no automatic connection to the realization of all others, the market interventions of no economic interest group have any privileged role in removing economic injustice or increasing economic disadvantage. However benevolent their intentions, the market interventions of consumer groups, tenant associations, labor unions, federations of worker cooperatives, and associations of public enterprises may just as well worsen as alleviate the maldistribution of wealth and economic opportunity. The same may be said of private business associations and landlord groups, however darkly their motives be painted.

The role of monopoly in economic interest group market intervention underscores this ambiguous and uncertain outcome. As we have seen, the creation of a monopoly is the basic tool economic interest groups dispose of for promoting their economic welfare in the marketplace. Contrary to common belief and the narrow focus of anti-monopoly agitation, the creation of cartels is not peculiar to private enterprises. It equally underlies the organization of labor unions, tenant associations, consumer groups, leagues of worker self-managed firms, and federations of public enterprises. In every case, a particular economic interest group gathers under its control a type of economic factor, so as to use its exclusive hold to limit the options of opposing economic groups and pressure them to accept certain terms of exchange. Although the conventions of bilateral agreement remain observed till the end, a thorough monopoly reduces the market freedom of other commodity owners to a largely formal prerogative, consisting in the freedom to take or leave the one offer of that type being made in the market. Hence, the success of an economic interest group in mobilizing the defining assets of its members can translate into a diminishing of the market freedom of others, transferring elsewhere the lack of economic opportunity it overcomes in its own backyard. In this respect, economic interest group activity not only fails to solve the problem of economic injustice, but creates novel difficulties of its own.

These added problems include the inability of economic interest groups to guarantee the rectitude of one anothers' activities, within and without their own organizations. Although economic interest groups can exacerbate economic injustice simply by abiding by the rules of civility, they can further violate civil rights by failing to adhere to those rules as they apply to their market interventions. An economic interest group may maintain discriminatory membership policies, excluding individuals because of some extraneous factor such as race, religion, gender, or sexual orientation, even though they share the same economic aims. Its organization can be tainted by internal corruption, where certain members use its activities to promote their own welfare at the expense of the common interest of the membership. Or, it may simply breach the canons of civil law and market autonomy by violating the freedom of other members of the economy, subjecting them to violent coercion, fraud, theft, discrimination, and other injustices.

What makes these possibilities particularly significant is that they may pertain to any economic interest group and that economic interest groups are structurally incapable of either precluding or righting these wrongs. Joint market initiatives to dissuade or penalize offending economic interest groups are hamstrung by the same limits that prevent any economic interest group from guaranteeing the economic welfare of its own members or of society at large. Although private economic pressure may take its toll, it provides neither a reliable deterrent nor a reliably effective penalty, nor for that matter, an objectively certified instrument for determining the guilt and punishment of economic interest group violators. On the other hand, the civil courts offer a remedy only for those violations that infringe upon property and household rights. When it comes to wrongs that impede the corporate rights specific to economic interest group activity, legal remedies are only available if additional legislation has been enacted covering these rights and civil courts have accordingly widened their jurisdiction to try cases falling under the new laws. In that event, individuals and economic interest groups can appeal to the courts to counter some of the new abuses that economic interest groups introduce. However, even these judicial measures cannot remedy the economic disadvantage that results from purely legal market activities. Such economic wrong remains perennially impervious to corporate action, while perennially arising from the very activities in which economic interest groups themselves partake.

For all these reasons, economic interest groups do not resolve the problem of economic injustice. They may play a deserved role in combating impediments to their members' economic opportunity, but their inability to ever eliminate these hindrances is as marked as their predilection to exacerbate them. Nevertheless, the limits of corporate action indicate what more must be done to achieve economic justice. Negatively speaking, they reveal that a just economy needs more than markets, civil enforcement of property, household, and corporate rights, and legal and market interventions by economic interest groups. Positively speaking, they call for a further intervention in the market, overcoming the particularity of corporate action with an enforcement of economic opportunity doubly universal in character. What is required is an enforcement of welfare as univeral in extension as it is in application. Instead of restricting its efforts to promoting the shared interest of some particular group, it must tend to the welfare of all members of the economy. By the same token, it must administer its relief not through the voluntary, contingent initiatives of private groups whose every success depends upon the independent market decisions of others, but through a mandatory public regulation, representing the concerted resolve of civil society and depending for its efficacy upon no one's private consent. The rights of economic opportunity rooted in market freedom demand this supplement to corporate action—a public welfare administration, extending assistance to every disadvantaged commodity owner, enjoying a common civil authority to which all owe respect, and empowered to secure everyone's economic freedom to satisfy self-chosen commodity needs through personally elected occupation.

When Hegel introduces the "police" as the counterpart of "corporations,"[7] he brings into discussion this same civil institution whose public regulation of the market is an imperative of economic justice. Admittedly, Hegel does include under the office of the "police" the public apprehension and punishment of criminals, which might better be discussed under the heading of the "Administration of Justice."[8] Further, Hegel errs in analyzing the "police" before examining "corporations." Since the limits of corporate activity both justify and define the remaining tasks of the public administration of welfare, it makes more sense to treat these civil institutions in the reverse order which we have followed. Be this as it may, Hegel's turn to the "police" does direct us to the central problems of public regulation of the market on which the justice of a just economy finally hinges.

10

The Normative Principles of Public Intervention in the Market

The Mandate for a Public Welfare Administration

By now it should be evident that market relations, either alone or supplemented by civil law, economic interest groups, and the private efforts of individuals and households, cannot realize the economic freedom of all and eliminate the economic injustice consisting in unequal economic opportunity. Yet, does this failure justify a public welfare administration to regulate the market? As Hegel has pointed out, two antithetical views challenge its introduction. One holds that public authority has no need nor any right to intervene in the market because every commodity owner already directs his conduct according to the needs of others as a condition for engaging in market activity.[1] The other maintains that public authority should not just intervene in the market, but directly superintend all social affairs, excluding markets entirely. What gives these views their significance is that they represent two competing entitlements, both rooted in the freedoms of a civil economy. The first objection reflects the civil right of individuals to work for their chosen livelihood as they please, whereas the second reflects the civil right of the public to have properly done what is essential to the welfare of all. Taken together, these entitlements mandate that, to paraphrase Hegel, market freedom should not be such as to jeopardize the general good, which in civil terms, represents the exercised economic autonomy of all together with the secured realization of their other rightful freedoms.[2] Yet, why need these entitlements be combined?

The right to public regulation

To begin with, why should the right to participate in the market as one pleases be constrained by the seemingly competing entitlements of public welfare? What right does public authority have to curtail the economic autonomy of individuals by intervening in the market? Hegel offers a series of responses, which, though not always on the mark, still direct us to the appropriate answer.

Addressing the right of public authority to regulate prices, Hegel points to the need for a conscious supervision standing above producers and consumers to enforce a fair balance between their sometimes colliding interests when the market fails to bring them automatically into harmony. What gives public authority the right to intervene in single cases and take such measures as fixing prices of the commonest necessaries of life is the fact that the regulated goods are offered not to a particular individual but to a universal buyer, the public at large. Marketed goods have this feature, Hegel maintains, by being publicly offered for sale and, in the case of common necessaries, by being in absolutely universal daily demand.[3] Claiming that this makes the price, quality, and safety of marketed goods a common concern, Hegel concludes that public authority thereby is entitled, and indeed, obligated to defend the public's right not to be price-gouged, defrauded, or endangered by what they buy.[4]

Why the public offering of marketed goods, or, in the case of common necessaries, the need of everyone for a certain good, should give license to public regulation constraining the economic autonomy of producers and sellers is, however, far from self-evident.

In a similar vein, Hegel maintains that public authority must step in to undertake such public works as installing street lights, constructing bridges, caring for public health, and other endeavors that serve the welfare of all.[5] Admittedly, market activity may not adequately furnish such public goods, but does that justify imposing upon individuals in order to finance and produce them?

Does the dependence of the larger branches of industry upon foreign conditions beyond the grasp of the individuals employed by and managing those enterprises justify the public care and direction that Hegel advocates?[6] Or, for that matter, does the possibility that families will fail to give their children the care and education they need to take their place in the market justify the public institution of compulsory care and education,[7] any more than does individuals' ability to lapse into sloth and dereliction give public authority license to compel them to accept aid and employment, as Hegel elsewhere maintains?[8]

Hegel's misguided justification of public regulation

In justifying all these examples of public intervention, Hegel appeals to a public responsibility that might seem extraneous to the market autonomy he wishes to uphold. Yet, what allows him to avoid embracing the polar claims of laissez-faire and total public administration of society is his conviction of the inherent connection between market autonomy and public responsibility for private welfare. Hegel's account of this connection provides the linchpin for all his justifications of a public administration of welfare that comes not to bury, but to redeem the market. However, although his account offers a legitimation of certain duties of the public administration of welfare, it still skirts by the crux of the matter.

Hegel's central argument is that the establishment of the civil economy gives individuals their market autonomy only at the expense of severing them from all the security and sustenance that family and nature could otherwise provide, and that this imposes rights and duties upon civilians and civil authority alike. Prior to the rise of a market economy, Hegel observes, the family served to provide for individuals, furnishing them with the skills and means enabling them to earn their living or, in the event of disability, giving them care and subsistence. Similarly, individuals could still obtain sustenance to some degree through direct access to the resources of nature, which were not yet separated from individuals by the wall of universal commodity ownership. With the advent of the market economy of civil society, where individuals interrelate in terms of nothing but their interdependent need and commodities, and where all conceivable objects of property have been drawn within the barriers of commodity ownership, the livelihood of individuals is set free from the shelter of household ties and natural abundance. In gaining self-subsistence as independent commodity owners, individuals become children of civil society, dependent upon what opportunities the market provides.[9] By divorcing the sustenance of its members from the secure confines of family and nature, the market subjects them to the economic necessity of having to labor for it, owe their entire livelihood to it, and do everything that involves needs, goods, and services by its means.[10]

Submitting individuals to these social compulsions as the price for granting them their market freedom, the civil economy can well be said to have as many claims upon individuals as they have rights against it.[11] Given how Hegel here describes the consequences of the rise of the market economy, these claims seem to consist simply in the social necessity to seek the satisfaction of one's needs by conforming to the market needs of others, just as the rights against civil society seem to consist simply in the honored freedom to come to market and enjoy the opportunity to engage in commodity exchange. However, Hegel maintains that these rights and duties signify much more. Because civil society supersedes the sustaining role of the family and nature, Hegel claims, the individual has economic rights and duties just as he had household rights and duties in the family. For Hegel, this quite literally puts civil authority in the position of taking the place of the family where the economically disadvantaged are concerned. Because the market economy is responsible for depriving individuals of the natural means of acquisition and breaking their exclusive bond to household autarchy, when it leaves its poor without the means for viable market participation, it leaves them without any further opportunity to acquire the skills and education needed for earning a living, as well as without proper health care, shelter or any of the services that could deal with the vices arising from their plight. For this reason, Hegel maintains, civil authority must provide its members with the kind of care that the family would otherwise have furnished.[12] This gives each civilian the right to demand a living from civil society, just as it gives civil society the right to compel individuals to protect themselves from their own license and undertake those activities by which they can provide for their own livelihood.[13]

Hegel's justification of a public administration of welfare as a family surrogate depends upon the truth of two claims: 1) that the sustenance provided by the family and by direct access to the gifts of nature is something to which individuals remain entitled in civil society, such that civil society has the responsibility to ameliorate any impediments to that sustenance that the civil economy introduces, and 2) that the responsibilities of the public administration of justice extend no farther than the rights and duties tied to what nature and household provide. Admittedly, as Hegel himself argues, if the family can be structured as an institution of freedom, whose members have rights and duties specific to their household roles, then civil society is obligated to insure that market relations not undermine the conditions for household autonomy. Similarly, although, as Hegel points out, man can claim no right against nature, to the degree that nature is a desacralized, rightless object subject to human domination, and hence bereft of duties to man,[14] persons do have a right to the natural prerequisites of their autonomy, a right of distress (*Notrecht*) that entitles them to the means of survival even when that overrides particular property entitlements of others.[15] In this respect, civil society is again obligated to provide its members with the means of life required for rational agency and intervene in the market when necessary to achieve this aim. However, these civil responsibilities do not give public authority any mandate to regulate market activity in order to guarantee individuals the wider rights specific to economic autonomy. The needs whose satisfaction individuals are entitled to in their capacity as persons and family members are not equivalent to those defined by the conventions of the market and its economic opportunity. Individuals can have their survival needs met and be fully able to perform their role in the family yet still be economically disadvantaged. If public authority is to be both responsible for and authorized to remedy the wrongs specific to economic injustice, the public administration of welfare must have legitimacy as more than a surrogate family.

Public regulation and the interrelation of economic right and duty

What supplies the requisite justification of the public administration of welfare is the fundamental connection between right and duty that Hegel emphasizes throughout his analyses of the different spheres of right. Because economic right, like any other right, consists in an exercise of freedom to which all agents are entitled, it equally entails the universal duty to respect the same exercise of freedom by others. This respect, which all bearers of right are obligated to pay as well as entitled to receive, consists not just in a theoretical recognition, but in a practical commitment to curtail particular actions of one's own when necessary to permit others to exercise their right. Naturally, the duty to restrict one's own exercise of freedom in behalf of that of others cannot extend to curtailing all one's exercise of that mode of autonomy. In that case the duty-bound agent would sacrifice its entitled freedom in behalf of others, leaving that freedom no longer a universal right, but a privilege others are left to enjoy. Hence, by definition, right entails the duty to restrict *particular* exercises of one's entitled freedom.

Applied to the economic right to satisfy self-chosen needs through action of one's choosing, the connection between right and duty signifies that market agents are duty-bound to restrict their economic activity in conformity to whatever partial regulation is necessary to extend equal economic opportunity to all. As we have seen, the workings of the market entail economic disadvantage while neglecting to provide the preconditions for both the economic and noneconomic freedoms to which individuals are entitled. Consequently, economic right gives civil society the responsibility and mandate to intervene in the economy for the sake of realizing the various modes of freedom of its members. By the same token, economic right gives every economic agent the duty to accept the impositions on its economic freedom that public authority must take to extend equal economic opportunity to all and protect the other freedoms to which they have a right. These impositions have legitimacy to the degree that they do nothing but realize the economic and other freedoms of all and do so by means of particular curtailments of market activity that are applied in a lawful, that is, impartial and equal way to the relevant economic factors.

This consequence of the inherent connection between economic right and economic duty makes manifest why the alternatives of laissez-faire and an entirely publicly managed economy are equally one-sided and unjust. Whereas laissez-faire neglects the economic duty that economic right entails as part and parcel of its reality, a publicly ordered economy neglects how the economic duty to regulate and to submit to public regulation is entirely in the service of economic right. As Hegel points out, if public organization supplants the market allocation of goods and services by providing for everything and determining everyone's labor, the individual's occupation is no more mediated through private choice and personal interest than are individual need and consumption.[16] In that case, the economic injustices of the market are replaced by a total elimination of economic freedom, which, although rationing jobs and goods to all, deprives everyone of their economic rights to decide how they will earn and consume.

The tasks of the public administration of welfare

Since the market responsibilities of public authority do not transcend the imperatives of economic and noneconomic right, what defines the tasks of public intervention in the economy is the character of economic autonomy and how it impinges upon the other institutions of freedom. With right, that is, the respected exercise of self-determination, providing the substance of justice, economic wrong consists in the infringement of economic freedom, and by extension, in the infringement by economic factors of noneconomic modes of self-determination. Accordingly, the problems of economic injustice have one general solution: affording to every member of society the opportunity to exercise the freedom of interest at play in market activity, while ensuring that that realization of equal economic opportunity conforms to the demands of the other spheres of right. This formulation supplies the public administration of welfare with a more determinate mission only when the structures of economic freedom and the other institutions of self-determination are considered in more detail. Nevertheless, its abstract mandate already fundamentally narrows the possible options.

To begin with, the mandate of economic justice proscribes any public enforcement of welfare that eliminates markets and the economic interest activity they make possible, or that curtails the property and household rights that commodity relations presuppose. As we have seen, insofar as the right to satisfy personally chosen needs through a self-selected occupation can only be exercised in reciprocity with others through market participation, the public enforcement of economic welfare must retain commodity relations together with their prerequisites, regulating rather than outlawing markets.

This demands much more than satisfying Marx's motto, "From each according to his ability, to each according to his needs." That solitary law of the communist utopia, which enters into effect when all family, market, and political institutions have withered away, predicates work and need upon nothing but the technique of automated production and the monological arbitrariness of natural liberty. Instead of freely satisfying needs in function of the economic autonomy of others, communist man simply toils as he can and takes what he wants, enjoying this license thanks to the magic productivity of technology. Hence, even if Marx's motto could be practiced, it would deprive work and need of their normative character, which depends upon inclusion in the reciprocal relations of right and duty that only institutions of conventional, nonnatural freedoms can supply. Although Marx may long to see justice wither away as man casts off his institutional roles and strips down to his species being, the imperatives of justice are ends in themselves, not expendable means to recoup a natural essence.

Admittedly, the jurisdiction of civil law does extend to securing the survival needs of human species being and the conditions for human choice insofar as these themselves comprise, at least in the case of human agents, the basic preconditions for self-determination of any sort. This imperative to secure the natural preconditions of free agency is what is at stake in the right of distress, which falls within the enforcement of property rights and personhood. However, economic justice extends beyond this right of survival to the civil right to enjoy an equal opportunity to earn a conventional livelihood by freely participating in commodity relations. Guaranteeing this specifically economic freedom to satisfy self-chosen needs through personally selected occupation in reciprocity with others is a much more ambitious undertaking than providing for human survival and the fulfillment of our species being.

Taken even in its most general formulation, the imperative of economic right mandates public intervention on at least four basic fronts.

Two of these fields for public action go hand in hand, due to the basic character of market freedom. In order for individuals to exercise their economic autonomy and satisfy their market needs, the commodities they choose to need must be available for exchange and they must own commodities of some sort needed by the owners of those commodities that they need to acquire. Because neither of these conditions is automatically fulfilled by the autonomous workings of the market, the enforcement of civil law, or the interventions of economic interest groups, public authority is obligated to step in and secure both of these correlative bases for the exercise of economic freedom.

On the one hand, the public administration of welfare must ensure that the market offers all members of society a sufficient and affordable supply of the commodities they need. Given the open character of market need, commodity ownership, and commodity production, this imperative entails intervention upon both the production and marketing of commodities. Of course, guaranteeing that needed commodities are in adequate and affordable supply only secures economic welfare if individuals have enough exchangeable commodities of their own to permit a reasonable match between what they can afford and what they choose to need.

Hence, at the same time that the public welfare administration tends to bringing to market sufficient quantities of reasonably priced commodities, it must also tend to supplying individuals with the assets they need to satisfy their wants in reciprocity with others. Given the diverse modes of earning that market relations involve, these assets can include such varied commodities as marketable skills, land, the means for producing items for rent or sale, produced goods themselves, or simply money. Having such assets or being able to competently employ them in the marketplace further depends on obtaining the requisite education and training, maintaining good health, refraining from falling into dereliction, and being free of unrenumerated housekeeping responsibilities that keep one from entering the market. None of these advantages, however, are automatically provided by one's own efforts, the family to which one belongs, or the market's own operations. Consequently, in obliging public authority to provide all with the assets allowing them to exercise their market freedom, economic right equally obliges public authority to establish compulsory education, to provide sufficient health care and day care services for all, and to aid those who, due to their own license, sink into indigence together with their dependents. In each case, what is imperative is providing individuals with the prerequisites for exercising their economic autonomy.

In this sense, Hegel is right to maintain that civil society displays the character of a universal family, possessing the right and duty of superintending education, health care, and other aspects of upbringing insofar as these bear upon a child's ability to become a member of society and function in the market.[17] This involves not only overriding the arbitrary and contingent preferences of parents when these are detrimental to the child's attainment of social autonomy, as Hegel notes,[18] but also counterbalancing the advantages and disadvantages children enjoy due to the different care and resources that their families can provide. As Rawls suggests, since these differences in upbringing can effect individuals' eventual economic opportunities in ways for which they are not responsible, public authority is obliged to counteract these tendencies.[19] Similarly, to the degree that differing natural endowments and handicaps affect the economic opportunities of individuals independently of their choice, the effects of these natural differences must also be counteracted through public action whenever necessary to insure equal economic opportunity.[20]

The need for public supervision holds true even when individuals' own license is responsible for reducing themselves to indigence. Individuals may be endowed with the liberty to undermine their own autonomy, but this is not a liberty to which they are entitled. On the contrary, since the exercise of right is an end in itself, individuals who enjoy the right to exercise the freedoms of property ownership, moral responsibility, household autonomy, market freedom, and political self-determination equally have a duty to maintain the prerequisites of these freedoms so far as they can. Hence, slipping into dereliction through one's own weakness is a wrong just as much as is attempting suicide. Because righting such a wrong consists in reestablishing the subjective conditions for exercising economic autonomy, individuals who put themselves in such a plight can be obliged by public authority to enter whatever programs are necessary to set them back on their feet as independent masters of their own livelihood. For this reason, Hegel is justified in maintaining that civil society has the right and duty of acting as a trustee for those whose extravagance destroys the economic security of themselves and their families[21] as well as the right and duty to press reluctant but able individuals to provide for their own livelihood.[22]

Broad as these imperatives are, the mandate of public initiative is not exhausted by public efforts to supply the market with needed goods and to provide individuals with what they must possess to exercise their market autonomy. Although the above described measures address the current problems of economic welfare as they locally effect individuals, they leave unsecured both the more universal prerequisites for economic freedom and the prerequisites for the other structures of right.

The universal prerequisites for economic freedom consist in the factors of common interest to the economic welfare of both present and future generations, such as economic infrastructures and the well-being of the environment in its capacity as a background condition for economic welfare. Insofar as market activity, civil law, and economic interest group activity cannot be counted on to provide for these factors of common interest either for present or future generations, public authority is obliged to insure that sufficient investment is made for economic infrastructures and that the environment is protected from the sort of despoilation that undermines the exercise of economic rights.[23] Since economic rights are not relative to any temporal ordering, public authority must fulfill these tasks with an eye to the welfare of both present and future generations.

By contrast, the requirement of providing for the preconditions of noneconomic rights pertains particularly to affording the internal and external prerequisites for political freedom, whose organs of government provide the ultimate guarantee for the other institutions of freedom. Two basic tasks are here entailed: 1) securing national sovereignty by providing adequate financing for national defense and the conduct of foreign affairs, and 2) providing the means for the proper internal working of self-government. The second task includes financing government offices and activities as well as financing the nongovernmental means of self-government, such as political parties and political campaigns. These efforts must aim at providing all citizens with equal political opportunity. To this end, public authority must also intervene upon the economy to prevent unequal economic leverage from being used to the political advantage of particular individuals or economic groups, as well as to prevent economic conflicts from disrupting the process of self-government. Although this intervention may largely overlap with the public efforts to diminish economic disadvantage, it has distinctly political aims that, as we shall see, are not always realized simply by achieving equal economic opportunity.

It should be acknowledged that Rawls's division of the public administration of welfare into allocation, stabilization, transfer, and distribution branches provides a framework for handling most of the tasks outlined above, even if he fails to justify his principles of justice and the economic institutions that allegedly accord with them. His allocation branch, which keeps the price system properly competitive by curtailing monopoly power and inefficient pricing,[24] could help furnish individuals with an affordable supply of the commodities they need, as well as channel resources so as to provide adequate earning opportunities and proper investment in public goods. Similarly, his stabilization branch, which aims at maintaining reasonably full employment in conformity with freedom of occupation, joins in providing the earning opportunities by which individuals can exercise their right to satisfy commodity needs of their own choosing.[25] The transfer branch, which guarantees to all a certain minimum standard of living,[26] helps enforce equal economic opportunity, provided it gives individuals the preconditions for exercising their economic autonomy, rather than imposing an administrative rationing. Finally, the distribution branch, which uses taxation and other levies both to insure a just allotment of wealth and to finance the public institutions of justice,[27] contributes a further effort in behalf of equal economic opportunity and the organs of economic and noneconomic right. Granted the general suitability of these efforts, when it comes to specifying how these interventions should be performed and whether they exhaust the imperatives of justice, what plays a determining role are not social contract principles, but the interaction concept of economic freedom in its concrete development.

The Challenge of Economic Wrong

It is not difficult to see how the imperatives of economic freedom oblige public authority to undertake the above described interventions. However, what is less clear is what measures can be taken to address these tasks, or more importantly, whether any public measures can successfully curb the economic wrongs plaguing market institutions. For it might seem that economic injustice is so engrained in commodity relations that no public intervention in the market can achieve equal economic opportunity without undermining the very institutions in which economic freedom has its exercise. Granted the identity of freedom and justice, economic justice would then be rendered an illusion, whose unrealizability would strip market institutions and the civil society they inhabit of all legitimacy and preclude any prescriptive economics.

The two horns of the dilemma: the conventional characters of market needs and occupations

What makes this possibility loom so large is the radical scope of economic right and the conventional needs and occupations it involves. Economic wrong is by no means limited to depriving individuals of the material requirements for the physical and psychological conditions of free agency. All members of society are entitled to those naturally and monologically defined requirements of subsistence because, as persons, the preconditions of their personhood warrant public protection as much as their property. However, in their capacity as economic agents, individuals enjoy an entitled welfare that extends beyond their mere survival needs. Because commodity relations provide them with an economic role in which they exercise a conventional, mutually respected autonomy by means of freely chosen needs and occupations, their economic right extends to earning a conventional livelihood in function of their economic self-determination. Social arrangements where given levels of consumption and occupations are set independently of the will of individuals may satisfy their survival needs. However, economic wrong will still persist so long as individuals remain deprived of the opportunity to satisfy market needs of their own choosing through personally selected occupation.

The difficulty has two sides. On the one hand, the economic needs to whose satisfaction individuals are entitled are conventional wants, multiplied and refined as far as the complementary choices of individuals can go. Hence, as we have seen, the poverty underlying economic injustice involves an inability to satisfy a conventional standard of living with no fixed limit. This puts the public administration of welfare in the seemingly thankless position of coping with a limitless economic deprivation.

On the other hand, just as economic right extends to needs for commodities of a completely unnatural diversity and plenitude, its exercise rests on occupations that are equally diversified and dependent upon the market decisions of others. As Hegel points out, this conventional diversification and specialization of employment entails the thoroughgoing subdivision and restriction of particular jobs, leaving individuals tied to compartmental occupations, not only restricting their economic activity to an often rote, fragmented employment, but leaving their economic opportunities severely limited by their specialized training and experience and the diverse requirements of other sorts of employment.[28] Although this may so sap the time and energy of certain individuals as to leave them unable to enjoy their broader freedoms and take advantage of the intellectual benefits of civil society, it does not automatically entail such consequences, as Hegel erroneously maintains, foreshadowing Marx's polemic against the bourgeois division of manual and intellectual labor.[29] Economic activities may be endlessly variegated and simplified, but by itself this need not diminish personal incomes nor prevent individuals from participating after work in other avocations, intellectual or not. What the conventional multiplication and refinement of earning activities does carry with it is a one-sided training and experience that leaves individuals all the more dependent upon market demand and all the more unable to adapt to the contingencies of shifting market conditions. Consequently, the public administration of welfare must contend with opportunities of livelihood as fickle and capricious as the needs they address. Somehow, public authority must solve the stupefying puzzle of affording every economic agent opportunities of earning in sufficient unnatural diversity to match both market demand and the particular qualifications, assets, and preferences that prospective earners bring to the market. This predicament renders the civil freedoms of need and occupation two horns of a dilemma, each seemingly casting in doubt the possibility of ever publicly remedying economic injustice.

Inadmissible therapies for economic wrong

What compounds the problem is the inadmissibility of the two most familiar therapeutic proposals: 1) treating economic wrong by putting the disadvantaged on the public dole, administratively allotting them goods and jobs, and 2) eliminating inequality of economic opportunity by imposing complete equality in personal wealth.

The wrongs of private and public doles

The first of these proposals cannot remove economic justice for reasons Hegel has made famous[30] and experience continues to confirm. Whether the poor be doled out means of livelihood directly from private benefactors or from public sources, the problem is the same. In either case, the needy would obtain subsistence without earning it through their own independent efforts. As Hegel points out, this would grate against the recipient's feelings of independence and self-respect. More importantly from a juridical point of view, it would violate civil society's principle of economic right according to which individuals are entitled to satisfy needs of their own choosing through personally selected earning activities in reciprocity with others.[31] None of the various arrangements of such assistance can escape this problem.

If being on private or public dole involved receiving particular goods through the unilateral decision of external benefactors, this would deprive recipients of choosing what commodities they want. This deprivation would not be removed if the recipient had a voice in running the private or public agency involved, as would occur in a democratic commune or a democratically governed public authority. In either case, the terms of the allotment would be decided by the majority rather than by the independent personal decision of the recipient.

If, instead, being on the dole meant receiving monetary payments with which to purchase consumer goods, the recipients would gain an opportunity to choose what items to buy. However, they would still be left without an opportunity to engage in the normatively valid activity of earning a civil livelihood.

The same would be true even if the poor get assigned wage-earning jobs, instead of receiving unearned goods or income. In this case of indirect rather than direct distribution of the means of livelihood, public assistance would allow disadvantaged individuals to acquire income through their own effort and be in a position to buy what they choose with their new earnings. Nevertheless, the full freedom to which economic right entitles each individual would still be lacking. For although the poor would now enjoy the opportunity to purchase what they need by means of their own labor, the selection of their job would still be out of their hands.

Without doubt, unilaterally assigning the poor commodities and employment can remove the material side of their deprivation. Nonetheless, doling out goods, money, and jobs to the poor is not equivalent to realizing their economic right to participate freely in commodity relations. So long as the disadvantaged are rationed goods and employment without the mediation of their own choice, these means of subsistence remain instruments of oppression, substituting an administered necessity for the economic freedom whose deprivation they should be removing.

The economic wrong of imposing an absolute equality of wealth

Given how differences in wealth can undermine the equal economic opportunity to which each member of civil society is entitled, and how economic justice consists in realizing economic autonomy, it might seem that economic injustice can be better handled, and indeed, decisively conquered by publicly enforcing an absolute equality of wealth. For if the public welfare administration could impose equal commodity ownership, ensuring that each member of society disposes over either the same specific assets or the same total purchasing power, would not economic disadvantage be abolished?

This option appears all the more warranted given how traditional objections to radical economic egalitarianism lose their force once the exclusive normativity of freedom is acknowledged. With economic right conceived in terms of equal economic opportunity, the Aristotelian appeal to differences in merit has no bearing upon the claims of economic justice. Admittedly, ensuring equal access to market activity does extend equal treatment to individuals who may have entirely unequal merit according to teleological standards of virtue. However, this is no violation of economic fairness, when the only qualification that counts is autonomous agency and the only inherent economic good is the exercise of self-determination in regard to needs and occupations.

Utilitarian objections, such as those that Hume inveighs against the Leveller demand for equal distribution of wealth, are similarly irrelevant. The enforcement of equal wealth may eliminate self-enrichment as an incentive to diligence and productivity, leading to a decline in the total wealth of society and in the aggregate happiness it brings.[32] Further, preventing resurgences of unequal commodity ownerships may involve such rigorous monitoring and supervision of economic transactions as to require an expensive and unwieldly administrative machine.[33] Be this as it may, such difficulties are of little concern to economic justice provided they do not undermine the equal opportunity that the leveling of wealth presumably provides.

Hume's critique comes closer to the mark when he points to two rather incongruous threats to freedom that he finds entailed in the public maintenance of equal wealth. On the one hand, he asserts that an equalization of wealth would sap the authority of the public administration required to maintain it, undermining the civil protection of person and property.[34] Although Hume supplies no argument as to why political authority need rest on economic privilege, the demarcation of civil society from the state, with its differentiation of social and political freedoms, runs counter to any such claim. For if the legitimacy of the state rests on its being both the organ of its citizens' political self-determination and the guardian of their nonpolitical freedoms, then political authority is not only independent of social inequality, but undercut by any economic advantage that has political ramifications.

What Hume perceives to be economic equality's other threat to freedom is more to the point. Hume argues that any effective public enforcement of radical equality would require that government have eyes, ears, and coercive power in every corner where exchange and production take place. Hence, individuals would only gain equal ownership at the expense of submitting to an all-pervasive supervision ready to degenerate into the most thoroughgoing tyranny.[35] Although Hume describes the danger as if it consisted in an invitation to further tyranny, extending to the other domains of life, he does draw attention to the decisive issue: namely, the question of whether public enforcement of total equality of wealth carries with it a pernicious restriction of economic autonomy. If it does, then radical egalitarianism provides a cure that kills the patient, destroying the economic freedom it is intended to extend to all.

Naturally, the degree to which public maintenance of equal wealth impinges upon economic autonomy depends on how it is accomplished. If the public welfare administration imposed equal wealth by restricting the commodity ownership of individuals to the same set of particular goods and assets, it would deprive them of their freedom of need. Instead of being at liberty to choose what needs to satisfy and what means of satisfaction to obtain, individuals would here be compelled to accept whatever is publicly mandated. Further, since they would be prohibited from using the particular utilities they are allotted to obtain a different distribution, individuals would equally lose their freedom to participate in market transactions, be it as a producer or renter of marketed goods, a wage earner, or a buyer and seller in general.

These impositions upon economic autonomy might seem avoidable if the public administration of welfare insures that everyone has not the same collection of particular goods, but an equal amount of wealth, as measured by its current exchange value. In that case, individuals would retain the freedom to choose which commodities to acquire by using their equal purchasing power as they please in the market. Further, they would seem to retain their freedom of earning as well, since all would be at liberty to employ their assets in the market as they see fit, subject only to a subsequent readjustment of their personal wealth if they either lost or gained purchasing power relative to others. Since this readjustment would aim at maintaining equal amounts of exchange value, it could best be administered through the monetary transfers of a positive and negative taxation, where individuals retain the prerogative to choose both what to relinquish to obtain the money for their tax bill and what to acquire with whatever income supplements they receive. In this way, individuals would seem to exercise a relatively unscathed market autonomy, while enjoying the leveled economic opportunities that equal purchasing power provides. Further, it could well require no more cumbersome a public supervision than what tax agencies already practice.

Nonetheless, does this measure really eliminate economic injustice and realize everyone's economic right to pursue freely chosen, yet interdependent needs and occupations? Is the imposition of an absolute equality of wealth upon participants in markets tantamount to the achievement of equal participation in the structures of economic freedom?

Two factors weigh against identifying strict equality of wealth with economic justice. One is inherent in the basic structure of commodity exchange, whereas the other we have seen Hume identify in utilitarian fashion and Rawls redescribe in the contractarian terms of the difference principle.

To begin with, given the diverse economic aspirations that markets permit individuals to pursue according to personal preference, equal purchasing power is not a necessary condition for equal economic opportunity. Since 1) individuals can satisfy their needs in reciprocity with others only by wanting different goods, owning different commodities, and pursuing occupations that complement one another, 2) exchange value is determined through the free agreement of market agents so long as market autonomy is retained, so that the purchase power required to satisfy desired wants can always fluctuate, and 3) economic right leaves individuals at liberty to desire different commodites, occupations and different standards of living, imposing uniform wealth can well restrict, rather than promote, everyone's economic freedom. Rigorously enforced, equal wealth impinges upon economic self-determination whenever there are individuals whose chosen wants require greater purchase power to satisfy, but do so without jeopardizing the desired economic options of others. In all such cases where differences in wealth are congruent with differences in desired economic pursuits, where, in other words, inequalities of purchase power do not hinder economic self-determination, the imposition of strict equality in wealth entails particular restrictions of economic freedom that do not serve its universal realization.

Such cases might appear to be so marginal or so dependent upon unforeseeable caprice that prudence would warrant enforcement of equality of wealth as the most practical way of ensuring equal economic opportunity. However, this reasoning ignores another cardinal aspect of commodity relations: namely, that eliminating relative personal enrichment as a possible incentive for economic activity may well interfere with allocating resources so as to provide sufficient affordable products, desired occupational opportunities, compensation for the handicapped, adequate protection of the environment, and proper investment in public goods for maintaining the economic and noneconomic freedoms of present and future generations. Although enforcing equality of wealth does not formally prohibit individuals from pursuing economic activities that can lead to unequal distributions of purchasing power, prior to the readjustments that public authority will make, it does, practically speaking, proscribe all economic opportunities where individuals can use their initially equalized purchasing power to acquire relatively greater wealth. Given the preferences of individuals, this can readily result in a decline in productivity, shortages of labor and capital in economic sectors and localities where some premium is needed to attract either, a consequent decrease in the amount and affordability of marketed commodities, a complete unavailability of goods whose production and marketing depends upon a monetary incentive, and a general atrophy of economic growth that may limit the options of economic freedom when this by no means serves the cause of equal economic opportunity.

Naturally, public authority can always step in and directly mobilize labor and capital when the market fails to provide for their adequate allocation, due to its own arbitrariness or to the constraints of rigorous equalizations of wealth. However, whenever a public command system of allocation is introduced, it is at the expense of the economic freedom that might otherwise be exercised if certain incentives were retained. Hence, if the aim of public intervention is to promote the exercise of economic self-determination, it is inadmissible to substitute a public command system for inequalities of wealth that enlarge the economic opportunities of all.

As we have seen, Hume raised this issue in castigating the Levellers' egalitarianism as a threat to the productivity and prosperity on which public happiness depends. Rawls offers his difference principle in response to this same problem, aware, however, that what counts is not the threat to happiness, but the threat to equal opportunity. To his credit, Rawls recognizes that rigid egalitarianism in respect to wealth can jeopardize the conditions of economic and noneconomic freedom for present and future generations, and that inequality of wealth should be tolerated so long as it promotes the exercise of these freedoms. As Rawls rightly points out, this applies not only to permitting certain inequality in incomes, but also to allowing inequalities in property holdings and inheritance so long as these contribute to the economic opportunity of the relatively disadvantaged.[36] Although Rawls characterizes the problem in terms of fairly distributing primary goods with which individuals can achieve whatever ends they please subject to the constraints of justice, his discussion of economic justice revolves around problems pertaining to equal economic opportunity in the market. However, Rawls is unable to justify his toleration of limited inequality of wealth. As argued in Chapter 3, Rawls fails both because his difference principle presupposes markets when it should be prior to all particular social arrangements and because he is unable to justify the normative necessity of markets by relying upon his only other available resource, the principle of equal liberty. The latter is of no avail because Rawls's account of liberty is institutionally nonspecific and his justification of the principle of equal liberty rests upon a choice procedure that takes that principle for granted.

Once the legitimacy of markets is established in virtue of their role as constitutive institutions of economic self-determination, Rawls's failure can be overcome. The difference principle can now be recast in explicit and due regard for the normativity of commodity relations, free from the pitfalls of contractarian theory. On these terms, the public administration of welfare receives its guiding principle for enforcing economic equality: that what is imperative is tolerating only those inequalities of wealth whose reduction would reduce the level of equal economic opportunity and the exercise of economic freedom in which it consists, as well as jeopardize the conditions for noneconomic institutions of freedom, taking into account on both scores the rights of present as well as future generations.

Complications of the Permissible Approach

Obliged to follow this imperative, instead of administering doles and rigidly equalizing wealth, the public administration of welfare must meet the challenge of economic injustice with a more flexible approach. Yet without doling out goods and jobs or eliminating every last inequality of purchase power, can public institutions provide everyone with enough exchangeable assets and enough market opportunities to exercise their economic freedom? Can public authority still accomplish the double duty of guaranteeing each individual the means of self-determined livelihood, such as a marketable labor power, sufficiently trained as the individual elects, and whatever else is needed to earn a conventional living in exchange with others, while insuring that corresponding earning opportunities and commodities abound in affordable supply? And if some economic disadvantage must always persist, does this render all talk of a just economy empty rhetoric?

Four problems, largely intimated already, seem to present perennial difficulties, given the approach that economic right ordains for the public administration of welfare. These are the problems of ever guaranteeing satisfaction to the artificially multiplied and refined needs of the market, of furnishing freely chosen livelihoods to the unemployed without exacerbating overproduction, of restraining the tendencies toward monopoly endemic to commodity relations, and of coping with the inequalities of wealth that market activity continually produces.

The discrepancy between personal need, market demand, and market supply

No matter what measures are taken to provide everyone with fair earning opportunities, it seems impossible for the public welfare administration ever to guarantee a match between the chosen needs of individuals, their purchase power, and market supply of the desired commodities. Because markets free the quantity and variety of needs and goods from the confines of natural subsistence, adding a conventional multiplication and differentiation limited only by the market decisions of individuals, commodity owners are at liberty to seek a conventional standard of living whose commodity needs may well exceed what they can afford and what the market has to offer.

This discrepancy leaves public authority with two options. On the one hand, it can circumvent the problem by restricting the freedom of need and imposing limits upon how low a standard of living will be publicly guaranteed and how high a standard of living will be publicly permitted. In doing so, however, the public welfare administration will be striking at the market autonomy of individuals, something that can only be warranted if the imposed restrictions somehow promote economic and noneconomic freedoms alike. Whether this requirement could possibly be satisfied is something that will be considered later.

If, on the other hand, public authority refrains from restricting the freedom of need, it must address all sides of the discrepancy between chosen needs, purchasing power, and market supply. As we have seen, public intervention is imperative because the "self-regulation" of the market is unable to guarantee either that supply will match consumer demand or that particular individuals will have purchasing power sufficient to meet their chosen needs. However market enterprises be owned and managed, unless public authority steps in, particular needed commodities may not be produced at all, or may be manufactured without desired specifications and quality, just as over- and underproduction may occur not just in particular sectors, but throughout the economy. Hence, the public welfare administration is obliged to reduce the discrepancy between market need and market supply by regulating economic resources so that the market is furnished with as many needed commodities at as affordable prices as possible. This involves combating inflation, and in that connection, insuring a sufficiently stable currency. At the same time, steps must be taken to insure that individuals have earning opportunities providing purchasing power as closely matching their needs as possible. What complicates matters is not just the open-ended character of preferred needs, but the fact that among the commodities that may be in under- or oversupply is labor power. Either situation easily jeopardizes individuals' possibility of obtaining a desired standard of living by means of a desired occupation.

Unemployment and overproduction

Perhaps the most vexing problem bearing upon the satisfaction of market need is how to eliminate unemployment without exacerbating overproduction. To the extent that individuals enjoy the economic right to satisfy freely chosen needs through a freely chosen occupation in reciprocity with others, unemployment is an economic injustice that public authority has a duty to eliminate. As we have seen, it is not sufficient to leave the jobless on the public dole. Unemployment insurance may give its recipients purchasing power with which to satisfy some of their chosen needs, but unless it is a transient measure, necessitated by the technicalities of transferring from old to new job opportunities, it does not help realize the able's right to exercise an occupation of their choice.

Hegel's warning

Hegel has suggested just how intractable a problem unemployment is for civil society in his famous remarks on the deadly linkage between public provision of work and increased overproduction. As Hegel points out, providing work for the unemployed may be more in keeping with economic right than putting them on a direct dole, but it increases the volume of production.[37] Yet, the economic evil which engenders so much unemployment is precisely an excess of production and a lack of a proportionate number of consumers. Although putting the unemployed to work might seem to increase market demand by providing new recipients of income, it cannot balance the added production it creates. Hence, public works only exacerbate the overproduction that makes workers redundant in the first place.

Although Hegel does not elaborate on why this must be so, there are two reasons that support his conclusion. First, if those put to work are paid at public expense, whatever market demand their incomes appear to add is actually drawn from other sectors of the economy, through whatever means are used to raise revenue for the public welfare administration. Hence, while public works add to the supply of produced commodities, they add little if any new demand. Second, even if those put to work are employed in self-supporting enterprises, the consumer demand their incomes represent cannot help match the aggregate market price of what they produce unless their products are sold at equal or less than their costs of production. Yet, if their enterprises operate either at a loss or without profit, market competition may make them less and less economically viable, with the result that they become a further drain on the economy, reducing its overall productivity and market strength to the economic detriment of its members. Either way, Hegel seems supported in his conclusion that civil society is not rich enough to check unemployment, despite the excess of wealth overproduction represents. The market may give rise to a wealth of luxury without limit, yet its own resources prove insufficient to check the poverty of the unemployed and their transformation into a rebellious rabble, possessing little motive to respect the norms of a civil society that offers them no opportunity to exercise economic autonomy.[38]

For Hegel, the inability of public authority to free the market economy of unemployment through public works leaves only one alternative solution: engaging in systematic colonization and imperialism.[39] Driven by its and the market's joint failure to create sufficient internal demand for increasing production, public authority is compelled to look beyond the limits of its own economy to combat unemployment. Imperialism, broadly conceived as the public effort to mobilize foreign markets for the economic welfare of the home economy, provides a way of overcoming the problem of insufficient demand. A particular civil society can unload its overproduction and receive in return otherwise unobtainable means of subsistence by using its public power to open and corner additional markets in other lands, which either lack the goods it has overproduced or cannot compete in quality or price due to the backwardness of their industry.[40] By means of publicly sponsored systematic colonization, on the other hand, a particular civil society can directly attack domestic unemployment by giving the jobless the opportunity to settle outside the mother country. This not only provides the disadvantaged with a new chance for exercising their economic autonomy, but creates a new source of demand and a new field for investment for the colonizing society.[41]

Although imperialism and colonization may well have these effects, so salutary from the point of view of the mother economy, the two salient points of Hegel's argument are questionable. To begin with, it is far from evident that any public effort to combat unemployment by putting people to work in the domestic economy will only worsen the employment situation by increasing overproduction. Further redundancy could seemingly be avoided if public projects put the unemployed to work in fields of industry in which, relative to supply, demand is strong enough to absorb new production. In that case, public works projects could conceivably become self-financing profit or non-profit enterprises providing increased employment and economic growth without overproduction. Conversely, even if Hegel is right that unemployment can be remedied only by public measures in foreign lands, both the justice and the long-term viability of this solution can be questioned. If the foreign territories are already inhabited, then justice would require respecting the rights and welfare of the indigenous people, which could so restrict imperial and colonial undertakings, that their value for the domestic economy could disappear. On the other hand, if the opening and mobilization of foreign markets and the promotion of colonization could be handled with justice to all concerned, it still might be doubted whether these efforts really solve unemployment and overproduction or merely transplant them abroad. The opening of foreign markets and the establishment of colonies may simply create new market economies afflicted with the same inability to generate sufficient market demand to sustain full employment. In that case, Hegel's foreign remedies would only magnify the domestic problems to international proportions.

Rosa Luxemburg's radicalization of the problem

Hegel's conclusions may be discreditable, but the problem he raises cannot be ignored. This is all the more true in face of the argument Rosa Luxemburg presents in the *Accumulation of Capital*,[42] an argument that radicalizes the systemic dilemma presented by overproduction. If Luxemburg finally fails to drive her point home, she at least helps put in perspective the magnitude of the challenge confronting the public administration of welfare.

Like Hegel, Luxemburg maintains that a market economy cannot internally generate the demand necessary to fuel economic expansion and forestall overproduction. Significantly, Luxemburg attempts to show that this applies to the market economy as a whole, so that even if public works in particular sectors could create new jobs without creating redundant production, there would still be no internal way to eliminate all domestic overproduction and the unemployment it involves. Moreover, like Hegel, Luxemburg argues that the market economy is compelled to turn to foreign economies and employ imperialism and colonization in order to obtain additional demand with which to reduce overproduction, increase employment, and generate increasing wealth. However, Luxemburg parts company with Hegel by arguing that the move to foreign economies is no solution at all, because once they serve their purpose they become transformed into market economies themselves which suffer from the same inability to create the expansion of demand upon which economic growth depends. Hence, the more the market economy draws upon other nonmarket economies to cure its overproduction, the more it extends market relations and eliminates the external sources of demand without which the market accumulation of wealth must collapse. Thus, whereas Hegel treats imperialism and colonization as workable treatments for economic injustice, Luxemburg views them as necessary outgrowths of a market dynamic by which the universalization of commodity relations brings the expansion of wealth to an absolute halt, threatening the general breakdown of the market system.

To prove her point, Luxemburg relies upon the schemas of the expanded reproduction of social capital which Marx develops in the incomplete manuscript that Engels assembled into the second volume of *Capital*. In adopting this model, Luxemburg shares Marx's basic assumptions that the process of capital accumulation totally absorbs the system of commodity relations, that exchange values and revenues all ultimately rest upon the capital-labor relation and the expenditure of labor within capital's production process, and that hence the laws of reproduction of the market economy can be conceived as laws for the accumulation of the total capital of society, where what exclusively enters in are labor-produced values and exchanges of the resulting products and revenue among capitalists and their wage laborers. Incorporating these presuppositions, the schema of expanded reproduction conceives the annual accumulation of the total social capital in terms of the interrelation of the two major branches of industry: the capital goods sector, made up of the capitals producing means of production, and the consumer goods sector, comprising the capitals producing consumer goods. These branches of social capital are treated as if they form a closed system in which there are neither savings out of wages nor lending between sectors. Moreover, in much of the analysis, Luxemburg follows Marx's example in presupposing an absence of technical change, expressed in a constant organic composition of capital and a fixed rate of surplus value, as well as an absence of fixed capital, whose replenishment requires spurts, rather than continual increments of investment. As Luxemburg and Marx would both admit, the assumptions of no lending between sectors, fixed organic composition of capital, and constant rate of surplus value all run counter to the dynamic of competition, whose tendency to equalize profit rates and market prices equally involves transfers of capital from one sector to another, continual revolutions in the technique of production, and altering rates of profit, not to mention the complications created by the immobility of fixed capital.[43] Nevertheless, these assumptions are not decisive for her argument, nor do they represent its chief stumbling block. The key commitments rather lie in Luxemburg's acceptance of the labor theory of value and its correlative identification of commodity relations with relations of private capital employing wage labor.

On these terms, the system of social capital will reproduce itself without any expansion if two conditions are met. The first is that the capitalists in both sectors replace all the means of production they consume during the year and the use value and value of the consumed means of production of both sectors equals the use value and value of the product of the capital goods sector. The second is that workers and capitalists spend their entire revenues on consumer goods and the value of the products of the consumer goods sector equals the total wages bill and surplus of both sectors. In that case the social product will be purchased in its entirety with the social revenue generated in its production and distribution, and its consumption will set in motion another round of production on the same scale as before.

If, however, there is to be an accumulation of the total social capital, then the capitalists in both sectors must not just replace the annually consumed equipment and material, but invest some of their surplus in additional means of production. This will allow them to expand their wealth only if consumer spending increases in line with the increased production in the consumer goods sector resulting from the investment in more means of production, which funds the expansion of the capital goods sector. Expanded reproduction cannot occur unless this additional demand is provided, allowing the capitals producing consumer goods to gain a profit with increased annual revenues, and thereby enabling the capitals producing means of production to obtain greater revenues for themselves by profitably selling more material and equipment to the producers of consumer goods and to those of their own ranks who must increase production to meet this growing demand for capital goods.

Luxemburg maintains that this is impossible because the consumer spending of the capitalists and workers of both sectors cannot provide any of the additional demand needed to purchase the newly added production that expanded investment has created. Their consumer purchase power is limited in value to the aggregate variable capital and the portion of the surplus that is not reinvested. Hence, Luxemburg concludes, it can only cover a portion of current costs of production and not provide any of the additional demand needed to purchase the newly added production that has been created by investing the surplus that the capitalists do not themselves consume.

It might be supposed that this problem can be overcome insofar as the expanded investment creates its own new demand through the revenues received by the producers of the additional means of production, the wages their workers receive, and the revenues and wages obtained in the consumer goods sector thanks to the resulting additional consumer spending of workers and capitalists from the capital goods sector. However, Luxemburg rejects this solution, maintaining that it leaves unexplained where the demand comes from that fuels the expanded investment in the first place. The purchase power at hand at the outset of each round of accumulation is simply insufficient. Consequently, if the capital of the economy is to accumulate on a global scale, as the social capital must do to retain its identity as self-expanding exchange value, it must move beyond its own closed system and seek additional demand from noncapitalist economies. Yet, Luxemburg argues, once the capitalist economy breaks open noncapitalist markets, it inexorably undermines their traditional economic organization and transforms them into organs of an expanded system of capitalist relations, burdened once again with the same realization problem which drove it beyond itself. The more the capitalist economy pushes into noncapitalist areas to fuel its own expansion, the greater becomes its own need for external markets and the more limited becomes their extent. The whole process of capital accumulation therefore irrevocably drives toward its own collapse, inescapably reached when capitalism has become a world-embracing closed system, having assimilated the noncapitalist economies upon which it must feed.

Luxemburg's reasoning might appear easily dismissible by the sort of objections raised by Joan Robinson and Paul Sweezy. Robinson claims that Luxemburg's analysis is incomplete because it ignores two factors that allow capitalism to rescue itself from its realization problems: the internal inducement to investment provided by competitive pressures to take advantage of technical progress and the rise in real wages that accompanies the development of capitalism.[44]

Sweezy pursues this second point, noting that Luxemburg's argument rests on the dogmatic presupposition that the purchase power of workers can never realize surplus value. This assumption entails, he maintains, that the consumer spending of workers must remain fixed, contrary to the fact that capital accumulation typically increases variable capital and thereby allows workers to realize part of the surplus value through their added spending. Once Luxemburg presumes that consumption cannot increase, it follows that expanded reproduction cannot be fueled by additional production of capital goods either, since, Sweezy implies, that would ultimately presuppose increased demand for consumer goods. However, once the assumption of the constancy of consumer spending is dropped, Luxemburg's whole argument comes crashing down.[45]

Further, Luxemburg's appeal to noncapitalist consumers cannot solve her poblem since, Sweezy observes, they cannot be sold any goods unless some of their own are purchased in return. Hence even if such trade were undertaken, it could not realize surplus value. The portion of the social capital representing surplus value would only alter in form, trading its shape as exported products for that of imported goods. In any event, since the turn to external markets is due to a shortfall of domestic consumer spending, there could hardly be any demand for imported goods in the first place.[46]

Luxemburg could well reply to all but the last of these objections with the same refrains she employs in criticizing the solutions to capital's realization problem offered by her contemporaries. She need not deny that competition may make increasing investment in capital goods a precondition of market success for individual firms. What she would question is whether this in any way alters the global situation of consumer demand, upon which investment is ultimately predicated. Given the assumptions of the reproduction schemas, so long as the disposable income of workers and capitalists cannot cover the portion of surplus value in the value of consumer goods, producers of consumer goods will lack the revenue to invest in additional capital goods, and producers of capital goods will accordingly lack the funds to underwrite their own expansion.

Similarly, even if wages were to increase, they could not eliminate the realization problem, since whatever surplus is left is always that element of the total production that exceeds the value of the expended constant and variable capital.

As for Sweezy's final objection, Luxemburg could reply that non-capitalist economies could trade with capitalist economies without exporting goods of equivalent value if the former had obtained means of exchange in commodity transactions not incorporated in the circuit of capital accumulation. However, this last riposte would contradict Luxemburg's acceptance of the labor theory of value and its correlative identification of commodity relations with the system of capital accumulation, leaving Sweezy able to observe that Luxemburg would have proved not the impossibility of a closed capitalist system, but the impossibility of capitalism altogether.[47]

What ultimately undermines Luxemburg's argument are the simplifications and assumptions built into the reproduction schemas on which she relies. To begin with, the schemas make it appear that the aggregate investments in capital equipment, raw material, and labor in each sector precede the aggregate sale of their portion of the social product and the realization of their profit. On this basis, the problem of additional consumer demand becomes a stumbling block, since it is presumed that additional purchase power must already be at hand in order for part of the surplus to be reinvested in added means of production. However, once one drops this consolidation of market transactions into temporally discrete stages in the capital circuits of the two aggregate branches of production, and takes due account of how expanded investment occurs in a staggered form, allowing increased wages and surplus to be already available to fuel further expansion, the realization problem is no longer insurmountable.

What further facilitates expanded reproduction is the availability of credit and the independence of the exchange value of wages, profits, and products from the conditions of production, both of which are dogmatically ruled out by the reproduction schemas. Because neither the technical arrangement of production nor the prices at which the factors of production were purchased unilaterally mandate the prices at which the product is finally sold nor the purchasing power wages and profits can command, the limits on accumulation cannot be inflexibly set by the production-determined parameters of Marx's reproduction schemas.

These considerations do not mean that imbalances in the growth of demand and investment cannot occur in particular sectors or throughout the economy at large, such that accumulation comes to a halt and disaccumulation enters in. However, they do signify that market relations do not preclude economic growth and that the search for external markets need not be a self-fulfilling prophecy of economic doom. Admittedly, so long as there are markets, the problem of overproduction can always surface and exacerbate the difficulties of providing freely chosen job opportunities to the unemployed. However, overproduction is not a fatal problem for economic justice, condemning commodity relations to deepening crisis and rendering public efforts to reduce unemployment exercises in futility. Hegel's warning and its radicalization by Luxemburg are best taken as extreme reminders of difficulties in maintaining economic welfare that must be perennially confronted.

The problem of monopoly formation

In addressing economic disadvantage without canceling the avenues of economic freedom, the public administration of welfare seems trapped between unforeseeable and unlimited demands for commodities and employment and equally unforeseeable and uneliminable outbreaks of under- and overproduction, involving shortages and surpluses of goods and labor. What contributes to these difficulties while creating its own obstacles to the general exercise of economic freedom are the tendencies to monopoly that are endemic to the opportunities provided by the civil economy. These tendencies have two basic forms of different extents: one is internal to individual enterprises, arising through the uneven concentration of capital among particular firms, whereas the other operates on an intra-enterprise basis through the joint undertakings of economic interest groups. As we have seen, both types of monopoly come into existence through nothing more than the exercise of the prerogatives to which members of markets and civil institutions are entitled. Nevertheless, whether a monopoly be exercised by a single firm or by a plurality of market participants in consort with one another, it can, although it need not, hinder the ability of other market participants to exercise their economic autonomy. It may do so by maintaining inflated prices, rents and interest rates, by hindering the entry of others into similar fields of business, by restricting options of employment, and by generally limiting the economic choices of others. As we have also seen, neither market relations, nor civil law, nor economic interest groups activity can be counted on to break the hold of existing monopolies, nor to bar their formation in the future.

Yet, if public intervention is to control the extent of monopolies for the sake of maintaining the freedom of equal economic opportunity, together with noneconomic freedoms, it can never eliminate the roots of monopoly formation: market freedom and its associate economic interest group activity. Measures can be taken to restrict monopoly activity in the name of economic freedom, such as setting caps on the differential concentrations of capital that will be permitted in economic sectors, or limiting the extent to which common fronts can be made in setting prices, wages, rents, and interest rates, or in directing purchasing power or marketing labor power. Yet this can never be more than a partial control of monopoly power so long as public authority tolerates any differences in the concentration of capital and any economic interest group interventions in the marketplace. Latitude on either score provides opportunities of unequal economic leverage that can translate themselves into the economic disadvantage of others. As we have seen, the dangers of monopoly depend in no way upon how firms are owned and managed or what identity the colluding economic interest group has. Hence, excluding certain forms of ownership and management and banning market interventions by certain economic interest groups will not dispel monopoly power and the problems it creates.

Still, particular restrictions may well be compatible with the promotion of equal economic opportunity, even if their success is contingent upon unforeseeable market conditions and of fleeting duration. Nonetheless, a universal equalization of the size of enterprises in the same or related branches of commerce would no more promote the common exercise of economic freedom than an across the board prohibition of economic interest group activity in the market. In each case, the general curtailment of market autonomy entailed in such measures would be so great as to outweigh whatever widened options they provide. Caught between the extremes of leaving monopolies be and proscribing the bases of their formation, public authority seems condemned to a never-ending remedial control that always fails to achieve an abiding solution.

The recurrence of economic inequality

The prospects of public intervention seem no better in face of the disparities of wealth that ceaselessly emerge from the workings of the market, however it be regulated. As we have seen, the moment individuals exercise their freedom to engage in commodity relations, differences in earnings are bound to result, no matter how equal their assets be at the outset, nor how enterprises be owned or managed. This is not just because individuals bring different talents and degrees of diligence to their economic endeavors, as Hume emphasizes,[48] but equally because of individuals' dependency upon the capricious market decisions of others and the fluctuations of value to which this subjects every element of wealth. This is all the more true, given how no regulation of monopoly power that retains market freedom and the rights of economic interest groups can completely eliminate the resurgence of inequalities in the concentration of capital, labor power, consumer purchasing power, and other economic factors.

Hence, Hegel is not completely off the mark in raising the specter of a rabble of paupers, haunting the civil economy with the rebellious indignation of a poverty-stricken underclass, whose members are left idle or marginally employed, unable to satisfy their needs through free participation in the market, and dependent instead upon chance, public doles, or criminal activity.[49] The formation of such a rabble is not just a problem afflicting laissez-faire economies. Given the inability of public regulation of the market to prevent all recurrences of economic inequality, it appears that the abolition of an underprivileged "rabble" is not something that can ever be achieved through public measures retaining economic autonomy. Rather, it seems to represent a chronic social disease of varying intensity, requiring a never-ending public care. For this reason, Hegel can well claim that civil society always leaves opportunities for individuals to act on their own moral initiative in behalf of the economic welfare of others,[50] even though the public administration of welfare is needed precisely to rescue the disadvantaged from the contingent mercies of private aid.

11

The Limits of the Public Enforcement of Economic Welfare

The irrepressible discrepancies between civil needs and market supply and demand, the linkage of unemployment and overproduction, and the ineluctable recurrence of monopolies and economic inequality all cast their shadows upon the enforcement of economic welfare. If the just economy cannot free itself of these complications to the exercise of economic autonomy, how can it retain validity when its justice lies in providing the fairest possible economic opportunity in consonance with noneconomic rights? Does the abiding presence of economic disadvantage, which calls for a ceaseless public intervention upon market institutions, condemn economic justice to a hollow ideal, incapable of realization, and therefore, since ought implies can, to a contradiction in terms? Or, if the problems besetting the public enforcement of economic welfare do not rule out a just economy, how can they be handled without turning economic freedom against itself?

These types of questions are not the unique concerns of economic justice, but apply to every structure of right. If the persistence of economic wrong calls into question the status of economic justice, then it would be perfectly congruent for the reality of property rights, morality, family rights, and political justice to be thrown into doubt by the uneliminable incidence of property crimes, immorality, maltreatment of spouses and children, and political corruption and unconstitutional acts. Yet, it is evident that none of these realms of justice can exist without allowing for the possibility of violations of their norms. No machinery of criminal enforcement can eliminate crime, no tugs of conscience can preclude actions in bad faith, no resource within or without the family can prevent child abuse and the mistreatment of spouses, no more than any balance of powers can prevent state officials from misusing their positions. Hence, the problem is not whether institutions of justice fail to eliminate all wrong, but rather whether the residual recurrence of injustice is handled so that it is reduced to a minimum and neither disrupts the coexisting institutions of justice nor represents an unfairly shouldered burden. To the extent that justice consists in the common exercise of freedom, the question becomes whether the persistence of particular infringements upon self-determination eliminates the structures of freedom and falls unfairly upon certain groups. Hence, the persistence of economic injustice need not make the just economy an empty mirage. Rather, it raises the problem of determining how the recurrence of economic disadvantage can be minimized so as to maintain the general exercise of economic freedom without allowing the incidence of economic wrong to become an affliction to which some are specially fated.

The Fair Restriction of Need

To begin with, how can the unavoidable discrepancy between personal need and market supply and demand be fairly handled in consonance with the exercise of economic autonomy? As we have seen, no matter how much purchasing power and production are publicly promoted, it is impossible to guarantee the satisfaction of the commodity needs that individuals are at liberty to choose. Public authority is thus faced with the problem of restricting the needs whose satisfaction is guaranteed. How can this be done fairly without impugning market freedom?

This is not a problem of some zero-sum game, where the supply of commodities and income are fixed givens. Rather, since both market supply and demand are themselves tied to the rate of economic expansion, the public welfare administration is in a position to influence their amount. Still, there are limits to what can be done, defined by the present resources of the economy and the current market conjuncture. These empirically given conditions restrict the available options, and hence, public authority must take them into account in determining what conventional standard of living can be generally guaranteed. This determination does involve restricting the freedom of need in at least two ways. On the one hand, it limits the enforcement of welfare to a certain guaranteed livelihood, excluding a whole arena of needs that individuals may choose to pursue, albeit in vain unless their own means suffice. On the other hand, extending that limit to the optimum may well involve restricting the range of needs whose satisfaction is publicly permitted. For, in order to guarantee all the widest range of satisfaction, limitations on income and consumption are likely required, limitations governed by the principle that inequalities of wealth are to be tolerated only insofar as they do not hinder the general exercise of economic and noneconomic rights.

Neither of these restrictions involve violations of economic right any more than need public measures regulating the supply of commodities. Although they impose particular limitations upon the freedom of need, they do so without countervening the strictures of economic or noneconomic justice. This is because the public impositions of a guaranteed standard of living and an upper limit on personal consumption both apply to all commodity owners alike and leave all the opportunity to enjoy the economic freedom of satisfying personally chosen needs in reciprocity with others without having to jeopardize their other rights. There may now be a restricted choice of needs whose satisfaction is, on the one hand, publicly permitted, and on the other hand, publicly guaranteed, but these dual limits are determined solely to advance, not hinder everyone's opportunity to earn a personally selected livelihood, whose satisfied needs are still determined by personal preference. No matter how high or low be the guaranteed standard of living and the upper limits on personal consumption, every commodity owner still retains access to an area of possible satisfactions, within whose borders their freedom of need has room to play. Hence, the basic rule of foundation-free justice is obeyed: that right limit right, that the limitation of self-determination be governed by no other desiderata than the realization of freedom. The injustice of unsatisfied need still prevails, but it neither prevents the general exercise of economic and noneconomic rights, nor falls unfairly upon a condemned few.

The Fair Regulation of Economically Relevant Inequalities

The fair treatment of the recurring inequalities of economic opportunity involves analogous solutions. As we have seen, the exercise of economic freedom can be jeopardized by inequalities in natural abilities, personal license, training, and wealth. Yet not all of these factors seem burdened by problems of chronic injustice.

The fair treatment of inequalities in natural abilities and training

In particular, it might appear that where natural handicaps and differentials in training bear upon economic opportunity, they can be compensated without the problems of resurgent disadvantage that complicate the public enforcement of welfare. Individuals afflicted with incurable physical and mental disabilities can be given the care they need and benefits permitting them to exercise as great a portion of the freedoms of need and occupation as they are able. On the other hand, public welfare institutions can provide treatment to those whose disabilities are remediable, just as enterprises can be required to modify their working conditions and marketing procedures so as to provide economic opportunities to the handicapped. Similarly, individuals who are economically disadvantaged due to their lack of education and training can be educated and trained at public expense so that they can participate on an equal footing in the market. In each case, the basis of economic disadvantage appears to be removable.

However, the public cures are not entirely immune to relapses of economic malaise. Individuals can always be subject to mental and physical disease that once again puts them at an economic disadvantage. Moreover, the obstacles to economic opportunity that result from the recurrence of monopoly power and inequality of wealth can always put financial strains upon the physically and emotionally handicapped who incur special expenses in coping with their difficulties. Admittedly, public authority is obligated to guarantee all citizens affordable health care so as to enable them to exercise their economic and noneconomic rights, and this would seem to obviate any special problems arising from the recurrence of other economically relevant inequalities. Yet, preventing certain handicaps from impeding economic opportunity may require such huge expenditures of resources that a tension arises between the greater opportunities won by the handicapped beneficiaries and the loss of opportunity incurred by others who must subsidize the measures taken. And this tension may be magnified by the perennially shifting state of the economy. In such instances, how can conflicts between the economic rights of the handicapped be weighed fairly against those of others whose economic welfare hangs in the balance?

In the case of inequalities of education and training, the problem is perhaps more obvious. Although public authority can always educate and train individuals whose lack of knowledge and skill puts them at an economic disadvantage, it can never eliminate the outbreak of discrepancies between the kinds of trained labor power that are in supply and the need for other skills that revolutions in technique and changing market wants may precipitate. Hence, no matter what training is given individuals at public expense, there can be no guaranty that they or others will not find themselves in desperate need of retraining. Thus, inequalities in education and training will continually recur. The problem, then, is how can they be treated justly?

Once again, the principle of fair treatment of abiding economic wrong consists in reducing the infringements of economic freedom to a minimum and sharing the burdens so that no individuals are perennially subject to unusual obstacles to their economic opportunity. This must be accomplished with due heed to the noneconomic rights and economic welfare of present and future generations.

In the case of remediable mental and physical handicaps whose treatment becomes a drain on the economic welfare of others, the just policy lies in channeling sufficient resources to overcome the handicapped's economic disadvantage until the point is reached where either the economic welfare of others falls below that of the handicapped or further efforts are only counterproductive for the handicapped themselves. In either case, the channeling of resources should be undertaken as much in conformity with economic autonomy as possible, so that, instead of unilateral expropriations of particular goods and services, reliance be made upon fiscal measures that leave to individuals and enterprises the choice of which assets to relinquish. Then the limitations upon economic freedom will be part and parcel of its realization.

As for handling the recurring economic disadvantages resulting from unequal education and training, the same principle suffices. Although there will always be some individuals in need of retraining, regardless of how thorough public education efforts may be, their predicament will be justly borne so long as the public welfare administration extends to them as much publicly assisted training as possible, provided efforts do not place others in economic straits worse than that of the publicly assisted, or further undermine the welfare of the latter or that of future generations.

The fair treatment of inequalities of personal license

The recurring economic inequalities resulting from varying degrees of personal license require a wholly analogous resolution. Once again, the problem involves the emergence of an impediment to economic autonomy that public authority cannot abidingly remove. No matter how doggedly public welfare institutions provide individuals with all the external means for pursuing a freely chosen independent livelihood, the economic welfare of certain individuals will end up in jeopardy owing to their own license or that of those on whom they are economically dependent. As we have seen, the basis of public obligation to provide compulsory aid to those who suffer at their own hands is simply that no one is entitled to undermine their own rightful freedoms. For this reason, Hegel can aptly maintain that civil society has the right and duty of acting as a trustee for those whose extravagance destroys the economic security of themselves and their dependents.[1] Since what counts is the exercise of economic autonomy, private dissipation becomes an economic wrong when it begins to subvert the economic opportunity of individuals and their dependents.

However, so long as the public welfare administration insures that aid is provided on an equal basis to all who victimize their own economic independence, the chronic recurrence of the problem among certain individuals is no mark of economic injustice. The fact that they continually fall into economically disadvantageous straits, despite public efforts on their behalf, merely testifies to subjective predilections for which the economy can bear no responsibility.

The fair treatment of inequalities of wealth

More far-reaching is the problem of fairly handling the inequalities of wealth that continually recur so long as commodity relations are retained. As we have seen, not all differences in income or wealth contribute to economic disadvantage.

On the one hand, certain inequalities may not entail any unequal infringements upon economic autonomy. Even though individuals may have very divergent incomes and assets, they may still satisfy their commodity needs and occupational aspirations to the same degree. This is always possible since market relations free commodity owners from the common natural confines of human wants and toils by giving them the opportunity to choose their own needs and which and how many commodities they will accordingly attempt to earn, as well as the opportunity to choose both their occupation and the degree to which they will pursue it. Given how commodity owners have varying preferences, both from one moment to the next and in contrast to one another, and given how commodity exchange is predicated upon differences of commodity needs and ownerships, one would even expect that individuals' chosen needs will most likely be satisfied through unequal distributions of wealth.

On the other hand, certain inequalities of income and commodity ownership that do favor the economic options of the more affluent may still contribute to the diminution of economic disadvantage by channeling resources advancing the economic opportunities of the less affluent and/or the noneconomic freedoms of all in present or future generations.

Where, however, recurring inequalities of wealth do create economic disadvantage, public authority must intervene to enforce the welfare of those whose relatively lesser means leave them unable to exercise their economic autonomy on a par with others. This may mean remedying the results of its own past interventions. For even if public authority has reduced the accumulation of resources by individuals, private corporations, worker cooperatives or state enterprises whose wealth has given them a market advantage, this regulation may well lead to new unequal distributions of wealth that give some an over-bearing market power to conclude advantageous transactions, while reducing others to a relative penury from which few economic opportunities beckon. As we have seen, this problem of the perennial incidence of disadvantageous inequalities of wealth cannot be conquered by imposing strict equality in personal assets, both because inequality of wealth is only unjust if it imposes unfair barriers to someone's desired market participation and because strict equality imposes restrictions upon the exercise of economic freedom that do not contribute to the latter's realization or to that of noneconomic rights. If however, economic right does mandate that all market participants be guaranteed sufficient means to earn an independent livelihood of their own choosing, how can an economy be just when every permissible public measure leaves room for new inequalities of wealth that carry with them economic disadvantage?

Once again, it is not the possibility of future economic wrong but rather the way it is shouldered that determines the justice of the economy. So long as new outbreaks of disadvantageous inequalities of wealth are not the perennial scourge of the same sectors of the economy and so long as public authority addresses each new incidence with the same commitment to reestablish the conditions of equal economic opportunity, the recurrence of disadvantage does not rob an economy of legitimacy. Instead, it makes the task of public intervention an ongoing mission that must continually readjust its efforts to cope with the new market contingencies which no public plan can ever foresee.

In each round of the continuing struggle to remedy unjust inequalities of wealth, what mandates the type and extent of public intervention is the current market conjuncture and the economic resources at hand. These determine the standard of living and occupational opportunity that all can be publicly guaranteed, as well as the upper limit of personal wealth that can be publicly tolerated. Since the aim of intervention is always the promotion of economic freedom, the elimination of recurring disadvantage should avoid as much as possible any restrictions upon the market activity and commodity ownership of individuals and enterprises. Hence, if at all feasible, nonrestrictive initiatives should be undertaken to remove the unequal opportunity created by unequal wealth. Such measures could include self-financing public works offering affordable commodities and widened earning opportunities to the disadvantaged, public loans that pay for themselves, and other devices that compensate for the limited opportunity of the less affluent without directly restricting the options of the more economically advantaged.

Whenever economic conditions make it impossible for these undertakings to surmount the disadvantage caused by inequality of wealth, then the enforcement of economic welfare will require publicly transferring wealth from the economically privileged to the economically underprivileged. Given the open character of commodity relations, the latitude in the ownership and organization of capital, and the diverse possibilities of class membership and monopoly power, the identity of the advantaged and disadvantaged need not have any abiding pattern allowing for a set rule of redistribution. On the contrary, the economic agents enjoying privileged market opportunities due to their unequal wealth may be individuals belonging to any of the economic classes or enterprises under any form of ownership and management. Indeed, given the unrivaled possibilities for the monopolization of wealth created by the nationalization of industry and commerce, public enterprises may well be the most supremely overprivileged economic entities from whom wealth should be redistributed.

Furthermore, given the various ways in which the economic welfare of individuals may depend upon the relative affluence of enterprises, the reestablishment of equal opportunity must take account of the relation between the unequal concentration of wealth among enterprises and the economic disadvantage rooted in the inequality of personal wealth, not forgetting the impact of any transfers upon the noneconomic rights of present and future generations. How then can wealth be redistributed so that no one's economic freedom is unduly curtailed?

Whatever identity the privileged and disadvantaged may have, transferring wealth between them through the public expropriation and public dole of particular assets will not best serve the fair promotion of their economic rights. As we have seen, that form of redistribution would unnecessarily deprive beneficiaries and benefactors alike of their full rights to choose what commodities to acquire and relinquish. In addition, by transferring specific goods, it would make it virtually impossible to ensure that all benefactors and beneficiaries give and receive wealth on the same terms. Similarly, any transfer of wealth taking the form of the requisition and bestowal of services in kind would unnecessarily impinge upon the freedom of occupation and unfairly penalize those who serve with greater ability and diligence than others.

Hegel points out these problems and suggests the method for re-distributing wealth that avoids them, while insuring the greatest fair-ness and respect for the exercise of economic freedom: redistribution not through transfers of goods and services, but through monetary taxation and reimbursement.[2] By redistributing wealth through trans-fers of money, in accord with assessments of the monetary worth of individual wealth, public authority can achieve two imperatives of eco-nomic justice at once. On the one hand, it allows public authority to fix quantitatively the relative economic opportunity of individuals as well as the losses and gains to be administered. This allows for a just and equitable handling that avoids the unequal treatment entailed when assessments and transfers are made in terms of concrete services and particular goods. For, as Hegel suggests, if assessment depended upon concrete ability, and redistribution involved particular services, the more talented, industrious individuals would bear a burden out of proportion to their relative economic standing,[3] whereas if assessment and transfer addressed particular goods, neither would accurately re-flect the most general measure of economic opportunity, disposable exchange value.[4] On the other hand, reliance on taxation allows the equitably determined transfer to be mediated through the choice of all parties concerned. By virtue of taxation, the economically privileged, be they individuals or private or public enterprises, are allowed to fulfill their economic duty to the disadvantaged without relinquishing their freedom to decide what commodities to exchange and what ser-vices to render in obtaining the money they must pay. Similarly, mon-etary reimbursements leave the disadvantaged with the full prerog-ative to decide how to translate the abstract form of wealth they have received into particular goods and earning opportunities. On both sides, the freedoms of economic right are retained as fully as the re-establishment of equal opportunity allows.

The singular advantages monetary taxation and reimbursement brings to the redistribution of wealth extend to the other forms of public intervention that are required to insure adequate supply of affordable commodities, employment opportunities, public goods and other factors ingredient in economic welfare. Hence, wherever possible, monetary incentives and disincentives should be employed to promote economic justice, in place of administrative appropriations of particular re-sources that unfairly fall upon certain agents and unnecessarily curtail their economic prerogatives.

In each case, the level of public fiscal regulation depends upon current economic conditions that are inherently contingent, due to the arbitrary character of market activity and the economy's susceptibility to external influences. There is no normative restriction to the amount of money that can be charged and disbursed by public authority so long as economic freedom is upheld in conformity with noneconomic rights and the legitimate expectations of future generations. Thus, in the case of redistribution of wealth among individuals and enterprises, any degree of taxation is permissible provided it serves to eliminate economic disadvantage without compromising the present and future condition of the other institutions of freedom. The equalization of wealth among individuals and among enterprises may not be an end in itself, but there is still no a priori limit to how strict an equality is required to maintain fair economic opportunity.

In carrying out such redistribution, it must not be forgotten that inequalities of income need not reflect the inequalities of wealth that bear upon the varying economic opportunities of individuals. Individuals with equal incomes may have completely unequal economic options if their personal wealth diverges, just as individuals with greatly unequal incomes may have equivalent economic opportunities if differences in their personal wealth balance out the discrepancies in their current incomes. Hence, the public welfare administration must neither assess the relative economic position of individuals according to their income, nor rely on income taxes as the primary means for reestablishing equal economic opportunity. Since what counts are the respective levels of personal wealth, which depends as much upon inheritance, gifts, frugality, and fortunate investment as upon income, the basis of assessment and the object of progressive taxation should be wealth, not income.

The Fair Balance of Private and Public Enterprise

In dealing with all the factors complicating the enforcement of public welfare, no issue has aroused greater controversy than that of the proper balance of private and public enterprise. Four basic alternatives stand in contention: 1) that economic justice is best served by public ownership and management of all enterprises; 2) that the extent of private and public enterprise is a matter of indifference; 3) that public enterprise is permissible only in desired undertakings where private enterprise is either not viable or uncooperative; and 4) that private enterprise ought to reign supreme throughout the economy.

The first view, that enterprises should be exclusively public, might seem totally at odds with economic freedom and its market realization. However, as Rawls points out, a centrally planned economy without private enterprise may yet retain markets for consumer goods and labor.[5] In that case, individuals still enjoy an opportunity to exercise their freedom of occupation and their freedom of need.

Although this mitigates one of the common objections against an exclusively public enterprise economy, the principal rationales for supplanting all private with public enterprise are cast in doubt by two further points that Rawls raises. It is commonly argued that public enterprise is an imperative of economic justice because private enterprise neither provides for public goods that serve the common interest, nor allows for the elimination of economic disadvantage. As we have seen, unregulated private enterprise indeed cannot be counted upon to provide for public goods. However, as Rawls argues, public ownership of the means of production hardly guarantees that more economic resources will be devoted to public goods, nor that public expenditures for public goods are better made employing public rather than private enterprises.[6] A regime that has nationalized all industry and commerce may well devote its economic resources to the aggrandizing ambitions of its party elite, leaving its people in relative poverty, aggravated by neglected consumer goods and service industries plagued by inefficiency, low quality production, and undersupply. On the other hand, as Rawls observes, there seems little reason in principle why a publicly regulated economy involving private enterprise cannot fairly provide for equal economic opportunity.[7] The foregoing discussion should underline how this is possible.

Hence, since public and private enterprise both are compatible with markets, thereby sharing their benefits and liabilities, and both offer no automatic provision of public goods, it is tempting to accept Rawls's conclusion that it is a matter of indifference from the standpoint of justice whether public or private enterprise prevails. What counts, it would appear, is rather whether adequate background institutions regulate the economy so that fair equal opportunity and noneconomic rights are upheld for present and future generations.

This conclusion would hold if it were true that the degree of private and public ownership has no necessary bearing upon the exercise of economic and noneconomic freedom. Public ownership of all enterprises may still allow a certain room for the freedom of occupation and the freedom to choose what commodities to need to the extent that labor markets and consumer goods markets are retained. However, both these freedoms are limited insofar as all those occupations involving private enterprise are prohibited, as is the right to choose to need commodities involved in private enterprise such as labor power, raw materials and instruments of production, rentable commodities, money to lend, and capital in general. These limitations would apply not only to the forms of private enterprise involving individual, family or share-holding corporate ownership, but equally to worker self-managed cooperatives. So long as public enterprise exclusively prevails, the needs, occupations, and economic interest group activities specific to all these varied modes of private enterprise would be precluded in favor of a universal proletarianization.

Since, contrary to Marxist claims, the varied forms of private earning need not generate irremediable economic injustice, it would be wrong to curtail the exercise of economic freedom they involve. Hence, it is an imperative of economic justice that every form of private enterprise respecting the rights of individuals be permitted, subject to whatever public regulation is necessary to maintain equal economic opportunity and the noneconomic institutions of freedom for present and future generations.

Moreover, exclusive public enterprise establishes a degree of monopoly power pernicious to the limited economic freedoms still provided by the retention of labor and consumer goods markets. As Michael Oakeshott points out,[8] nationalization of the economy undermines the freedom of contract in the sale of labor power by limiting the employment options of individuals to one and only one employer. To enjoy real, rather than formal proprietary right over their labor, individuals must have a genuine choice between independent potential employers, which implies that there be private ownership of factors of production other than labor power.[9] Although a nationalized economy could still, in principle, permit independent trade unions, the right to strike, and other economic interest group activities open to wage laborers, the ability to bargain over the wage and working conditions would be greatly undercut by the absence of any other employers.

The same would be true of the options of consumers. Although they too could, in principle, organize their own consumer interest groups and mobilize their purchasing power in consumer boycotts, their ability to counter the unified control of public producers would be severely handicapped by the total absence of any other suppliers of consumer goods and services. Both as wage earners and as consumers, the members of the nationalized economy would have their market choices limited by the most extensive monopoly power possible.

That democratic management of the state economy might give everyone an equal voice in determining economic planning would not remove this problem. There would still be an unbridgeable gap between the univocal voice of collective decision with its promotion of a centralized national welfare[10] and plural personal preferences for needs and occupations. In effect, complete public ownership of enterprises would subject the ordering of society to direct political control, so that even if the political domain remained a sphere of freedom, it would preside over an economy in which the forms of social autonomy have virtually withered away. Subverting, to paraphrase Oakeshott, the division of labor between market and political controls,[11] the elimination of private enterprise brings to collapse the distinction between civil society and the state, which is so necessary to the full exercise of freedom. Although it might be doubted whether the resulting extension of state administration automatically threatens political freedom, as Oakeshott, following Hume, suggests,[12] the blow to social self-determination is enough to make it an imperative of economic justice that the hegemony of public enterprise be broken.

What then, is the just balance between public and private enterprise? If public ownership is to be retained, should it be restricted to beneficial ventures that private enterprise cannot undertake without reverting to detrimental monopolies, leaving public monopoly as the only alternative?

Michael Oakeshott advances this view as part of a political economy of freedom whose basic principle consists in making competition effective wherever possible.[13] Well aware that effective competition is a product not of laissez-faire, but of systematic public regulation, Oakeshott makes its maintenance the key to economic justice to the extent that it guarantees the greatest diffusion of power within society, making possible the exercise of social freedom as well as preserving the division between social and political controls, on which the full development of freedom depends. For these reasons, Oakeshott argues that private monopoly should be suppressed, whether it take the form of labor or enterprise cartels, and that whatever public monopolies are necessary should be reduced and simplified as much as possible.[14] Whether this creates the most efficient arrangement for meeting human wants is secondary to the normative considerations of social and political freedom.

To begin with, it must be granted that Oakeshott is correct in maintaining that justice requires the establishment of public enterprises in those cases where economic undertakings are legitimately needed, but where private enterprise cannot function without taking monopoly forms that are detrimental to economic welfare or the nonpolitical rights of present and future generations. As we have seen, markets are prone to neglect facilities necessary for the flourishing of the institutions of freedom. This may occur as much due to the arbitrary unwillingness of private investors as owing to market conditions that make the required undertakings economically unfeasible for private enterprise. When such facilities go wanting and public incentives are unable to mobilize sufficient private participation to address the problem, public authority has the obligation to take matters into its own hands and establish public enterprises furnishing the needed public goods. Hence, the fourth alternative, that the economy be restricted to private enterprise, is unjust.

Be this as it may, do Oakeshott's strictures prescribe the proper limits of public enterprise? To begin with, is there not a need for public enterprise whenever private investment is not forthcoming for undertakings beneficial to freedom even though prospects are not gloomy and public incentives are made available? It would seem that public enterprise is permissible, and indeed, obligatory, in any such circumstance where private enterprise could be viable, but does not enter the breach out of the willful caprice market autonomy allows.

In at least two respects, Oakeshott draws the line too narrowly by restricting public enterprise to only those cases where public welfare requires ventures that private enterprise cannot feasibly tackle and that require a public monopoly to be pursued. On the one hand, public enterprise is also called for when other public measures fail to attract private participation in worthy undertakings that are feasible for private enterprise. On the other hand, the public enterprises that are established need not be state monopolies. They may rather enter into economic sectors where private enterprises already operate, albeit without completely fulfilling public needs.

Further, the concerns properly raised by Oakeshott by no means rule out public enterprise in fields where the limits of private participation pose no problem for the economic and noneconomic rights of present and future generations. Granted the virtues of taxation, is there anything wrong, for instance, with launching profitable public enterprises as an alternative means of raising public revenues? Or, for that matter, is any injustice done if public enterprises enter into competition with private firms irrespective of any further agenda?

What decides the issue is once again whether any of these public undertakings unnecessarily limit the exercise of economic and noneconomic freedoms of present and future generations. Of course, any such public ventures may fall prey to the same abuses of monopoly power to which any enterprises may be prone once they reach a certain level of relative size and performance. However, if public enterprises can be regulated, like all other firms, so that their monopoly power is curtailed, need they impinge upon the economic opportunities of individuals? Indeed, might they not even contribute to a swell of economic growth, which, subject to the proper regulation, increases economic welfare for all?

Certainly, the establishment of public enterprises in economic sectors where private enterprise can function does not automatically impose barriers to the exercise of economic freedom, nor to the well-being of the institutions of noneconomic freedom. However, certainly, if such public enterprises begin to take a commanding position in one sector or the other, and their monopoly power is not dispersed by public intervention, they will present the threat to social freedom of which Oakeshott warns. Since the point at which economic leverage becomes monopoly power depends upon market contingencies that can only be known empirically, there is little more to be said in general than this: public enterprise is tolerable only to the degree that it contributes to the exercise of economic and noneconomic freedom. As we have seen, public enterprise can provide this service solely in conjunction with private enterprise.

The Contingent Success of Public Intervention

Whatever be the balance between private and public ownership, the predominant forms of enterprise, the activities of economic interest groups, the ministries of civil law, or the mercies of public welfare institutions, public intervention remains a chronically needed undertaking, whose own measures warrant continual revision in face of the ever changing state of the economy. The contingencies inherent in the freedoms of commodity relations and in the market's liability to influence by external events renders public regulation a continually recurring imperative, whose achievements can never be final enough. The most extensive public efforts may be made to adjust supply and demand, redistribute wealth, counter monopoly formation, and otherwise enforce equal economic opportunity, yet so long as market autonomy is maintained, the outcome remains hostage to unforeseeable meetings of wills, sure to frustrate any rigid projections of would-be social engineers and their econometricians. If the economy were ordered by a single agency, then public administration could hope for as high a degree of planned success as the technical proficiency of its administrators and economic subjects allows. However, because the just economy can never supplant commodity relations without annulling the freedoms in which economic justice lies, its workings remain determined by the independent, yet interdependent decisions of autonomous market agents. Their multilateral initiatives defy all unilateral planning and prognostications, to the continual embarrassment of economists who treat the economics of the market as if it were not a science of freedom. Hence, how soon any given public measure will restore equal opportunity and how long it will be before economic disadvantage rears its head again are questions for which no a priori answer can be given.

The just economy is therefore perennially at risk, always in danger of outbreaks and resurgences of economic injustice. Yet, the same contingencies that leave it at risk also make the success of current public intervention an irrepressible possibility. As we have seen, this predicament does not cast in doubt the reality of economic justice. That public intervention in the market enforces the economic rights of individuals without ever eliminating the conditions that foster economic disadvantage is no more a mark of defeat than the inability of the police and courts to bring the enforcement of property entitlements to the point of removing the possibility of crime. Far from undermining the legitimacy of the economic order, the perennial public campaign for economic justice is one of the just economy's constitutive occupations.

Insofar as this occupation is addressed equally to all members of the economy, as a matter of binding public responsibility, its basic guidelines are eminently suited to legal enactment. Hence, the activities of the public welfare administration properly comprise a legal enforcement of economic welfare, resting on an extension of civil law beyond the jurisdictions of property and household entitlements to that of economic right. Public regulation of the market may take the form of continually revised interventions reacting to the contingent state of the economy, but it still has a lawful character determined by the basic imperatives entailed in the concept of economic freedom. As a consequence, the public welfare administration can and is obliged to execute laws mandating the enforcement of equal economic opportunity. Implementing them will require an intervening judgment determining what specific public measures best respond to the given market contingencies. As with any other execution of law, these measures require an attention to perceived circumstances, precluding any direct derivation from legal statute. Nevertheless, the basis of implementation remains the laws of public welfare, positing in legal form the rational imperatives of economic justice.

In this way, then, the public welfare administration of civil society subjects the market economy to a public regulation enforcing the economic freedom of all. The market remains the underlying institution upon which action is taken, just as was the case with the legal enforcement of property and household rights and the corporate activities of economic interest groups. Subject to these interventions, the market economy becomes the just economy, providing economic self-determination with its institutional realization. In this capacity, it functions as the institutional base of a just society, offering the freedom of interest a legitimate sphere presupposed and referred to by all other civil institutions.

However, the commodity economy does not thereby become the determining base of civil society, as Marx forewarned. Because economic justice depends upon public regulation of the market, freeing society from subservience to capital or any other economic factor, the just economy is a commodity economy that remains subordinate, rather than determinative of the other institutions of the just society. When, counter to the requirements of the realization of the freedom of interest, social institutions fall under the domination of markets, society cannot be free. It makes little difference whether it is private capitalists, worker self-managed cooperatives, or government enterprises that preside over a market that has become the determining base of society. So long as the public subordination of commodity relations is not achieved, economic justice remains an unfulfilled specter haunting public life.

The Political Regulation of the Just Economy

Although the civil regulation of the market economy is a prerequisite for the realization of economic freedom, the subordination of commodity relations to public welfare regulation is not enough to put the just economy in its proper place. If economic institutions are to realize noneconomic as well as economic rights, then it is equally important that the economy not subvert the other institutions of freedom. Above all, economic relations must conform to the demands of the institutions of political freedom, which have primacy by being the ultimate guarantor and arbiter for all other spheres of right.

There are two sides to this political subordination of the just economy. On the one hand, public regulation must insure that the institutions of political freedom are provided with the economic resources they need to operate. As we have seen, this involves provisions for both the conduct of foreign relations and the conduct of domestic government. Regarding the conduct of foreign relations, the economy must be managed so as to provide the means for self-defense and the promotion of just international goals. As for the conduct of domestic government, the economy must supply adequate resources to permit state offices to carry out their policies.

On the other hand, economic relations must be regulated so as to guarantee that all citizens are provided with fair access to the economic resources necessary for their own political participation. Differences in economic position must not be allowed to become instruments of political privilege, and conflicts of economic interests must not be allowed to interfere with the exercise of political freedom and national sovereignty.

Whereas the public administration of welfare is charged with regulating the economy chiefly to enforce the goals of social justice, the regulation here in question is of a different sort. Instead of intervening upon the market to promote economic freedom, what lies at issue is an intervention specifically aiming at the promotion of political freedom.

It might seem that this regulation of the economy for purely political ends is redundant. For if the public welfare administration succeeds in enforcing equal economic opportunity as fairly as possible, are not the economic bases of political inequality eliminated? Would not all citizens have sufficiently equal financial resources to make their political voice count as forcefully as anyone else? This would be true if the economic bases of equal political opportunity perfectly corresponded to the economic bases of equal economic opportunity. Yet is the elimination of economic disadvantage equivalent to the removal of all economically determined political disadvantage?

Admittedly, to a certain degree, there is congruence. Since effective political participation in a democracy depends to no small extent upon mobilizing financial resources to fund campaigns and influence public opinion, public efforts to eliminate economic disadvantage would presumably tend to equalize the means individuals have available to underwrite the political activities they support.

Nonetheless, differences in wealth and economic position that are tolerable to fair equal opportunity, need not be equally indifferent to political opportunity. To begin with, inequalities in wealth that promote the economic opportunities of all may still allow individuals with more assets to have a greater political clout that in no way contributes to the political opportunities of the less affluent. Similarly, unequal concentrations of capital among enterprises and limited monopoly combinations that do not contribute to economic disadvantage may give certain firms or groups of economic agents proportionally greater means to finance political campaigns than those other market participants whose economic welfare they do not threaten.

Moreover, individuals or groups who may have equal financial resources may still, owing to their economic roles, have an unequal power to influence the course of political events. Proprietors and employees of the mass media may, thanks to the regulation of the public welfare administration, have no economic advantage over others, yet still be able to use their economic position to wield very unequal control over the chief instrument for influencing political opinion. For instance, owners of newspapers, radio stations, and television networks, be they private individuals, families, shareholders, or the state, may use their proprietary position to determine editorial policy so as to advance their own political views with far greater force than those who are in the position of consumers of the mass media. Alternately, employees of mass media enterprises, whose earnings may even put them among the economically disadvantaged, may still make use of job actions, strikes, and other strategies based in their workplace role to influence what the mass media can disseminate, to the political disadvantage of others. The same opportunities for unequal political influence fall to any other individuals whose occupations play a special role in the mounting of political activity.

Hence, if equal political opportunity is to be realized, public authority must counteract these economic factors, which the public enforcement of equal economic opportunity hardly touches. This means that the just economy is only worthy of its title if it is subject to a continual political supervision that intervenes upon the market to prevent commodity relations from interfering with the equal political opportunity of citizens and the affairs of state. Like the social supervision that regulates the market to maintain economic freedom, this political intervention must cope with all the unforeseeable contingencies that market activity entails. Since the state of the economy bears upon the resources available to the state for its domestic and international activities, any public scheme for fairly allotting campaign resources must consider its economic ramifications. Nevertheless, in doing so, what remains of paramount importance is not economic welfare, but the political welfare of self-governing citizens. If the demands of equal political opportunity require more radical equalizations of wealth and the concentrations of capital among enterprises than do the requirements of economic opportunity, then justice requires restricting particular realizations of economic freedom for the sake of the more fundamental ends of political self-determination. This may increase economic disadvantage, but if it promotes the equality of political opportunity, on which all freedoms ultimately rest, it remains a limitation of economic autonomy wholly consistent with its realization.

In these respects, the just economy is no more the determining base of the state than that of civil society. Its justice instead rests upon its public subordination to the requirements of civil and political freedom. These requirements do not entail the elimination of market autonomy, but only particular restrictions whose legitimacy resides in their promotion of the institutional system of freedom. When, however, economic factors begin to disrupt the exercise of political self-determination and subordinate the state to economic ends, the economy forfeits its validity, no matter how egalitarian it may be.

The just economy is therefore a product of continual political as well as civil vigilance. Although it provides a discrete sphere for realizing its own intrinsic rights, the just economy remains an element of a greater political whole, whose primacy must never be ignored.

NOTES

Introduction

1. See Adam Smith, *The Wealth of Nations* (New York: Random House, 1937), pp. 13, 259.
2. David P. Levine, *Economic Studies: Contributions to the Critique of Economic Theory* (London: Routledge and Kegan Paul, 1977), pp. 198, 236.
3. Karl Marx, *Capital* (New York: International Publishers, 1970), vol. 1, pp. 46, 167.
4. Hannah Arendt, *The Human Condition* (Chicago: University of Chicago Press, 1958), p. 96 ff.
5. Martin Heidegger, *The Question Concerning Technology and Other Essays*, trans. W. Lovitt (New York: Garland Publishing, 1977), pp. 3–35.
6. Jurgen Habermas, *Theory and Practice* (Boston: Beacon Press, 1973), "Labor and Interaction," p. 142 ff.
7. C. B. Macpherson, *The Rise and Fall of Economic Justice and Other Papers* (New York: Oxford University Press, 1985), p. 14.
8. Ibid., pp. 1–8.
9. Ibid., p. 14.

1 The Systematic Exclusions of Economic Relations from the Domain of Justice

1. For a more complete discussion of praxis theory and its parallel to classical metaphysics, see Richard Dien Winfield, *Reason and Justice* (Albany: State University of New York Press, 1988), Chapters 1 and 2.
2. Edith Hamilton and Huntington Cairns, eds., *The Collected Dialogues of Plato* (Princeton, N.J.: Princeton University Press, 1973); V462c, p. 701; V449c ff., p. 689 ff.; V464a, p. 703; IV434b-c, p. 676.
3. Ibid., II369b-372d, pp. 617–19.
4. Ibid., I346d, p. 596.
5. Ibid., IX580e-581a, p. 807.
6. Ibid., IX589e-590a, p. 817.
7. Ibid., V743e, p. 1328; IX870b, p. 1430; see also VIII355b, p. 1601.
8. Ibid., VII801b, p. 1372.

9. Ernest Barker, ed. and trans., *The Politics of Aristotle* (New York: Oxford University Press, 1973), 1252a26–1252b1, p. 3.

10. Ibid., 1252b13–14, p. 4.

11. Karl Polanyi discusses this point in "Aristotle Discovers the Economy," in *Trade and Market in the Early Empires: Economies in History and Theory*, ed. Karl Polanyi, Conrad M. Arensberg, and Harry W. Pearson (Glencoe, Ill.: The Free Press, 1957), pp. 66, 78, 80–81.

12. Barker, *The Politics of Aristotle*, 1253b23–1254a3, pp. 9–10.

13. Ibid., 1254a3, p. 10.

14. Ibid., 1256a13–14, p. 19.

15. Ibid., 1256b26–30, p. 21.

16. Ibid., 1254a1–8, p. 10.

17. Ibid., 1257a, pp. 23–24.

18. Aristotle, *Nicomachean Ethics,* in *The Basic Works of Aristotle*, ed. Richard McKeon (New York: Random House, 1971), 1119b26–27, p. 984.

19. Barker, *The Politics of Aristotle*, 1258b, p. 30.

20. Ibid., 1255a, p. 14; Aristotle, *Nicomachean Ethics*, 1133a30–33, p. 1,011.

21. Barker, *The Politics of Aristotle*, 1328a35–36, p. 298.

22. Ibid., 1278a2–3, p. 108.

23. See Polanyi, "Aristotle Discovers The Economy," p. 88.

24. *The Basic Works of Aristotle, op. cit.,* 1130b30–1131a1.

25. This view is most notably advanced by C. B. Macpherson in his book, *The Political Theory of Possessive Individualism: Hobbes to Locke* (Oxford: Clarendon Press, 1962).

26. How liberal theory cannot consistently legitimate democratic government is discussed in Richard Dien Winfield's "The Reason For Democracy," *History of Political Thought*, vol. 5, no. 3, (Winter 1984):549–54.

27. See C. B. Macpherson, *The Rise and Fall of Economic Justice and Other Papers* (New York: Oxford University Press, 1985), pp. 6–7.

28. Thomas Hobbes, *Leviathan* (Harmondsworth, Middlesex, England: Penguin Books, 1968), p. 161.

29. Ibid., p. 295.

30. Thomas Hobbes, *Man and Citizen* (New York: Doubleday, 1972), p. 222.

31. Hobbes, *Leviathan*, pp. 294–95.

32. Ibid., pp. 295–96.

33. Ibid., p. 295.

34. Ibid., p. 299.

35. Ibid., pp. 300–301.

36. Ibid., pp. 290, 386.

37. Hobbes, *Man and Citizen*, p. 267.

38. Hobbes, *Leviathan, op. cit.,* p. 208.

39. Ibid., pp. 282–283.

40. Hobbes, *Man and Citizen*, p. 260; Hobbes, *Leviathan*, p. 376.

41. Hobbes, *Leviathan*, p. 208.

42. See Macpherson, *The Rise and Fall of Economic Justice*, p. 9.

43. Hobbes, *Leviathan*, pp. 151–52.

44. Macpherson, *The Rise and Fall of Economic Justice*, pp. 135–46.

45. Hobbes, *Man and Citizen*, p. 267.

46. Macpherson reverses these priorities and subordinates Hobbes's construction of the commonwealth to the needs of the primitive accumulation of capital. See Macpherson, *The Rise and Fall of Economic Justice*, pp. 141–43.

47. John Locke, *The Second Treatise of Government* (New York: Bobbs-Merrill, 1952), p. 21.

48. Ibid., pp. 17, 18, 109.

49. Ibid., pp. 25, 26.

50. Ibid., p. 22.

51. Ibid., pp. 22, 27, 28, 29, 105.

52. Ibid., p. 22.

53. Ibid., p. 29.

54. J. J. Rousseau, *The Social Contract and Discourses*, trans. G. D. H. Cole (New York: E. P. Dutton, 1950), p. 285.

55. Ibid., p. 289.

56. Ibid., p. 286.

57. Ibid., p. 292.

58. Ibid., p. 296.

59. Ibid., pp. 306, 307, 317.

60. Ibid., pp. 306–7, 311.

61. Ibid., p. 20.

62. Ibid., p. 77.

63. Ibid., pp. 77–78.

64. Ibid., p. 78.

65. Ibid., p. 66.

66. Ibid., p. 93.

67. Ibid.

68. I. Kant, *The Metaphysical Elements of Justice*, trans. John Ladd (New York: Bobbs-Merrill, 1965), p. 34.

69. Ibid., p. 35.

70. I. Kant, *Critique of Judgment*, trans. J. H. Bernard (New York: Hafner, 1951), p. 9.

71. Ibid., p. 46; I Kant, *Education*, trans. Annette Churton (Ann Arbor: Ann Arbor Paperback, 1960), p. 68.

72. Max Weber, *Economy and Society*, ed. Roth and Wittich (New York: Bedminster Press, 1968), vol. 1, p. 339.

2   Unsystematic Ethical Conceptions of the Economy

1. Adams Smith, *The Wealth of Nations* (New York: Random House, 1937), p. 14.
2. Karl Polanyi, "Aristotle Discovers the Economy," in *Trade and Market in the Early Empires*, ed. Karl Polanyi, Conrad M. Arensberg, and Harry W. Pearson (Glencoe, Ill.: The Free Press, 1957), pp. 68, 70.
3. David Levine argues this point in "Political Economy and the Argument For Inequality," *Social Concept*, vol. 2, no. 3 (September 1985):22.
4. Ibid., p. 23.
5. Ibid., p. 15.
6. Marx gives a detailed critical documentation of political economy's "natural" reductions in *Theories of Surplus Value*, 3 vols. (Moscow: Progress Publishers, 1968–1971).
7. David Levine provides a more systematic treatment in *Economic Studies: Contributions to the Critique of Economic Theory* (London: Routledge and Kegan Paul, 1977).
8. Adam Smith, *The Wealth of Nations*, p. 14.
9. Ibid., p. 259.
10. Ibid.
11. Ibid., p. lviii.
12. Ibid.
13. Ibid., p. 13.
14. Ibid., p. 15.
15. Ibid., p. 11.
16. Ibid., p. 17.
17. Ibid., p. 30.
18. Ibid., p. 259.
19. Ibid., pp. 47–48.
20. *Fichtes Werke-Band III* (Berlin: Walter de Gruyter, 1971), pp. 212–13, 241.
21. Kant, for example, argues this in his *The Metaphysical Elements of Justice*, trans. John Ladd (New York: Bobbs-Merrill, 1965), p. 93.
22. Kant, *The Metaphysical Elements of Justice*, pp. 79–80, 90–91.
23. Fichte, *Werke-Band III*, pp. 286, 388.
24. Ibid., pp. 214, 411.
25. Ibid., pp. 166–67.
26. Ibid., pp. 191, 214, 226, 241.
27. Ibid., p. 237.
28. Ibid., pp. 219, 232.
29. Ibid., pp. 232, 234, 235.
30. Ibid., pp. 440, 446–47.
31. Ibid., pp. 476, 504.

32. Robert Nozick, *Anarchy, State, and Utopia* (New York: Basic Books, 1974), pp. 207–8.

33. John Rawls, *A Theory of Justice* (Cambridge, MA: Harvard University Press, 1971), p. 302.

34. Ibid., p. 75.

35. Ibid., pp. 60–61.

36. Ibid., p. 302.

37. Ibid., p. 75.

38. Ibid., p. 195.

39. Ibid., p. 197.

40. Ibid., p. 199.

41. Ibid.

42. Ibid.

43. Ibid., p. 260.

44. Ibid., p. 357.

45. Ibid., p. 266.

46. Ibid.

47. Ibid., p. 273.

48. Ibid., p. 266–68.

49. Ibid., p. 270.

50. David Levine intimates as much in "Political Economy and The Argument For Inequality," p. 12, as does C. B. Macpherson in *The Rise and Fall of Economic Justice and Other Papers*, pp. 12–13.

51. See C. B. Macpherson, *The Rise and Fall of Economic Justice and Other Papers*, p. 13.

52. Rawls, *A Theory of Justice*, p. 359.

53. Ibid., p. 270.

54. Ibid.

55. Ibid., p. 271.

56. Ibid., p. 272.

57. Ibid.

58. Ibid.

59. Ibid., p. 302.

60. Ibid., p. 273.

61. Ibid., p. 281.

62. Ibid., p. 275.

63. Ibid., p. 273.

64. Ibid., p. 272.

65. Nozick, *Anarchy, State, and Utopia*, pp. 183–231.

66. Ibid., p. 178.

67. Ibid., pp. 178–80.

68. Alasdair MacIntyre, *After Virtue* (Notre Dame: University of Notre Dame Press, 1981), pp. 227–37.

69. Ibid., p. 231.

70. Ibid., pp. 231–32.

71. Ibid., p. 233.

72. Rawls, *A Theory of Justice*, pp. 120, 129–30.

73. Ibid., pp. 131–35.

74. Ibid., p. 130.

75. Ibid., p. 137.

76. Ibid., p. 143.

77. Ibid., pp. 92–93.

78. Ibid., p. 86.

79. Ibid., p. 92.

3 The Normative Confusions of Marx's Economic Theory

1. Karl Marx, *Economic and Philosophical Manuscripts of 1844*, trans. Martin Milligan (New York: International Publishers, 1964), p. 118.

2. Ibid., pp. 113–14.

3. Ibid., p. 65.

4. G. W. F. Hegel *Philosophy of Right*, trans. Knox (New York: Oxford University Press, 1967), paragraph 57.

5. Kant points out the incoherence of such a notion in his *Metaphysical Elements of Justice*, p. 98.

6. Marx, *Manuscripts of 1844*, pp. 78, 111.

7. Ibid., p. 132.

8. Marx and Engels, *The German Ideology*, ed. C. J. Arthur (New York: International Publishers, 1970), p. 42.

9. Ibid., p. 42 ff.

10. Marx, *Wage-Labor and Capital*, trans. Harriet E. Lothrop (New York: Labor News Company, 1902), p. 35.

11. Ibid., p. 36.

12. Marx and Engels, *The German Ideology*, p. 52.

13. Marx, *A Contribution to the Critique of Political Economy* (New York: International Publishers, 1970), pp. 20–21.

14. For a critical analysis of analogous attempts by Marx's epigones, see Richard Dien Winfield, "The Dilemma of Labor," *Telos*, no. 24 (Summer 1975); and Winfield, "The Young Hegel and the Dialectic of Social Production," *Telos* no. 26 (Winter 1975–76).

15. Karl Marx, *Grundrisse*, trans. Martin Nicolaus (New York: Vintage Books, 1973), p. 242.

16. Ibid., p. 177.
17. Ibid., p. 405.
18. Ibid., p. 528.
19. Ibid., p. 242.
20. Ibid., p. 881.
21. Karl Marx, *Capital* (New York: International Publishers, 1968), vol. 1, p. 36.
22. Marx, *Grundrisse*, p. 881.
23. Ibid., p. 267.
24. Ibid., p. 267.
25. Ibid., p. 320.
26. Ibid., p. 646.
27. Marx, *Capital*, vol. 1, p. 177.
28. Ibid., pp. 183–84; Marx, *A Contribution to the Critique of Political Economy*, p. 36.
29. Marx, *Capital*, vol. 3, p. 820.
30. *Marx-Engels Studienausgabe II (Das Kapital, I. Auflage 1867, I. Buch Kapitel 1)* (Hamburg: Fischer Taschenbuch Verlag, 1971), p. 241.
31. Marx, *Capital*, vol. 1, pp. 81–82.
32. Ibid., p. 71.
33. Marx, *Capital*, vol. 2, p.34.
34. Marx, *Capital*, vol. 3, p. 325.
35. Ibid.
36. Marx, *Grundrisse*, p. 196.
37. Karl Marx, *Grundrisse der Kritik der politischen Okonomie* (Frankfurt: Europaische Verlagsanstalt, 1972), p. 903. (The Nicolaus translation excludes the *Anhang* from which all citations to the German text are here taken.)
38. Marx, *Capital*, vol. 1, p. 73.
39. Ibid.
40. Ibid., pp. 72–73.
41. Marx, *Grundrisse der Kritik der politischen Okonomie*, p. 903.
42. Ibid., p. 904.
43. Ibid., p. 903.
44. Ibid.
45. Marx, *Capital*, vol. 1, pp. 583–84.
46. Marx, *Grundrisse der Kritik der politischen Okonomie*, p. 904.
47. Marx, *Grundrisse*, p. 171.
48. Marx, *Grundrisse der Kritik der politischen Okonomie*, pp. 907–8.
49. Marx, *Capital*, vol. 1, pp. 74, 79.
50. Ibid., p. 73.
51. Ibid., p. 75.
52. Ibid., p. 38.

53. Ibid., pp. 168–69.
54. Marx, *Critique of Political Economy*, p. 45.
55. Marx, *Capital*, vol. 1, pp. 72–73.
56. Ibid., p. 72.
57. The prime initiator of this theory of reification is Georg Lukacs, whose *History and Class Consciousness* makes commodity fetischism a key principle for understanding bourgeois society.
58. Marx, *Capital*, vol. 1, p. 167.
59. Ibid., p. 44.
60. Ibid., p. 167.
61. Ibid., p. 78.
62. Ibid., p. 177.
63. Ibid.
64. Ibid., pp. 183–84.
65. Ibid., p. 184.
66. Ibid., p. 46.
67. Ibid., p. 186.
68. Ibid., p. 38.
69. Ibid., pp. 46, 71.
70. Marx, *Critique of Political Economy*, p. 31.
71. Marx, *Capital*, vol. 1, pp. 46, 71.
72. Ibid., p. 39.
73. Ibid., p. 71.
74. Ibid., p. 323.
75. Ibid., p. 44.
76. Ibid., p. 197.
77. *Marx-Engels Studienausgabe II*, p. 222.
78. Marx, *Capital*, vol. 3, p. 632.
79. Ibid., vol. 3, p. 791; *Capital*, vol. 1, p. 217.
80. Marx, *Capital*, vol. 1, p. 235.
81. Ibid., p. 195.
82. Marx, *Capital*, vol. 3, p. 820.
83. Ibid.
84. Ibid.
85. Marx, *Capital*, vol. 1, pp. 18–19; Marx, *Grundrisse*, p. 101.
86. Marx, *Capital*, vol. 1, p. 581, fn. 1.
87. Ibid., pp. 612–13.
88. Marx, *Capital*, vol. 3, p. 177.
89. Marx, *Capital*, vol. 1, p. 8.
90. Ibid., p. 76.

91. Marx, *Capital*, vol. 2, pp. 81–82; Marx, *Capital*, vol. 3, p. 617.

92. Marx, *Critique of Political Economy*, pp. 31–32.

93. Marx, *Grundrisse*, p. 88.

94. Marx, *Capital*, vol. 3, p. 876.

95. Marx, *Capital*, vol. 1, p. 114.

96. Marx, *Grundrisse*, p. 107.

97. Marx, *Capital*, vol. 3, p. 287.

98. Marx, *Grundrisse*, p. 107.

99. Ibid., pp. 103–5, 105–6.

100. Hegel, *Philosophy of Right*, p. 266.

101. Marx, *Grundrisse*, p. 109.

102. Ibid., p. 99.

103. Ibid., p. 107.

104. Ibid., p. 717.

105. Ibid., p. 253.

106. Ibid., p. 712.

107. Marx, *Capital*, vol. 1, pp. 81–82.

108. Marx, *Capital*, vol. 3, p. 791.

109. Marx, *Critique of Political Economy*, p. 20.

110. Marx, *Grundrisse*, p. 245.

111. Friedrich Nietzsche, *On The Genealogy of Morals*, trans. Walter Kaufman and R. J. Hollingdale, (New York: Random House, 1969), p. 70.

112. Marx, *Capital*, vol. 1, p. 585.

113. Ibid., p. 581, fn. 1; pp. 612–13.

114. Ibid., p. 480 ff.

115. Ibid., p. 734 ff.

116. Marx, *Critique of Political Economy*, p. 19.

117. Marx, *Grundrisse*, pp. 108, 227–28.

118. Ibid., pp. 253, 331.

119. Ibid., p. 712.

120. Ibid., p. 228.

4   Hegel's Mandate for the Just Economy

1. G. W. F. Hegel, *Philosophy of Right*, trans. Knox (New York: Oxford University Press, 1967), remark to paragraph 189.

2. Ibid., paragraphs 1 and 29.

3. Hegel treats the choosing will as a theme in his theory of Subjective Spirit under the heading, "Practical Spirit."

4. Ibid., *op. cit.,* remark to paragraph 71.

5. Ibid., remark to paragraph 261.

6. Ibid., paragraph 37.

7. Ibid., paragraph 260 and remark to paragraph 261.

8. Ibid., paragraph 127.

9. See Karl Polanyi, *The Great Transformation* (Boston: Beacon Press, 1957), Chapter 4, pp. 43–55.

5   The Elementary Structure of Market Freedom

1. Hegel, *Philosophy of Right*, trans. Knox (New York: Oxford University Press, 1967), remark to paragraph 190.

2. G. W. F. Hegel, *Vorlesungen Uber Rechtsphilosophie IV*, Edition Ilting (Stuttgart-Bad Cannstatt: Frommann-Holzboog, 1974), p. 475.

3. Ibid., p. 476.

4. Hegel, *Philosophy of Right*, paragraph 194.

5. Ibid., paragraph 192.

6. Hegel anticipates these relations in describing the use of property in paragraph 63 and its addition in the *Philosophy of Right*.

7. Ibid., paragraph 195; Hegel, *Vorlesungen Uber Rechtsphilosophie*, vol. 4, p. 605.

8. Hegel, *Vorlesungen Uber Rechtsphilosophie*, vol. 3, p. 598.

9. This development is anticipated in paragraph 77 of the *Philosophy of Right* and treated thematically in paragraph 192.

10. Eugen v. Bohm-Bawerk discusses how this problem afflicts Marx's theory in "Zum Abschluss des Marxhschen Systems," in *Aspekte der Marxschen Theorie 1*, ed. F. Eberle (Frankfurt-am-Main: Suhrkamp, 1973).

11. Karl Marx, *Capital* (New York: International Publishers, 1970), vol. 1, p. 73 f.

12. Hegel, *Philosophy of Right*, paragraph 196.

13. Marx, *Capital*, vol. 1, p. 71 ff.

14. Ibid., p. 38 ff.

15. Hegel, *Vorlesungen Uber Rechstphilosophie,* vol. 3, pp. 630–31.

16. Hegel, *Vorlesungen Uber Rechstphilosophie*, vol. 4, pp. 228–29; Hegel, *Philosophy of Right*, paragraphs 204, 299, addition to paragraph 63.

17. Ibid., paragraphs 204, 299.

18. Hegel, *Vorlesungen Uber Rechstphilosophie*, vol. 4, pp. 228–29.

19. Ibid., Addition to paragraph 63.

20. Ibid.

21. Hegel, *Vorlesungen Uber Rechstphilosophie*, vol. 3, pp. 630–31.

22. Marx, *Capital*, vol. 1, p. 166 ff.

23. Marx, *Capital*, Chapters 6 and 7.

6   The Place of Capital in the Market Economy

1. Karl Marx, *Capital* (New York: International Publishers, 1970), vol. 1, Part 8, "The So-Called Primitive Accumulation."

2. Hegel, *Philosophy of Right*, trans. Knox (New York: Oxford University Press, 1967), paragraph 189; Hegel, *Vorlesungen Uber Rechstphilosophie*, Edition Ilting (Stuttgart-Bad Cannstatt: Frommann-Holzboog, 1974), vol. 3, pp. 619–20, 630–31; vol. 4, pp. 626–27.

3. Hegel, *Philosophy of Right*, paragraph 196.

4. Hegel, *Vorlesungen Uber Rechtsphilosophie*, vol. 4, p. 496.

5. Hegel, *Vorlesungen Uber Rechtsphilosophie*, vol. 3, p. 607.

6. Hegel, *Vorlesungen Uber Rechtsphilosophie*, vol. 4, pp. 240, 493; Hegel, *Philosophy of Right*, paragraph 67.

7. Hegel, *Philosophy of Right*, paragraph 198; Hegel, *Philosophy of Mind*, trans. Wallace and Miller (New York: Oxford University Press, 1971), paragraph 525; Hegel, *Vorlesungen Uber Rechtsphilosophie*, vol. 1, p. 314; vol. 4, p. 502.

8. Hegel, *Vorlesungen Uber Rechtsphilosophie*, vol. 3, p. 609; vol. 4, p. 502.

9. Hegel, *Vorlesungen Uber Rechtsphilosophie*, vol. 3, pp. 607, 609.

10. Ibid., pp. 607–9; Hegel, *Philosophy of Right*, paragraph 197.

11. Hegel, *Philosophy of Right*, paragraph 198; Hegel, *Philosophy of Mind*, paragraph 526; Hegel, *Vorlesungen Uber Rechtsphilosophie*, vol. 3, p. 610.

12. Hegel, *Philosophy of Right*, paragraph 198; Hegel, *Vorlesungen Uber Rechtsphilosophie*, vol. 4, p. 502.

13. Hegel, *Philosophy of Right*, paragraph 198, Hegel, *Philosophy of Mind*, paragraph 526; Hegel, *Vorlesungen Uber Rechtsphilosophie*, vol. 3, p. 611.

14. Hegel, *Vorlesungen Uber Rechtsphilosophie*, vol. 3, p. 611.

15. Ibid., p. 612.

16. Ibid., p. 611; vol. 4, p. 503.

17. Hegel, *Philosophy of Right*, paragraphs 199 and 200.

7   Classes, Estates, and Economic Justice

1. Hegel, *Philosophy of Right*, trans. Knox (New York: Oxford University Press, 1967), paragraph 201; Hegel, *Vorlesungen Uber Rechtsphilosophie*, Edition Ilting (Stuttgart-Bad Connstatt: Frommann-Holzboog, 1974), I pp. 314–315, III p. 621, IV p. 511.

2. Hegel, *Philosophy of Right*, paragraph 206; Hegel, *Vorlesungen Uber Rechtsphilosophie*, vol 1, p. 322; vol. 3, pp. 635, 638.

3. Hegel, *Philosophy of Right*, paragraph 201; Hegel, *Vorlesungen Uber Rechtsphilosophie*, vol. 3, pp. 632–34.

4. Hegel, *Philosophy of Right*, paragraph 203.

5. Ibid.

6. Ibid.

7. Ibid., addition to paragraph 204.

8. Hegel, *Vorlesungen Uber Rechtsphilosophie*, vol. 3, p. 628.

9. Hegel, *Philosophy of Right*, paragraphs 203, 305, and 306, addition to paragraph 204.

10. Hegel, *Vorlesungen Uber Rechtsphilosophie*, vol. 1, p. 315.

11. Hegel, *Philosophy of Right*, paragraph 203; Hegel, *Philosophy of Mind*, trans. Wallace and Miller (New York: Oxford University Press, 1971), paragraph 528.

12. Hegel, *Philosophy of Right*, addition to paragraph 203.

13. Hegel, *Vorlesungen Uber Rechtsphilosophie*, vol. 3, p. 626.

14. Hegel, *Vorlesungen Uber Rechtsphilosophie*, vol. 4, p. 515.

15. Ibid., p. 517.

16. Hegel, *Philosophy of Right*, paragraph 303.

17. Hegel, *Vorlesungen Uber Rechtsphilosophie*, vol. 3, p. 632.

18. Hegel, *Philosophy of Right*, addition to paragraph 296.

19. Hegel, *Vorlesungen Uber Rechtsphilosophie*, vol. 4, p. 521.

20. Hegel, *Philosophy of Right*, paragraph 205.

21. Hegel, *Philosophy of Right*, paragraph 204.

22. Ibid.

23. Ibid., addition to paragraph 203.

24. Ibid., paragraph 250; Hegel, *Vorlesungen Uber Rechtsphilosophie*, vol. 3, p. 629, vol. 1, p. 315; Hegel, *The Philosophy of Mind*, paragraph 528.

25. In the *System der Sittlichkeit*, for instance, Hegel limits the process of production to the activity of a particular Estate, echoing Plato. Manfred Riedel discusses this in *Studien zu Hegels Rechtsphilosophie* (Frankfurt am Main: Suhrkamp, 1970).

26. Hegel, *Philosophy of Right*, paragraph 204.

27. Hegel, *Vorlesungen Uber Rechtsphilosophie*, vol. 3, pp. 630–31, vol. 4, p. 520.

28. Ibid., vol. 3, pp. 628–631, vol. 4, p. 520; Hegel, *Philosophy of Right*, paragraph 204.

29. Hegel, *Philosophy of Right*, paragraph 243.

30. Ibid., paragraph 245.

31. Ibid., paragraph 251.

32. Ibid., paragraph 250.

33. Ibid., paragraphs 298 and 301.

34. Ibid., paragraphs 303–12.

35. Ibid., paragraph 308.

36. Ibid., paragraphs 305–7.

8   Commodity Relations and the Enforcement of Economic Justice

1. Hegel, *Philosophy of Right*, trans. Knox (New York: Oxford University Press, 1967), paragraphs 82 ff. and 102.

2. For this reason, there can be no precluding the sorts of conflicts that involve vio-

lations of person and property even in a communist society where market relations are eliminated and a free abundance of goods prevails. Hence, "the association of free producers" must either resign itself to a state of anarchy where licence has free sway or resurrect civil institutions of law and justice, together with the political structures to enact, authorize and execute the needed legislation.

3. Hegel, *Philosophy of Right*, paragraphs 209–29.

4. Ibid., paragraphs 200, 230, 236 and 237.

5. Ibid., paragraph 200.

6. Ibid.

7. Karl Polanyi discusses these problems at length in *The Great Transformation* (Boston: Beacon Press, 1957), particularly in Chapters 14-16, pp. 163–200.

8. Hegel, *Philosophy of Right*, addition to paragraph 255.

9. Carole Pateman, *Participation and Democratic Theory* (New York: Cambridge University Press, 1970), p. 110.

10. Hegel, *Philosophy of Right*, paragraph 255.

9 The Limits of Private Intervention in the Market

1. Hegel, *Philosophy of Right*, trans. Knox (New York: Oxford University Press, 1967), paragraphs 230–56.

2. Ibid., paragraph 252.

3. Ibid., paragraph 256.

4. Ibid., paragraph 250.

5. Ibid., paragraphs 252–53.

6. Michael Oakeshott discusses this point in "The Political Economy of Freedom," in *Rationalism in Politics and Other Essays* (London: Methuen, 1962), p. 54.

7. Hegel, *Philosophy of Right*, paragraphs 231–49.

8. Ibid., paragraphs 232–34.

10 The Normative Principles of Public Intervention in the Market

1. Hegel, *Philosophy of Right*, trans. Knox (New York: Oxford University Press, 1967), addition to paragraph 236.

2. Ibid., addition to paragraph 238.

3. Ibid., paragraph 236.

4. Ibid.

5. Ibid., addition to paragraph 236.

6. Ibid., paragraph 236.

7. Ibid., paragraph 239.

8. Ibid., addition to paragraph 240.

9. Ibid., paragraph 238.

10. Ibid., addition to paragraph 238.

11. Ibid., paragraph 238.

12. Ibid., paragraph 241.

13. Ibid., addition to paragraph 240.

14. Ibid., addition to paragraph 244.

15. Ibid., paragraph 127.

16. Ibid., remark to paragraph 236.

17. Ibid., paragraph 239 and addition to paragraph 239.

18. Ibid., paragraph 239 and addition to paragraph 239.

19. John Rawls, *A Theory of Justice* (Cambridge, MA: Harvard University Press, 1971), pp. 74, 301, 511.

20. Rawls raises this point in ibid., pp. 74–75.

21. Hegel, *Philosophy of Right*, paragraph 240.

22. Ibid., addition to paragraph 240.

23. Ibid., paragraph 235.

24. Rawls, *A Theory of Justice*, p. 276.

25. Ibid.

26. Ibid.

27. Ibid., pp. 277–78.

28. Hegel, *Philosophy of Right*, paragraph 243.

29. Ibid.

30. Ibid., paragraph 245.

31. Ibid.

32. David Hume, *An Enquiry Concerning The Principles of Morals* (Indianapolis: Hackett, 1983), p. 28.

33. Ibid.

34. Ibid.

35. Ibid.

36. Rawls, *A Theory of Justice*, pp. 277–78.

37. Hegel, *Philosophy of Right*, paragraph 245.

38. Ibid., paragraphs 244, 245.

39. Ibid., paragraphs 246 and 248, addition to paragraph 248.

40. Ibid., paragraph 246.

41. Ibid., paragraph 248.

42. Rosa Luxemburg, *The Accumulation of Capital* (New York: Monthly Review Press, 1968).

43. Joan Robinson points out this discrepancy in her introduction (pp. 13–28) to *The Accumulation of Capital*, pp. 16–17.

44. Ibid., p. 28.

45. Paul Sweezy, *The Theory of Capitalist Development* (New York: Monthly Review Press, 1968), p. 204.

46. Ibid., p. 205.

47. Ibid.

48. Hume, *An Enquiry*, p. 28.

49. Hegel, *Philosophy of Right*, paragraph 244, addition to paragraph 244.

50. Ibid., paragraphs 207, 242.

11   The Limits of the Public Enforcement of Economic Welfare

1. Hegel, *Philosophy of Right*, trans. Knox (New York: Oxford University Press, 1967), paragraph 240.

2. Ibid., paragraph 299, remark to paragraph 299, and addition to paragraph 299.

3. Ibid., addition to paragraph 299.

4. Ibid., paragraph 299.

5. Rawls, *A Theory of Justice* (Cambridge, MA: Harvard University Press, 1971), p. 271.

6. Ibid., p. 270.

7. Ibid., pp. 280–81.

8. Michael Oakeshott, *Rationalism in Politics and Other Essays* (London: Methuen, 1962), p. 45.

9. Ibid.

10. Ibid., p. 53.

11. Ibid., p. 52.

12. Ibid., pp. 52–53.

13. Ibid., p. 55.

14. Ibid., pp. 56–57.

INDEX